COPING WITH AFRICA'S FOOD CRISIS

· FOOD IN AFRICA SERIES ·

Series Editor: *Art Hansen*
  Center for African Studies
  University of Florida

COPING WITH AFRICA'S FOOD CRISIS

edited by
Naomi Chazan and Timothy M. Shaw

Lynne Rienner Publishers • Boulder & London

Published in the United States of America in 1988 by
Lynne Rienner Publishers, Inc.
948 North Street, Boulder, Colorado 80302

and in the United Kingdom by
Lynne Rienner Publishers, Inc.
3 Henrietta Street, Covent Garden, London WC2E 8LU

Library of Congress Cataloging-in-Publication Data
Coping with Africa's food crisis / edited by Naomi Chazan and Timothy M. Shaw
    p. cm. — (Food in Africa series)
  Bibliography: p.
  Includes index.
  ISBN 0-931477-84-0 (lib. bdg.)
  1. Food supply—Government policy—Africa—Case studies.
2. Agriculture and state—Africa—Case studies. I. Chazan, Naomi, 1946– . II. Shaw, Timothy
M. III. Series.
HD9017.A2C65 1988
338.1'9'6—dc19   87-26849
                                                    CIP

British Library Cataloguing in Publication Data
A Cataloguing in Publication record for this book is available from the British Library.

Printed and bound in the United States of America

The paper used in this publication meets
the requirements of the American National
Standard for Permanence of Paper for   ∞
Printed Library Materials Z39.48-1984.

Contents

Tables

Acknowledgments

This collection is a result of long-standing professional collaboration plus a relatively recent concern with broad development issues. The professional interaction between the two coeditors and between both of them and Lynne Rienner has a lengthy genesis and is renewed often at African Studies Association (ASA) annual conferences. The development concern was in fact first articulated at the December 1983 meeting of the ASA in Boston, when the coeditors organized a pair of panels on "Popular Strategies for Coping with the Food Crisis in Black Africa." Happily, Lynne Rienner Publishers was able to share the novelty and vitality of the panels with us, and after considerable gestation this edited selection of much revised papers is the result. We appreciate the encouragement and patience of the original panelists and eventual contributors alike.

In addition, Naomi Chazan would like to thank the staff of the Africa Research Program of the Center for International Affairs, Harvard University, and especially its director, Dov Ronen, for the intellectual and logistical support that helped bring this book to fruition; and Tali, Shai, and Barry Chazan, for providing in many ways the support so essential for scholarly pursuits. Tim Shaw acknowledges and appreciates the continuing assistance and indulgence of Jane Parpart and the energy and proficiency of Evelyn Flynn. It has also been a pleasure to work with Lynne Rienner Publishers, particularly Lynne Rienner and Gia Hamilton, and our copy editor, Beverly Armstrong.

We hope that in all of this, the resilience of Africa's people is neither overlooked nor eroded. Their survival and well-being continues to be our primary concern.

Naomi Chazan, Jerusalem
Timothy M. Shaw, Halifax

About the Contributors

Naomi Chazan is senior lecturer in political science and African studies and head of the African Studies Department at the Hebrew University of Jerusalem. She was recently visiting professor at Radcliffe College and at Harvard University.

Cyril Koffie Daddieh is visiting professor of government at Colby College in Maine. He holds a PhD from Dalhousie University.

Michael Ford is associate professor of politics at Hampshire College in Massachusetts.

Kenneth Good is associate professor of political and administrative studies at the University of Zambia.

Frank Holmquist is professor of politics at Hampshire College, where he has been associate dean of the School of Social Science.

Jon Kraus is professor of political science at the State University of New York, Fredonia.

Carol Lancaster is at the Institute for International Economics in Washington, D.C. She was previously director of the African Studies Program at Georgetown University.

Barbara Lewis is professor of political science at Rutgers University in New Brunswick, New Jersey.

Michael F. Lofchie is professor of political science and director of the African Studies Center at the University of California, Los Angeles.

Janet MacGaffey is research associate at the Institute for the Study of Human Issues in Philadelphia. She is author of *Entrepreneurs and Parasites: The Struggle for Indigenous Capitalism in Zaire* (Cambridge, 1987).

Timothy M. Shaw is professor of political science and director of the Centre for African Studies at Dalhousie University, where he also coordinates the International Development Studies program.

·PART 1·
Popular Responses

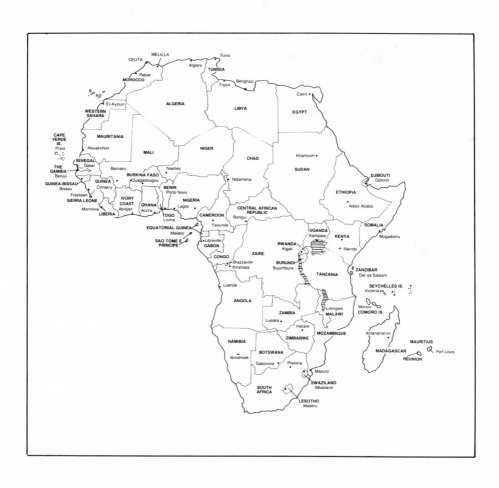

·1·

The Political Economy of Food in Africa

NAOMI CHAZAN
TIMOTHY M. SHAW

Governments, especially in unstable post-colonial West Africa, come and go. The major problems they profess to tackle remain. As the Lagos Plan of Action reminds us, "Africa is unable to point to any significant growth rate or satisfactory index of general well-being in the last 20 years." The Lagos plan—key words "collective self-reliance"—aimed to be an "agonising but frank reappraisal" of social and economic development efforts. A central issue in the Plan is that of food production. The international agencies regularly bombard each other with statistics on this issue . . . : on average, diets in Africa provide 6 per cent less energy than the minimum required for sustained healthy living; the current food supply situation in twenty-two African countries is so bad that over 150 million people may soon face hunger and malnutrition. . . .

It is vital, when considering the whole dreadful spectra of food shortages, to distinguish between natural calamities and political action. Political choices are made by people, can be pinpointed, and have in some cases incontestably left other people hungry. There is nothing inevitable or hopeless about food shortages.[1]

The structural weaknesses of African agriculture are well known: low production and productivity, and rudimentary agricultural techniques. This situation obviously gives rise to insufficient agricultural growth, especially of food production, in the face of rapid population growth, and has resulted in serious food shortages and malnutrition in the continent.[2]

The economic crisis is especially evident in agriculture, and is reflected in output figures. Export crop production stagnated over the past two decades. . . . Total food production rose by 1.5 per cent per year in the 1970s, down from 2 per cent in the previous decade. But since population was rising rapidly—by an annual average of 2.5 per cent in the 1960s and 2.7 per cent in the 1970s—food production per person was stagnant in the first decade and actually declined in the next. Imports of food grains (wheat, rice and maize) soared—by 9 per cent per year since the early

1

1960s—reinforcing food dependency. Food aid also increased substantially. Since 70 to 90 per cent of the population earns its income from agriculture, the drop in production in this sector spelled a real income loss of many of the poorest.[3]

· THE VARIABILITY OF FOOD POLITICS ·

The political economy of food has taken on a special importance with the intensification of the food crisis in Africa in the 1980s. Per capita food production in the early part of this decade dropped at an alarming rate[4] (see Table 1.1). Prices of essential commodities soared, and food distribution networks were often incapable of meeting even the most basic of needs. Over half the states on the continent experienced acute food shortages (see Table 1.2). Too many of the citizens of these countries were on the brink of outright starvation.

Manifold explanations have been offered to account for the food crisis, and alternative panaceas or strategies have been proposed. Some observers have favored interpretations rooted in the environment, in natural disasters, and in ecological constraints.[5] Some have highlighted the changing structure of economic production and exchange.[6] Others have insisted on the paramountcy of migration patterns, demographic movements, and social considerations.[7] And still others have stressed the international dimensions of Africa's food insecurity: shifts in world prices for primary exports, the rising cost of imports, multinational involvement in agribusiness, growing external dependency, and the unequal incorporation of the continent into the global economy.[8] But regardless of the variety of perspectives permeating the literature, it is becoming increasingly apparent that much of the responsibility for Africa's inability to feed itself, a problem symptomatic of a much broader economic crisis (oil shocks, negative terms of trade, exchange problems), lies with the failure of governments.

"There is, indeed, no such thing as an apolitical food problem."[9] Inappropriate policies, a preference for cash-cropping and production for export, high food subsidies, rural neglect, the urban bias of economic planners, corruption, sexist disregard of crucial female inputs into agriculture, and inefficiency have all combined to place politics at the center of the food problem.[10] The domestic and international facets of food politics not only help to explain existing trends, but also underline the importance of finding political remedies to food-related issues.[11] An almost axiomatic relationship has consequently emerged between hunger, politics, and instability.

The political economy of food cannot, however, be reduced to a simple correlation between poverty and political uncertainty, or, for that matter, between abundance and political stability. Such an approach does not help to explain differences in political patterns in countries undergoing extensive food difficulties. It neither assists in pinpointing the directions of political change, nor does it permit the presentation of policy prescriptions of other than a very general sort. Understanding of the political economy of food in Africa requires elaboration and refinement if it is to serve as the foundation for analysis and praxis.

. This concentration on the food nexus as indicative of a wider range of issues has emerged out of a reconsideration of the continent's troubled first two decades since independence. Symptomatic and symbolic of this reevaluation are two divergent treaties and strategies that have become the subject of considerable debate and disagreement: the Organization of African Unity's (OAU) Lagos Plan of Action and the World Bank's Agenda for Action. These divergent reactions to the continental crisis, which has intensified in an exponential manner since the early 1970s, treat both manifestations and causes, agreeing on the former but differing on the latter. In 1986 the OAU developed its Africa's Priority Programme for Economic Recovery (APPER), later discussed at the Special General Assembly on Africa, which sought to mesh to two approaches. Likewise, scholars and advisers disagree about explanations and prescriptions while concurring over symptoms: the interaction of population explosion, urbanization, and rural neglect; the tensions between production and distribution, between food and commodities, and between local consumption and export; and the dialectics of land, capital, labor, and gender.

In this introduction, we seek to go beyond existing definitions of food policies in an attempt to understand some of the variable connections between food-related problems (as reflective of economic trends) and political patterns in contemporary Africa. We will assume, therefore, that the political economy of food cannot be restricted to the analysis of national and global interchanges alone. The food problem directly affects the fate of groups and individuals; their responses are as much a part of food politics as those of their governments. In our analysis, we treat a variety of states and regimes as well as classes and regions.

People react to particular aspects of the food crisis in different ways. Three distinct manifestations of food insecurity are evident in Africa today. The first relates to the problem of food prices, which is closely linked to consumption patterns;[12] the second centers on issues of food availability;[13] and the third revolves around problems of real scarcity: of insufficient production. Each of these derives from different sources, affects specific groups in a variety of ways, evokes unique coping mechanisms, possesses its own specific political ramifications, and spawns quite separate patterns of political conflict. The implications, therefore, of responses to each type of food crisis vary significantly;[14] and although observable reactions to food problems usually involve some combination of these issues, the full impact of these reactions can only be understood by a prior analysis of each type separately.

We focus our discussion on the political causes, manifestations, responses, and outcomes of these three forms of the food crisis in Africa. We argue that the type of political conflict evident in given locations is closely related to the nature of poverty in that setting. By venturing beyond the formal underpinnings of the political economy of food and expanding our analysis to incorporate popular responses as well, we may be able not only to shed more light on the complexity of the food crisis on the continent but also to offer some thoughts on the range of possibilities for its resolution: to go beyond aggregate data to the politics of production, distribution, and consumption.

· FORMS OF FOOD POLITICS ·

The Politics of Food Prices

The most common food problem in Africa in the 1980s relates to the high cost of essential commodities. The problem is not one of scarcity, but of the inability of large segments of the population to pay the inflated price of a square meal. The saga of soaring food prices is familiar to many Africans: Whereas abundant food was frequently available at reasonable prices two decades ago, the reduction in food production and the growing dependence on imports (see Tables 1.3 and 1.4) has put many items beyond the reach of the average citizen. In some countries, the cost of a single meal that barely meets minimum requirements is sometimes twice or three times the approved minimum daily wage.[15] Food is ostensibly available, but many people are simply not able to afford to purchase it.

The inflationary spiral of food costs in an almost natural by-product of general policy preferences exhibited by many African governments since independence. Most African states have encouraged cash-cropping for export not only to augment government revenues but also to satisfy urban demands for Western goods. These moves have inevitably fostered a dependence of the rural producer on the pricing system determined at the state center and hence on the world market prices of specific commodities. The move away from production for consumption inevitably created a void in the flow of goods to the markets, a slack that was picked up by the expansion of food imports. The growth of imported consumption items, facilitated by the active intervention of multinational agricultural firms, changed consumption patterns in many African urban areas.[16] Shifts from roots (yams, cassava) to grains (wheat, ray) became commonplace in the continent's cities. The rising middle class shunned local foods, preferring Swiss cheese and pickles to gari and fufu.

By the 1970s new consumption patterns had become well entrenched. But as the price of imports leaped and export revenues dropped in the aftermath of the oil crisis, many governments were caught in a major policy dilemma: Should they increase producer prices to enhance local production, or should they raise government subsidies to satisfy urban demands for cheaper food?[17]

Country after country, while paying lip service to the need for rural revitalization, opted for the less risky course of establishing a complex system of price supports. The reasoning behind this strategy is fairly self-evident: The political cost of offending the urban population was much higher than that of incurring the wrath of the small farmer. "A major reason for the fact that official development policy has thus far aimed at squeezing as large a surplus product as possible out of petty producers lies in the fact that they are able to exercise the least political and institutional influence on the governmental decisionmaking process."[18]

The impact of this policy orientation was twofold. On the one hand, export production stagnated because cash-cropping became less and less worthwhile (see Table 1.5); and on the other hand, state coffers were depleted while state managers artificially propped up expensive food imports by overvaluing local currencies. The ensuing balance-of-payments problems increased external pressures to alter priorities.[19] Foreign creditors, and in particular the International Monetary Fund (IMF), demanded rigid austerity measures (including devaluation and higher producer prices) to rectify the distortion wrought by past food-pricing policies.[20] Since the late 1970s, therefore, food prices skyrocketed throughout the continent as government after government adjusted its policies to meet the dictates of external benefactors and, not coincidentally, of local farmers.

The end result of this complex but nevertheless fairly widespread process was to put many consumer items out of the grasp of large portions of the population. Life-styles were disrupted, expenditure structures were altered, and poverty proliferated. Most hard hit were the urban dwellers. Unskilled labor was unable to keep up with the cost of food; consequently, urban hunger became more commonplace. Gradually, skilled workers, salaried employees, and even the professional middle classes were hurt by the rapid expansion of the inflationary spiral. And in the rural areas, the high price of imports reduced the incentive to continue production for export. The pricing crisis has therefore affected classes and geographic areas differentially.

Economic policy responses, in these circumstances, have varied, as indicated in any comparisons between the Lagos Plan and Agenda for Action, with important implications for patterns of inequality. In the cities the struggle to find cheap food became a major preoccupation. People have learned to make do with less, to change their consumption habits, and to reduce, albeit reluctantly, their standard of living. They have sought out, indeed frequently elaborated, new sources of supply and, at times, alternative distribution networks. In most severely affected countries (such as Uganda, Zaire, Tanzania, and Ghana) rural-urban migration dropped, and urban-rural population shifts became more pronounced; there may yet be some positive fringe benefits. But, by and large, economic reactions to the high cost of food dealt less with production and accumulation and more with distribution and consumption. More people were suffering in the large cities and fewer were managing than in the past.[21]

In the rural areas some major changes in production and exchange have been evident (compare the alternative recommendations of the Lagos Plan and Agenda for Action). Large food producers raised their prices more quickly than did retailers and wholesalers.[22] Some peasants have shifted from export to food production to fulfill their own needs and, significantly, to take advantage of higher prices for foodstuffs. This reaction has severely affected export earnings and hence indirectly even further intensified inflationary pressures.[23]

The net effect of these responses has been, almost uniformly, to foster a renewed urban dependency on the countryside and to exacerbate class tensions in the city. The political expression of the rising frustration of the urban dwellers focused squarely on demands for changes in government policy. Lacking alternative sources of income or of food supply, inhabitants of major urban agglomerations have had little choice but to step up pressure on the state to alleviate the high cost of living. A rash of strikes and demonstrations against price hikes occurred throughout the continent in the first part of the 1980s. Thus, for example, in the spring of 1979 Liberia experienced riots that decried the raising of rice prices to producers. In Ghana, food prices were at the root of urban noncompliance in the late 1970s and early 1980s. Sudan experienced widespread demonstrations following an IMF-imposed 62 percent hike in sugar prices.[24] The Tanzanian leadership was subjected to increasingly vocal calls for greater government control over food prices. In Zambia, wildcat strikes among mine workers protested, among other things, recessionary moves made by the regime.[25] In Kenya, deteriorating standards of living in Nairobi furnished the backdrop for the abortive coup attempt of August 1982. Somali troops clashed with civilians in the northern part of the country after a demonstration was held to protest the ill effects of the economic crisis.[26] Even in relatively well-to-do Côte d'Ivoire (Ivory Coast), students have gone out on strike against the high cost of living.[27] The "state-centric" anger of urbanites may be contrasted with the "withdrawal" proclivities of rural elements: self-reliance in the countryside versus antagonism in the cities.

These political activities have provided a funnel for the expression of dissatisfaction with government measures and a significant outlet for the venting of popular demands for reform. Despite the salience of these outbursts, however, they have generally been confined to major cities and have been directed specifically at policymakers. These political responses have operated within the boundaries of the state and have reaffirmed (albeit in a negative way) the centrality of the state in ensuring adequate food supplies at a reasonable cost. The pattern of political conflict that has emerged therefore has been elitist in form and content (although the political implications must be assessed in light of the politics of other facets of the food crisis).[28] Political maneuvers marked by ethnic and class overtones have been concentrated at the state center, only sporadically breaking beyond the urban barrier. The political response to the food-price challenge has consequently charged the atmosphere in many African states, creating an immediate, albeit restrained, challenge to existing regimes. Yet, if current governments fail, then the ominous historical trends scenario of the Economic Commission for Africa (ECA) will surely materialize with myriad negative and problematic implications.

Given the proximity of these manifestations to the seat of power, few governments have been able to avoid tackling this type of discontent. Some have attempted to repress opposition, mostly as a temporary measure to avert chaos. But most administrations have eventually had to confront the pricing problem more directly. At this juncture, the paradoxes that have led to the present crisis have become more pronounced. Thus, the tendency to reintroduce price controls in order to assure minimum food supplies necessarily grants extra protection to consumers at the expense of producers. Price supervision may be politically wise, but economically it does little to promote increased production and hence lower prices in the long range. Even if a policy of price incentives (with all its political risks), as adopted by most countries in the mid-1980s, is set in train, it is unclear whether governments need encourage food production, to reduce dependency on foreign markets, or promote production in order to increase foreign-exchange resources and thereby augment the influx of cheap supplies from abroad.[29] These difficulties have heightened the dilemmas facing African governments in the short term, although there appears to be a growing consensus that higher prices for both exports and food items might eventually lead to greater availability and hence to more reasonable prices and more adequate consumption patterns over time.[30] Until the results of such policy adjustments begin to take root, however, it is not unreasonable to suggest that food prices will continue to foment dissent and that "IMF riots" will proliferate.

The Politics of Food Supplies

The food problem is closely linked to issues of food availability. Access to food products in many parts of Africa is glaringly unequal. Although frequently food is visible in the towns and in the countryside, it is simply not within reach of many segments of the population. The problem of hunger is all too often not one of scarcity but of the monopolization of productive assets by the powerful few.[31] Abundance and deprivation flourish side by side in many parts of the Sub-Sahara: The apportionment of basic sustenance does not conform to any equitable formula.

Lopsided food distribution patterns have evolved gradually during the past century. The introduction of cash-cropping alongside subsistence agriculture has fostered inequities in the countryside since the commencement of the colonial period. The process of rural differentiation—very acutely highlighted in areas of plantation agriculture—institutionalized the coexistence of mixed modes of production and, hence, of different modes of distribution as well. The uneven development of the countryside, propelled by a penchant for production for export at the expense of food cropping,[32] was supported not only by land tenure policies that bolstered relatively large independent producers, but also by the development of transportation and marketing networks with a heavy urban and coastal bias. Certain ethnic groups, geographic regions, and farmers' associations flourished under the aegis of colonial authorities concerned with raising exports and ensuring suitable standards of living in the metropolis.

The inegalitarian market structure devised and developed during the colonial period had international implications as well. Food security became as dependent on foreign-exchange reserves as on productive capability.[33] After independence, the propensity to manage access to food on the basis of criteria of power rather than need continued apace. The inherited structure of most economies was not altered by the successor elites, thereby linking pricing policy to structural inequalities. The transportation and marketing network was nurtured to meet bureaucratic and external demands first. The temptations of Western values established an environment that sanctioned official accumulation through malfeasance to the detriment of the creation of suitable local supply routes.[34] But much more perniciously, this attitude fostered a long period of neglect of agriculture in general and of food production in particular. Most African leaders simply ignored agricultural pursuits during the first heady years of independence, thus even further exacerbating the uneven supply of agricultural goods.[35]

The administrative inadequacies of food management were not always apparent when food supplies were fairly abundant. But as dependence on imports grew and food prices rose, access to supplies became noticeably circumscribed. Governments tightened their control over the movement of food, increased their monopolies over essential commodities, and attempted to centralize distribution processes. The close relationship between control over power and access to food was especially apparent in countries that have suffered from natural disasters. In the Sahel belt and the Horn of Africa, foreign food aid frequently never reached the areas most seriously affected by droughts. Similarly, the malnutrition and starvation in South Africa in the 1980s was as much a consequence of discriminatory relief efforts as of poor yields.[36] Two decades after independence, many Africans were confronted with the unsavory prospect of knowing that food was available but having no way of obtaining it.

The challenge of food accessibility relates directly to problems of maldistribution and lopsided accumulation. It is as much an issue of administration as of production.[37] Ample bread in some neighborhoods and no bread at all in other parts of a city has been a familiar sight in many African towns. Certain items did not appear in the marketplace but could be found at the dinner tables of government officials. All too often, totally useless items, such as Tabasco sauce, could be purchased easily, but no meat was available for a simple meal. In short, the politics of food supplies originates in power concentrations; the issue has consequently evoked power concerns.

Those most severely affected by the lack of access to food supplies have been those most removed from the centers of political life. In the urban areas, these are the workers and the lower echelons of salaried employees. In the rural portions, peasant producers and seasonal labor have been less likely to have access to food supplements than have independent farmers engaged in market production. On the other hand, individuals and groups at the conjuncture of production and exchange (both domestic and international) were in a far better position to oversee distribution and hence to procure vital foodstuffs. Everywhere, women and children have been relatively dependent and disadvantaged despite their centrality in agriculture.

The economic response to inadequate food supplies has focused on devising means of bypassing the formal marketing networks—that is, of moving beyond the state. The restructuring of exchange through the institutionalization of a parallel economy has become a common feature in Africa in the 1980s. Specific groups have embarked on this task in different ways. But in every country where nonformal economic processes are on the ascendance, the initiative may be traced back to those engaged in trade rather than in production, whether of foodstuffs or commodities. This group has spearheaded a series of activities aimed at reorienting accumulation and distribution patterns. The first of these activities is smuggling. Export goods and foodstuffs are transferred illegally from countries that offer lower prices to those that grant high payments or are themselves sources of required commodities. A familiar pursuit since independence, smuggling was especially rampant in the early 1980s. It was particularly noticeable in countries like Ghana, Uganda, Zaire, and Guinea, where access to food was circumscribed and essential supplies could be obtained only by resort to illicit transfers across international frontiers.[38]

Closely linked to smuggling is hoarding and black-marketeering. Hoarding occurs when official prices are low and the sale of particular items becomes unprofitable. Inflated prices on the black market appear when specific goods that are in great demand are unavailable through regular channels. The regulation of supplies to the parallel market has been facilitated by the creation of unofficial transportation monopolies that control the extraction of food from the rural areas.

These pursuits require a certain degree of organization. In countries where food supplies have been unpredictable—and where many individuals dabble to some extent in the black market—minimal organization is discernable. But as the severity of the problem of food accessibility has become more pronounced, the institutionalization of response patterns has increased to the point that full-fledged parallel distribution systems have emerged. *Kalabule* in Ghana and *magendo* in Uganda are just two examples of what is a much more prevalent phenomenon throughout the continent: the black market.[39]

Groups less conveniently located at the interface of production and exchange have evolved other means of gaining access to food. In rural and urban areas, home production for consumption purposes became commonplace, frequently with official approval.[40] Surplus goods, when available, were often marketed by the petty producer, and small self-contained points of exchange began to develop in the countryside. Recourse to renewed emphasis on mixed modes of production was hence a by-product of food unavailability.

Government personnel, on the other hand, sought to capitalize on their positions in order to funnel state resources to meet personal needs. Corruption, fraud, and embezzlement fast became the salaried technocrat's response to inadequate food supplies. By diverting official aid resources, and even operating budgets, to the parallel system, state managers were able to augment their own incomes and meet the needs of their families and dependents. Thus, many of those responsible for the skewed lines of food supply reacted to the situation by further exacerbating the problem.[41] At the same time, they helped to shift the structural emphasis to the rural areas, thereby contributing to the shifting balance between rural and urban areas.

Impoverished urban inhabitants were not, however, able to utilize these channels to obtain food, as their access to established or alternative power poles was limited in the extreme. Lack of food availability, most acutely felt in these circles, has therefore either driven people out of their countries (inducing widespread migration in the Horn of Africa, the Sahel, and parts of West, Central, and Southern Africa) or encouraged a return to the rural areas.[42] Those who remained in the cities were subjected to growing hunger or resorted to theft to avert starvation. The rising crime rate is but a meager indication of the desperation attendant upon the inequality of food distribution.

These diverse economic responses to the food supply challenge possess certain common features. First, the various reactions reflect the enormous effort expended on finding ways to bypass formal structures. These popular strategies have been antistate in orientation and substance. Second, they promote loyalty to the individual and the specific group above support for the system as such. Third, these economic devices are not inherently productive: They are predicated mostly on diverting existing resources rather than on augmenting supplies. Thus, the result of these responses has been generally to accentuate existing social cleavages and, in more extreme cases, to bolster the propensity of strong urban groups to prey on the countryside and to deplete its resources.

The highly politicized character of the food-availability issues has therefore fueled divisive political responses. Unequal access to food supplies has necessarily focused attention on who holds power as well as on how state power is used. Political agitation against food maldistribution consequently has centered on the social identities of officeholders. No longer content with demanding policy alterations, those protesting problems of food access have come out squarely against the existing leadership. The inequity of food distribution in many parts of Africa has raised the question of accountability to the forefront of the political agenda;[43] hence the "counterrevolutionary" imperative of both Plan and Agenda.

This concern has found multiple expressions. At the most basic level, it has involved a growing awareness of the extensiveness of government institutions in daily life.[44] This realization has usually been the precursor of more direct political action. In its initial stage, such action has taken the form of an unwillingness to cooperate with the government. In Mali, the black market in grain was directly responsible for the popular reluctance to support the government-supported Democratic Union of the Mali People.[45] In Ethiopia, irate Tigre militants kidnapped aid relief workers in April 1983. In other parts of the continent, participation rates dropped precipitously as more evidence of official malfeasance was uncovered.[46] Lack of cooperation sometimes, at a second stage, erupted into strikes and demonstrations aimed directly at changing the leaders responsible for inadequate food supplies. Protests of this sort were commonplace in Kenya and Zaire, in Ghana and Sierra Leone, in Uganda and Zambia.

At the third stage, dissatisfaction with those purportedly in charge of government actions led to attempted military takeovers. A rash of coup efforts (not always successful) was recorded throughout Africa at the beginning of the 1980s. In the last six months of 1983 alone, aborted coups were documented in Tanzania, Uganda, Ghana, Niger, and possibly also in Angola and Zimbabwe. And in Burkina Faso these pressures finally culminated in the radical putsch of August 1983. There appears, therefore, to be a close connection between recent military interventions and dissatisfaction with food accumulation and distribution patterns.[47]

Food entitlement questions have raised political consciousness and consequently evoked more generalized discontent. The pattern of political conflict in these circumstances has taken on distinctly communal characteristics. Specific groups—be they ethnic collectivities, occupational associations, religious organizations, or geographic communities—have undergone a process of politicization. The struggle for access to power and its concomitant control of allocations accentuated the differential interests of various social agglomerations. Previously fluid patterns of association and identification ossified under the growing pressure of instrumental concerns. The occupants of the state nexus became the object of distaste and distrust. Communal politics in this context sometimes possess a negative quality: Annoyance with officeholders outweighs a quest for more constructive alternatives. The thrust of political protest tends to center on the actions of a privileged few and a demand for supervision of their behavior. But the purpose of this quest for control over decision makers is not unidirectional. Some relatively well organized groups near the power apparatus may wish to supplant existing ruling coalitions in order to use the fruits of office for their own purposes. Many coups constitute attempts of this order. On the other hand, a long period of inequitable distribution may foment a more generalized disgust with all state-linked activities. Under these conditions, sentiment against the establishment in its entirety, regardless of political hue, becomes commonplace. Alienation is the breeding ground for populism and fatalism, for indifference and revolt. Its common feature is noncompliance, and it may, in the long run, augur a more fundamental and constructive reconsideration of power relations.

The threat posed by the responses—both political and economic—to inadequate food distribution is not only greater in scope than that presented by reactions to high food prices, it is also much more difficult to control. As the clash of interests became more pronounced, so too did the contradictions facing those in power. If they made moves to redress maldistribution, they incurred the risk of losing their own sources of support. If they continued to support the needs of their own cohorts, they further exacerbated existing divisions and circumscribed their administrative capacities. This dilemma is not new. But it is underlined when food resources, in any event scarce, are unevenly distributed: Class antagonisms intensify.

Under these conditions, official techniques to counteract noncooperation have veered toward the repressive. In Sudan, the response to President Numeiry's growing unpopularity was a palpable increase in coercion later met by a coup in 1985.[48] Ghanaian leaders during the past decade, despite the many differences between them, all resorted to authoritarian devices to stem the tide of disaffection. This has been true of the populist Jerry Rawlings regime, until the mid-1980s especially. In Kenya, a clampdown on the opposition accompanied the growing tide of popular dissatisfaction. In Zaire, Guinea, Angola, the Central African Republic, Uganda, and many other states, political detention became an unsavory substitute for constructive reallocations.[49]

Some governments favored more sophisticated strategies to deal with growing unrest. These have involved campaigns against traders and black-marketeers, the creation of investigative commissions to uproot corruption in the civil service, the closure of borders to curtail smuggling, and even the total takeover of distribution mechanisms in an effort to ensure the dispersion of minimal supplies.[50] In most instances, however, these measures were insufficient to overcome growing alienation and have generally been replaced by a greater openness toward market mechanisms.

Formal reaction to demands for greater accountability faltered on economic as well as on political grounds. Many governments have attempted decentralization and local self-reliance as a means of increasing food supplies.[51] But these schemes, in situations in which political commitment to leaders was at best equivocal, frequently dissipated, as they could not build on the perception of a common destiny[52]—the food crisis necessitated going beyond nationalism. The politics of food supplies may therefore require more fundamental structural revisions if the validity of existing organizations is to be reinforced.

At root, inadequate food supplies make the elimination of hunger difficult. Massive injections of food supplies are required to overcome shortages. As most African states were confronted with a situation of growing food scarcities, the prospect of obtaining the quantity of food needed to eliminate existing inequities and at the same time eradicate loci of hunger was extremely remote. Under these conditions, market mechanisms don't always work; or, alternatively, they work all too well, to the discomfort, even demise, of the poor. Thus, the poor become more marginalized and more politicized.[53] Without instituting broadly based changes in the structure of political relations, the dichotomous processes set in motion by uneven access to food resources may become even more pronounced in the coming years.

The Politics of Food Scarcities

The most fundamental and debilitating food problem in Africa has been that of increasing absolute shortages. Food production has barely kept up with previous levels, yet population growth is expanding at a most worrisome pace (see Tables 1.1 and 1.6). In most areas, supplies simply have not been able to meet existing needs. In places where agricultural output dropped, there has not been enough to feed those who in the past could eke a living out of the land. Undernourishment, malnutrition, rural impoverishment, and starvation have spread throughout the continent. By 1984, the enormity of this trend could no longer be ignored.[54]

Food scarcity is the final stage in the long process of agricultural neglect, mismanagement, and disinterest. All the factors involved in the creation of food-pricing and food distribution problems—including the preference for cash-cropping, plantation agriculture, urban growth, industrialization, and Western life-styles—may be found in abundance in the growing absence of food supplies. These difficulties have been compounded by astounding demographic increases, shifts in rural settlement patterns, rising urbanization, and misplaced development priorities. The roots of rural impoverishment may be attributed also to ignorance, to an inability to make use of technological advance, to meager agricultural inputs, and to poor training and extension services. These lacunae, when accompanied by natural disasters (and especially the widespread drought of 1984–1985), civil strife, and inadequate central guidance, have resulted in declining production rates (see Table 1.7) and virtually complete poverty.[55]

Food constraints deplete human energy, reduce motivation and initiative, limit production, and circumscribe prospects for amelioration. They radiate a ripple effect that further intensifies unequal access to food and causes the prices of the little that can be purchased to skyrocket; there is an exponential impact of malnutrition and marginalization. In short, the absolute lack of food both lies at the source of underdevelopment and constitutes its most debilitating outcome.[56]

The existential origins of food scarcities, though they affect everyone, lie undeniably in the rural areas. All too many African countries have, since independence, undergone a common cycle, which commenced with urban shortages and rural abundance, progressed to urban scarcity and rural maldistribution, and finally peaked with widespread urban and rural poverty. Lack of production means that absences proliferate and that food crises are transmuted into a collapse of the most fundamental of productive enterprises. When the rural areas are affected, the catastrophe that ensues is well-nigh immeasurable.

The food scarcity problem impinges, albeit unequally, on all sectors of society and on all social classes. Spatial and generational differences become more pronounced. Class divisions are highlighted. Ethnic, communal, and religious cleavages are highlighted. And gender inequities surface with greater intensity. Hunger fuels widespread social disarray and therefore provokes heterogeneous, often contradictory, reactions.

The economic responses to the shortage of food in the mid-1980s, therefore, centered on devising multiple means of sheer survival. Four facets of this quest for survival have become manifest. The first, originating among progressively impoverished urban groupings, is a renewed interest in agriculture and the land. In countries where food scarcity in the cities was acute, those who could afford to do so began to return to the countryside. In Ghana, for example, professionals, officials, and well-to-do businessmen purchased large tracts of land and commenced previously shunned farming activities. A new type of rice cultivator, poultry farmer, and cattle breeder has sprung up, shunting aside peasant producers and adversely affecting the labor market.[57] This middle-class system of disengagement from state sources of food supply is not unique to Ghana. It has been documented in Kenya, Zambia, Tanzania, Togo, Côte d'Ivoire, Senegal, Uganda, and Ethiopia.[58] In all instances, the revival of food cropping is viewed as a way of establishing independent, direct means of obtaining essential food commodities.

A second, and allied, method of survival is rural in derivation and implementation. Entire communities attempted to withdraw, independently, from the state nexus into a conscious form of economic self-encapsulation. "The original motivation for most types of self-development is a strongly felt deprivation, both materially (non-satisfaction of basic needs) and psychologically (alienation from a dominant society dependence on others)."[59] Local self-reliance was facilitated by the preservation of strong community ties, by the persistence of a philosophy of group solidarity defined in situational terms, by a perceived threat to survival, and perhaps by the emergence of an articulate leadership.[60] Instances of constructive disengagement from formal development schemes permeated rural Africa. In Ethiopia, herders began to grow their own food, as among the Afars, and altered their consumption habits substantially.[61] Villages in Cameroon sought out and developed their own sources of water when government supports failed. In Niger, peasants devised rattraps to protect their crops and subsequently increased yields.[62] Harambee villages in Kenya achieved some autonomy from government constraints. In Uganda, farmers returned to subsistence agriculture with renewed energy. Rural self-help schemes, autonomous of government control, flourished in the Casamance in Senegal, in remote areas of Zaire, in Ghana, and in Mozambique. "Today millions of people in the Third World have turned their back on official development strategies and are trying to improve their living conditions through their own efforts"[63]—a novel, non-Friedman, non-monetarist, definition of laissez-faire, which indicates renewed initiative, but hardly a full exercise of the exit option.

The process of productive withdrawal from the formal and nonformal markets was predicated on a growing need to produce in order to survive. Self-encapsulation therefore entailed a return to noncapitalist modes of production and a resurgence of traditional crafts and trades.[64] By developing a protective shield against outside intrusions, local communities attempted to guard against the ill effects of overexposure and overvulnerability to broader economic currents. Such efforts were most successful where local cohesiveness has been maintained, where natural resources are available, and where government intrusions have been minimized. In these cases, the constructive elements of self-reliance paved the way, with the injection of new skills and management techniques by returnees, for the possibility of overcoming acute food shortages.

But not all self-reliance efforts, however ingeniously pursued, were successful. In areas overrun by wars and pestilence or stricken by drought and natural disasters, shifts in local production did not constitute a viable option for the rural hungry. Undernourishment saps work capacity, and careful cultivation all too frequently results in meager yields. For a growing number of rural dwellers, withdrawal did not provide an answer to impoverishment. In these instances a third response surfaced: migration. Population movements occurred when local possibilities had been exhausted and no real prospects for minimal sustenance could be expected from remaining in place. The refugee problem in Africa has reached alarming proportions in the 1980s, with estimates of the number of refugees ranging between 5 and 10 percent of the entire population of the continent. The wandering hungry have gravitated to potential food distribution centers in neighboring countries, inevitably increasing pressures—already close to intolerable—on governments. The problem has been most severe, perhaps, in the Horn of Africa. Many of the "homelands" in South Africa fast became overpopulated refugee camps. And in West Africa and the Uganda-Zaire-Rwanda-Sudan area the flow of migrants has increased steadily.

Migration to avert starvation can attenuate hunger when the target of migration has the capacity to absorb and gainfully employ the newcomers.

Unfortunately, this has not always been the case. When relief efforts are insufficient or falter, a fourth response mechanism comes into play: helplessness and total dependence. Such revelations of utter despair, where famine reigns and survival is open to question, have become all too familiar.[65] In these situations, people are unable to help themselves. Having tried every possibility to no avail, they can do no more than put themselves at the mercy of others, the ultimate attempt to avoid the Malthusian "solution" of starvation.

These four major economic responses to the specter of starvation differ widely. Common to all, however, is the concerted search for alternatives to existing patterns of production and exchange. The changes induced by the need to cope with real scarcity are, by their very nature, radical. They evoke drastic shifts not only in priorities, but also in the organization of social life and in the structure of production. These attempted coping mechanisms possess nonstate qualities: They are not geared to counteract existing policies or to bypass the state. They tend to center exclusively on people and hence ignore political decisions and institutions. But because they also involve a quest from some assistance elsewhere, they tend to reinforce the need—and hence the notion—of central political organization.

The political ramifications of these processes therefore contain extremely heterogeneous elements. In some areas, where new groups have intruded into rural communities, political conflict at the local level has been on the rise. Class conflict in the villages has proliferated, displayed in such diverse ways as robbery or planned crop-burning.[66] Populism and antiestablishment trends, once confined to urban settings, have permeated the countryside. Elaborate patron-client relationships may, in these conditions, atrophy, and new possibilities of structural readjustment may emerge around techniques of individual and collective self-help.[67]

In areas where local survival efforts have been carried out on a communal basis, self-encapsulation has resulted in the reinvigoration and expansion of traditional institutions. Instrumental politics, revolving around local concerns, have thrived, often to the detriment of national considerations and alliances. The thrust of these activities has been twofold: to reinforce political cohesion around local authority figures and to detach local structures from interference by the state. In these cases, economic self-reliance has thus been followed by political involution as well.[68] Where this pattern of political response was commonplace, it was generally also accompanied by increased pressure on the already fragile state establishment. The unwillingness of local collectivities to entertain intrusions from above did not mean that demands for amenities ceased. On the contrary, in many of the communities that achieved some measure of self-reliance, requests for assistance actually escalated. This pattern has been documented in the case of the Harambee villages in Kenya and also in remote parts of Ghana.[69]

The resumption of the centrality of agriculture therefore frequently had the political effect of increasing expectations from the central government while simultaneously limiting its penetrative or implementative capacity. The contradictions inherent in this trend became particularly acute where refugee populations, unable to feed themselves yet not easily subject to state dictates, congregated. In these countries, both the demands on the state apparatus and the constraints on its operational capabilities escalated to new heights. These tensions were even further exacerbated in those cases in which survival techniques failed completely and entire groupings were helpless in the face of growing hunger.

The diverse political responses to the problem of food scarcity call into question the foundations of state power. The issue is no longer how power is utilized or who controls the state, but the validity of state power itself.[70] Food shortages provoked distinctly nonapathetic reactions that raise questions about the integrity of state networks in portions of the continent. The pattern of political conflict became more diffuse, multidirectional, and mass-oriented. By tugging on the system from many different angles, these responses necessarily altered patterns of identification and association and thereby rendered many official efforts less significant. "Scarcity thus underlines and exacerbates the main problems of governality in Middle Africa, namely social incoherence, overdeveloped state structures, insufficient state legitimacy, and inadequate state coercive power."[71]

In these circumstances, the options open to officeholders were very sparse indeed. Many governments, confronted with very real food shortages, have tried to institute stopgap measures such as immigration controls, expulsion of illegal aliens, and border closures.[72] Although these techniques may have had the effect of stemming the tide of migratory pressures, they have not provided solutions to the problems of internal food scarcity and disengagement. In order to deal with these manifestations of food politics, it has become necessary to come to terms with basic power concepts. Scarcely an administration in Africa today can properly afford to ignore the issue of rural poverty. And the tendency is, increasingly, to decentralize as a means of fomenting self-help schemes. Less government as a way of contending with movement away from the state is at times implemented because no other choices are available. Some governments encourage self-reliance up to a point, so long as it does not carry political implications. In other cases, benign support is extended, and in still other instances self-reliance (from above) has been adopted as a slogan for central development efforts.[73] Depending on the degree of acquiescence to existing coping strategies, government activities have ranged from active encouragement and emphasis on strengthening linkage arrangements to passive acquiescence to ongoing self-encapsulation measures: the dialectics of "laissez-faire" and "self-reliance."

The attractiveness of minimizing government involvement, advocated by many observers,[74] is not always as self-evident as it might appear on the surface. Prolonged inaction by the state in the name of self-reliance may increase the risk of even further reducing the importance and hence the effectiveness of the state mechanism. This device, moreover, even when carried out constructively, is effective only when local survival mechanisms do appear to alleviate acute food scarcities. When they do not, despite efforts to sustain food agriculture, governments may be compelled to intervene more directly. Some regimes have forwarded national self-reliance as a panacea in these situations.

But, although "local self-reliance can more or less function without governments, national self-reliance is an empty word when it is not rooted in local communities."[75] Inexorably, chronic food shortages have heightened external dependence and made hungry African states into supplicants for international handouts (see Table 1.8).

The threat posed by persistent food scarcities, if not handled expeditiously, is thus a prescription for real political impotence. When states are on the verge of total breakdown—an extreme condition that began to appear on the African stage—amelioration is a most lengthy process.[76] The chronic absence of food, left unattended, has set in motion processes that defy the limits of conventional political analysis. Hunger, starvation, and acute deprivation lead to loss of control and could, it is not too far-fetched to suggest, alter the bases of the existing international as well as national systems. The reversal of these trends has become a vital precondition for human well-being and global order.

The Cycle of Food Response and Reaction

The political economy of food in Africa progressed in three ever-widening waves. Food price issues, left unresolved, escalated into problems of inadequate supplies and then to questions of complete scarcities. The social groups affected expanded from the urban areas, gradually coming to encompass larger and larger portions of the population in the cities and in the countryside. Politically, therefore, the food crisis at first highlighted problems of policy, and then proceeded to raise more fundamental questions of accountability and governability. The linkage between these problems is far from haphazard: Failure to cope adequately with pricing issues impeded accumulation and distribution and then adversely affected production.

Because each specific problem evoked divergent economic and political responses, attempts to contend with one aspect of the political economy of food necessarily came into conflict with similar efforts to deal with other facets. Each African state, and especially those seriously affected by the food crisis, exhibited differing combinations of the various manifestations of response and reaction to the situation. Details of conditions in Ghana did not coincide with those in Zaire, which in turn diverged from conditions in Chad, Ethiopia, Lesotho, Uganda, Tanzania, Nigeria, or Niger. In each country, however, the constellation of historical, ecological, external, cultural, social, natural, and political factors at work came together to create a specific, complex, and distinctive type of food insecurity that yielded distinct political results.[77] It is this differentiated nature of poverty, and hence of political conflict, that supplies the framework for a more refined approach to policy reformulation and implementation.

• THE IMPLICATIONS OF FOOD POLITICS •

The political economy of food in African generates a subtle, complex, and multifaceted dynamic that commences with political causes, evokes political responses, and brings about a variety of political ramifications. "In something of a dialectical process, scarcity undermines institutional effectiveness, which in turn worsens the constraints of scarcity."[78] It is impossible to divorce hunger from politics or to avoid coming to terms with the political roots of scarcity on the continent. "Unless means can be found to resolve the paradox of power, to resolve the problems of national administrative structure . . . neither integrated rural development nor any other policy of rural reform will have much impact on economic conditions in the developing world."[79]

The direction of change implied by these processes varies: Certain states are being fortified, whereas others are being undermined; the capacity of some states has deteriorated rapidly, as others have expanded their grasp. Though the imperative of change is inescapable in all these situations, the possibilities that are presented follow many different courses.[80] Some of these options are illuminated by the particular patterns of food politics that have evolved in Africa in the 1980s.

The politics of food prices highlights the problem of appropriate policies. There is hardly a voice in Africa today that does not advocate greater concentration on rural and agrarian matters. But advances in these areas require increased participation in decision making, greater attention to producer needs, more efficient implementation, and a careful reassessment of contact with external sources of food items.[81] Hence the commonality between the Lagos Plan and Agenda for Action, as expressed in APPER. However, recognition of the centrality of agriculture does not lead to homogeneous prescriptions: Plan and Agenda advocate agricultural production for food and commodities and for internal consumption and external markets, respectively. The tension between basic human needs—"self-reliance"—and foreign exchange —"economic growth"—is profound. In this context, local organizations may play an increasingly important role. The alternative to a "willed future" embodied in the ECA's "normative scenario" (see Table 1.9) is ominous—a more unequal and attractive continent.

The politics of food supplies focuses interest on more fundamental structural rearrangements. Unless resources are more justly distributed and access to central goods reordered, antistate sentiments can whittle away any gains in the productive sector. The need for structural change extends beyond the boundaries of specific states: It is meaningless if it does not encompass continental and international institutions.[82] The basic reordering implied by problems of uneven distribution places emphasis on representation and public supervision as much as on participation. It therefore suggests an alteration of modes of control and of the bases of political action, a concern with good government.

The politics of food scarcity raises insufficiently addressed issues regarding the nature of the state in contemporary Africa. It highlights the paradox between the trend toward state collapse and the state's persistence, almost by default, nevertheless, because nonstate alternatives are found wanting. The diminution of government and the decentralization of decision making are clear by-products of growing problems of food production and other facets of the food crisis. And although the constructive aspects of this process cannot be belittled, the reduction of state intervention must be accompanied by a thorough rethinking of the role of the state in the economy and the society.[83] Such a drastic reconstruction has global ramifications as well: It may grant a greater role to nongovernment actors than has heretofore been entertained.[84] It is no longer possible to avoid the issue of governability at any level.

The three major manifestations of the political economy of food and the prescriptions they incorporate do not always interlock. There are inherent contradictions in dealing with all these issues simultaneously, and not every state must contend with their consequences together. Depending on the peculiarities evident in specific contexts, different trends are set in motion, and these will in all likelihood yield quantitatively distinct results, as the case studies in this book demonstrate. What unites these different processes is the fact that they all involve real alterations in the conceptualization, control, and uses of power. Without changes in the perception and operationalization of the power component in the African context, it is impossible to perceive of a concrete amelioration of material problems and their food concomitants.

Food insecurity in Africa developed in progressively deleterious stages that gradually enveloped growing numbers of people. Breaking the vicious cycle of hunger and scarcity means breaking the equally regressive cycle of political misdirection and impotence.[85] The two are inextricably linked. By highlighting their variable interactions and manifestations, it might be possible to make some meaningful steps toward attaining the most essential goal of providing adequate sustenance for survival and growth. As the Lagos Plan somewhat optimistically advocates in a spirit of economic Pan-Africanism: "The same determination that has virtually rid our continent of political domination is required for our economic liberation. Our success in exploiting our political unity should encourage us to exploit the strength inherent in our economic unity.... Africa's huge resources must be applied principally to meet the needs and purposes of its people."[86] The willingness, albeit belated and reluctant, displayed by Africa's ruling class to even contemplate such radical reformism is one indication of the political crisis brought about by agricultural decline.

TABLE 1.1 Growth of Population and Agricultural Production

	Average annual growth of population (percent)		Average annual growth rate of volume of production (percent) 1969-71 to 1977-79			Average annual growth rate of total production per capita (percent) 1969-71 to 1977-79		
	1960-1970	1970-1979	Food	Nonfood	Total	Food	Nonfood	Total
Low-income countries	2.4 w^a	2.6 w			0.9 w			-1.7 w
Low-income semiarid	2.3 w	2.3 w			1.1 w			-1.2 w
1. Chad	1.8	2.0	1.0	2.0	1.1	-1.0	0.0	-0.9
2. Somalia	2.4	2.3	0.6	-0.8	0.6	-1.7	-3.1	-1.7
3. Mali	2.4	2.6	1.0	9.8	1.4	-1.6	7.2	-1.2
4. Burkina Faso	1.6	1.6	2.0	7.2	2.1	0.4	5.6	0.5
5. Gambia^b	3.2	3.0	0.1	-	0.1	-2.9	-	-2.9
6. Niger	3.3	2.8	1.3	-7.8	1.3	-1.5	-10.6	-1.5
7. Mauritania	2.5	2.7	-1.3	-	-1.3	-4.0	-	-4.0
Low-income other	2.4 w	2.6 w			0.8 w			-1.8 w
8. Ethiopia	2.4	2.1	0.4	1.3	0.4	-1.7	-0.8	-1.7
9. Guinea-Bissau^b	2.6	1.6	1.4	0.0	1.4	-0.2	-1.6	-0.2
10. Burundi	1.6	2.0	2.7	1.8	2.6	0.7	-0.2	0.6
11. Malawi	2.8	2.8	3.1	8.6	4.0	0.3	5.8	1.2
12. Rwanda	2.8	2.8	3.9	4.7	3.9	1.1	1.9	1.1
13. Benin	2.6	2.9	2.5	-5.2	2.3	-0.4	-8.1	-0.6
14. Mozambique	2.2	2.5	-0.6	-4.7	-1.0	-3.1	-7.2	-3.5
15. Sierra Leone	2.2	2.5	1.4	4.9	1.7	-1.1	2.4	-0.8
16. Tanzania	2.7	3.4	1.9	-0.5	1.4	-1.5	-3.9	-2.0
17. Zaire	2.0	2.7	1.3	-0.6	1.2	-1.4	-3.3	-1.5
18. Guinea	2.8	2.9	0.5	-11.7	0.2	-2.4	-14.6	-2.7
19. Central African Republic	2.2	2.2	2.4	1.5	2.2	0.2	-0.7	0.0
20. Madagascar	2.1	2.5	1.8	0.7	1.7	-0.7	-1.8	-0.8
21. Uganda	3.7	3.0	1.7	-8.3	-0.5	-1.3	-11.3	-3.5
22. Lesotho	2.0	2.3	2.4	-7.0	1.4	0.1	-9.3	-0.9
23. Togo	2.7	2.4	-0.2	-4.2	-0.4	-2.6	-6.6	-2.8
24. Sudan	2.2	2.6	3.1	-3.9	1.8	0.5	-6.5	-0.8

	2.8 w	3.2 w			2.2 w			-1.1 w
Middle-income oil importers	**2.8 w**	**3.2 w**			**2.2 w**			**-1.1 w**
25. Kenya	3.2	3.4	2.9	7.5	4.0	-0.5	4.1	0.6
26. Ghana	2.4	3.0	-0.1	-4.5	-0.1	-3.1	-7.5	-3.1
27. Senegal	2.4	2.6	1.0	11.3	1.1	-1.6	8.7	-1.5
28. Zimbabwe	3.9	3.3	2.6	3.8	2.9	-0.7	0.5	-0.4
29. Liberia	3.1	3.3	3.5	0.2	2.7	0.2	-3.1	-0.6
30. Zambia	2.8	3.0	3.0	-0.9	2.8	0.0	-3.9	-0.2
31. Cameroon	1.8	2.2	3.3	1.8	3.1	1.1	-0.4	0.9
32. Swaziland[b]	2.2	2.6	3.7	14.6	4.6	1.2	12.1	2.1
33. Botswana[b]	1.9	2.2	1.1	2.0	1.1	-1.1	-0.2	-1.1
34. Mauritius[b]	2.2	1.4	1.9	3.9	1.9	0.6	2.6	0.6
35. Ivory Coast	3.7	5.5	4.6	1.8	3.8	-0.9	-3.7	-1.7
Middle-income oil exporters	**2.4 w**	**2.5 w**			**1.1 w**			**-1.4 w**
36. Angola	1.5	2.3	0.2	-13.3	-3.3	-2.1	-15.6	-5.6
37. Congo	2.1	2.5	-0.1	1.9	-0.1	-2.6	-0.6	-2.6
38. Nigeria	2.5	2.5	1.7	-1.3	1.7	-0.8	-3.8	-0.8
39. Gabon	0.4	1.2	0.1	-13.3	0.1	-1.1	-14.5	-1.1
Sub-Saharan Africa	**2.5w**	**2.7 w**			**1.3 w**			**-1.4 w**

[a]w = mean
[b]From World Bank file data

Source: World Bank, *Accelerated Development in Sub-Saharan Africa: An Agenda for Action* (Washington, D.C.: IBRD, 1981), pp. 167 and 176.

TABLE 1.2 Growth Rates of Agricultural Production, 1969–71 to 1977–79
(average annual growth rate in volume as a percentage)

4+	3–4	2–3	1–2	0–1	<0
Kenya	Cameroon	Benin	Botswana	Ethiopia	Angola
Malawi	Ivory Coast	Burundi	Chad	Gabon	Congo
Swaziland	Rwanda	Central African	Guinea-Bissau	Gambia	Ghana
		Republic	Lesotho	Guinea	Mauritania
		Liberia	Madagascar	Somalia	Mozambique
		Burkina Faso	Mali		Togo
		Zambia	Mauritius		Uganda
		Zimbabwe	Niger		
			Nigeria		
			Senegal		
			Sierra Leone		
			Sudan		
			Tanzania		
			Zaire		

Sources: FAO *Production Yearbook* tapes and World Bank, *Accelerated Development in Sub-Saharan Africa: An Agenda for Action* (Washington, D.C.: IBRD, 1981), p. 50.

TABLE 1.3 Growth of Production of Selected Food Crops
(in volume)

	Annual growth rate (percent)					
	Sub-Saharan Africa		Oil-exporting countries		Oil-importing countries	
Crop	1961–63 to 1969–71	1969–71 to 1977–79	1961–63 to 1969–71	1969–71 to 1977–79	1961–63 to 1969–71	1969–71 to 1977–79
Cereals						
Rice (paddy)	4.0	2.9	6.3	10.7	3.8	2.2
Wheat	3.8	–0.2	–1.2	–0.6	4.0	–0.2
Maize	5.2	1.3	5.1	0.9	5.2	1.4
Millet/sorghum	0.9	1.0	0.2	0.7	1.3	1.2
Roots and tubers	2.0	1.8	2.3	1.6	1.8	1.9
Pulses	3.3	1.1	5.2	0.0	2.8	1.4
Groundnuts	0.7	–0.9	–1.2	–14.0	1.7	2.7
Palm oil	1.7	2.2	0.1	2.7	3.7	1.6

Sources: FAO *Production Yearbook* tapes and World Bank, *Accelerated Development in Sub-Saharan Africa: An Agenda for Action* (Washington, D.C.: IBRD, 1981), p. 47.

TABLE 1.4 Growth of Imports of Selected Agricultural Commodities, 1961–63 to 1977–79 (in volume)

| | Annual growth rate (percent) | | | | | |
| | Low- and middle-income countries | | Oil-exporting countries | | Sub-Saharan Africa | |
Commodity	1961–63 to 1969–71	1969–71 to 1977–79	1961–63 to 1969–71	1969–71 to 1977–79	1961–63 to 1969–71	1969–71 to 1977–79
Cereals	7.4	6.8	21.5	18.2	9.0	9.5
Wheat	9.3	9.2	26.8	13.3	12.9	10.7
Rice	4.9	7.3	3.7	68.0	4.9	12.1
Maize	8.5	2.6	–	47.3	8.7	5.7
Dairy products	9.8	5.4	--	17.0	7.2	7.2
Sugar	2.1	–0.1	6.0	23.4	2.5	5.8
Meat	1.1	5.4	2.3	33.1	1.3	13.3
Animal and vegetable oils	11.6	5.4	9.1	70.3	11.5	13.0

Sources: FAO *TradeYearbook* tapes and World Bank, *Accelerated Development in Sub-Saharan Africa: An Agenda for Action* (Washington, D.C.: IBRD, 1981), p. 48.

TABLE 1.5 Growth of Agricultural Exports

| | Annual growth rate (percent) | | | | | |
| | Sub-Saharan Africa | | Oil-exporting countries | | Oil-importing countries | |
Export	1961–63 to 1969–71	1969–71 to 1977–79	1961–63 to 1969–71	1969–71 to 1977–79	1961–63 to 1969–71	1969–71 to 1977–79
Thirty main agricultural exports						
Volume	1.9	–1.9	–0.7	–8.6	2.6	–0.7
Unit value	2.3	16.2	3.1	16.8	2.1	16.1
Value	4.3	14.0	2.3	6.8	4.8	15.3
Value of other agricultural exports	4.6	8.9	33.4	–1.6	3.4	9.8

Sources: FAO *TradeYearbook* tapes and World Bank, *Accelerated Development in Sub-Saharan Africa: An Agenda for Action* (Washington, D.C.: IBRD, 1981), p. 46.

TABLE 1.6 Production of Major Crops

	Average annual volume of production				
				Rate of growth (percent)	
				1961–63 to	1969–71 to
	Thousands of metric tons				
Crop	1961–63	1969–71	1977–79	1969–71	1977–79
Cereals:					
Maize					
Sub-Saharan Africa	8,105	12,132	13,438	5.2	1.3
Oil exporters	1,136	1,691	1,814	5.1	0.9
Other countries	6,969	10,441	11,624	5.2	1.4
Millet					
Sub-Saharan Africa	8,083	8,875	9,178	1.2	0.4
Oil exporters	2,689	2,870	3,083	0.8	0.9
Other countries	5,394	6,005	6,095	1.4	0.2
Rice (paddy)					
Sub-Saharan Africa	3,473	4,735	5,936	4.0	2.9
Oil exporters	232	380	856	6.4	10.7
Other countries	3,241	4,355	5,080	3.8	1.9
Sorghum					
Sub-Saharan Africa	8,203	8,591	9,768	0.6	1.6
Oil exporters	3,700	3,632	3,768	–0.2	0.5
Other countries	4,503	4,959	6,000	1.2	2.4
Wheat					
Sub-Saharan Africa	923	1,243	1,220	3.8	–0.2
Oil exporters	36	33	31	–1.1	–0.8
Other countries	887	1,210	1,189	4.0	–0.2
Total Cereals					
Sub-Saharan Africa	31,518	37,701	41,669	2.3	1.3
Oil exporters	7,828	8,648	9,609	1.3	1.3
Other countries	23,690	29,053	32,060	2.6	1.2
Oils and Oilseeds:					
Coconuts					
Sub-Saharan Africa	1,350	1,451	1,563	0.9	0.9
Oil exporters	75	86	90	1.7	0.6
Other countries	1,275	1,365	1,473	0.9	1.0
Groundnuts (in shell)					
Sub-Saharan Africa	4,922	5,194	4,826	0.7	–0.9
Oil exporters	1,864	1,699	503	–1.2	–14.1
Other countries	3,058	3,495	4,323	1.7	2.7
Palm kernels					
Sub-Saharan Africa	806	711	664	–1.6	–0.9
Oil exporters	439	306	310	–4.4	0.2
Other countries	367	405	354	1.2	–1.7
Palm oil					
Sub-Saharan Africa	970	1,112	1,321	1.7	2.2
Oil exporters	573	579	718	0.1	2.7
Other countries	397	533	603	3.8	1.6

TABLE 1.6 (continued)

	Average annual volume of production				
				Rate of growth (percent)	
				1961–63 to	1969–71 to
	Thousands of metric tons				
Crop	1961–63	1969–71	1977–79	1969–71	1977–79
Other:					
Pulses					
Sub-Saharan Africa	2,973	3,861	4,207	3.3	1.1
Oil exporters	616	925	923	5.2	0.0
Other countries	2,357	2,936	3,284	2.8	1.4
Roots and Tubers					
Sub-Saharan Africa	57,042	66,694	77,026	2.0	1.8
Oil exporters	23,162	27,674	31,488	2.2	1.6
Other countries	33,880	39,020	45,538	1.8	1.9
Seed Cotton					
Sub-Saharan Africa	1,315	2,279	1,867	7.1	-2.5
Oil exporters	136	268	195	8.8	-3.9
Other countries	1,179	2,011	1,672	6.9	-2.3
Sugar					
Sub-Saharan Africa	1,415	2,303	2,806	6.3	2.5
Oil exporters	88	179	109	9.3	-6.0
Other countries	1,327	2,124	2,697	6.1	3.0

Source: World Bank, *Accelerated Development in Sub-Saharan Africa: An Agenda for Action* (Washington, D.C.: IBRD, 1981), p. 168.

TABLE 1.7 Yields of Major Crops

Crop	Average annual kilograms per hectare			Index of yields (1961–63 = 100)		Index of relative yields (world = 100)		
	1961–63	1969–71	1977–79	1969–71	1977–79	1961–63	1969–71	1977–79
Beverages:								
Cocoa								
World	273	330	329	121	121	100	100	100
Developing countries	273	330	328	121	120	100	100	100
Sub-Saharan Africa	257	319	278	124	108	94	97	84
Coffee								
World	442	476	497	108	112	100	100	100
Developing countries	440	475	496	108	113	100	100	100
Sub-Saharan Africa	367	410	355	112	97	83	86	71
Tea								
World	863	827	881	96	102	100	100	100
Developing countries	868	1,006	1,236	116	142	101	122	140
Sub-Saharan Africa	781	1,153	1,245	148	159	90	139	141
Cereals:								
Maize								
World	2,140	2,558	3,090	120	144	100	100	100
Developing countries	1,197	1,376	1,509	115	126	56	54	49
Sub-Saharan Africa	893	1,020	977	114	109	42	40	32
Millet								
World	561	617	636	110	113	100	100	100
Developing countries	527	575	568	109	108	94	93	89
Sub-Saharan Africa	600	586	561	98	94	107	95	88
Rice								
World	2,026	2,320	2,612	115	129	100	100	100
Developing countries	1,628	1,846	2,101	113	129	80	80	80
Sub-Saharan Africa	1,249	1,349	1,419	108	114	62	58	54
Sorghum								
World	912	1,103	1,320	121	145	100	100	100
Developing countries	638	734	965	115	151	70	67	73
Sub-Saharan Africa	751	693	701	92	93	82	63	53

Wheat								
World	1,179	1,524	1,784	129	151	100	100	100
Developing countries	998	1,193	1,443	120	145	85	78	81
Sub-Saharan Africa	785	1,255	1,084	160	138	67	82	61
Oils and Oilseeds:								
Groundnuts (in shell)								
World	874	926	979	106	112	100	100	100
Developing countries	822	840	882	102	107	94	91	90
Sub-Saharan Africa	832	776	797	93	96	95	84	81
Other:								
Pulses								
World	615	694	704	113	114	100	100	100
Developing countries	520	531	524	102	101	85	77	74
Sub-Saharan Africa	439	381	393	87	90	71	55	56
Roots and Tubers[a]								
World	10	11	11	110	110	100	100	100
Developing countries	7	9	9	129	129	70	82	82
Sub-Saharan Africa	6	7	7	117	117	60	64	64
Seed Cotton								
World	923	1,067	1,214	116	132	100	100	100
Developing countries	665	790	842	119	127	72	74	69
Sub-Saharan Africa	425	565	528	133	124	46	53	43
Sugar Cane[a]								
World	49	54	56	110	114	100	100	100
Developing countries	47	51	54	109	115	96	94	96
Sub-Saharan Africa	49	58	59	118	120	100	107	105
Tobacco								
World	1,117	1,138	1,256	102	112	100	100	100
Developing countries	817	835	984	102	120	73	73	78
Sub-Saharan Africa	767	732	828	95	108	69	64	66

[a]Metric tons per hectare
Source: World Bank, *Accelerated Development in Sub-Saharan Africa: An Agenda for Action* (Washington, D.C.: IBRD, 1981), p. 169.

TABLE 1.8 Agricultural Imports

Commodity	Volume			Average annual growth rate (percent)		Value (millions of dollars)		
	Thousands of metric tons			1961–63 to 1969–71	1969–71 to 1977–79	1961–63	1969–71	1977–79
	1961–63	1969–71	1977–79					
Rice								
Sub-Saharan Africa	464	680	1,696	4.9	12.1	63	91	619
Oil exporters	6	8	511	3.7	68.0	1	1	269
Other countries	458	672	1,185	4.9	7.3	62	90	350
Wheat								
Sub-Saharan Africa	394	1,043	2,352	12.9	10.7	30	81	473
Oil exporters	52	347	940	26.8	13.3	7	28	215
Other countries	342	696	1,412	9.3	9.2	23	53	258
Maize								
Sub-Saharan Africa	197	385	599	8.7	5.7	12	32	102
Oil exporters	()[a]	6	133	–	47.3	()[a]	1	26
Other countries	197	379	466	8.5	2.6	12	31	76
Cereals not elsewhere stated								
Sub-Saharan Africa	123	239	215	8.7	-1.3	9	21	40
Oil exporters	30	58	15	8.6	-15.6	2	6	3
Other ciuntries	93	181	200	8.7	1.3	7	15	37
Cereals, total								
Sub-Saharan Africa	1,177	2,346	4,862	9.0	9.5	114	225	1,234
Oil exporters	88	419	1,599	21.5	18.2	10	36	513
Other countries	1,089	1,927	3,263	7.4	6.8	104	189	721
Dairy products								
Sub-Saharan Africa	–	–	–	7.2	7.0	44	109	457
Oil exporters	–	–	–	–	17.0	13	27	201
Other countries	–	–	–	9.8	5.4	31	82	256

Sugar								
Sub-Saharan Africa	670	816	1,281	2.5	5.8	84	109	429
Oil exporters	68	108	581	6.0	23.4	9	17	216
Other countries	602	708	700	2.1	-0.1	75	92	213
Meat								
Sub-Saharan Africa	38	42	114	1.3	13.3	20	24	176
Oil exporters	5	6	59	2.3	33.1	3	3	96
Other countries	33	36	55	1.1	5.4	17	21	80
Animal and vegetable oils								
Sub-Saharan Africa	51	122	325	11.5	13.0	12	32	204
Oil exporters	1	2	142	9.1	70.3	( )[a]	1	81
Other countries	50	120	183	11.6	5.4	12	31	123
Total agricultural imports[b]								
Sub-Saharan Africa	—	—	—	(4.3)[c]	(3.5)[c]	749	1,137	4,227
Oil exporters	—	—	—	(1.5)[c]	(16.0)[c]	151	207	1,663
Other countries	—	—	—	(5.1)[c]	(2.8)[c]	598	930	2,564

[a]( ) = less than half the unit shown
[b]Includes products not listed above
[c]Estimated from an average of price increases for the imports shown in the table and applied to the value of total agricultural imports

Source: World Bank, Accelerated Development in Sub-Saharan Africa: An Agenda for Action (Washington, D.C.: IBRD, 1981), p. 171.

TABLE 1.9 Africa's Food Balance Projected

| | Historical trends scenario | | Normative scenario | |
	1978–1980	2008	1978–1980	2008
Cereals				
(in millions of metric tons)				
Total demand	74.8	203.1	74.8	224.0
Food	59.9	159.0	59.9	170.9
Industry	0.2	1.6	0.2	1.8
Feed	5.3	17.9	5.3	24.2
Seed	2.6	4.3	2.6	4.9
Waste	6.8	20.3	6.8	22.2
Total domestic production	58.4	144.2	58.4	190.4
Imports	20.9	58.9	20.9	33.6
Roots, tubers and pulses				
(in millions of metric tons)				
Total demand	85.1	216.1	85.1	202.3
Food	64.6	164.7	64.6	152.1
Industry	0.1	0.4	0.1	0.6
Feed	1.8	5.6	1.8	7.1
Seed	4.8	9.7	4.8	9.5
Waste	13.8	35.7	13.8	33.0
Total domestic production	88.2	216.5	88.2	203.5
Meat				
(in millions of metric tons)				
Total demand	4.7	13.6	4.7	13.6
Beef	2.3	5.0	2.3	5.0
Mutton	1.0	3.7	1.0	3.7
Pork	0.2	0.8	0.2	0.8
Poultry	0.8	4.2	0.8	4.2
Total production	4.3	13.7	4.3	13.6
Self-sufficiency ratio (SSR)				
(in percentages)				
In cereals	75.	71.	75.	85.0
In roots, tubers, and pulses	100.	100.	100.	100.6
In meat	93.	100.	93.	100.0
Per capita food consumption levels				
(in kg)				
Cereals	142.1	147.8	142.1	171.0
Roots, tubers, and pulses	153.3	153.3	153.3	152.5
Meat	11.1	12.6	11.1	12.6

Source: Economic Commission for Africa, *ECA and Africa's Development, 1983–2008: A Preliminary Perspective Study* (Addis Ababa, 1983), ECA projections and FAO printouts, pp. 27–28 and 64–65.

· NOTES ·

Many thanks to Frank Holmquist for his careful comments on an earlier draft of this chapter.

1. "Editorial: People Are to Blame," *West Africa* October 31, 1983, p. 2491.
2. OAU, *Lagos Plan of Action for the Economic Development of Africa 1980–2000* (Geneva: International Institute for Labour Studies, 1981, for OAU), p. 7.
3. World Bank, *Accelerated Development in Sub-Saharan Africa: An Agenda for Action* (Washington, D.C.: IBRD, 1981), p.3 (also known as the Berg Report).
4. See Sara Berry, "The Food Crisis and Agrarian Change in Africa: A Review Essay," *African Studies Review* 27 (June 1984): 59–112. According to the estimates of the UN Food and Agriculture Organization (FAO), per capita food production fell by 11 percent during the 1970s. See "Drought Not Cause of African Famine," *Weekly Review*, August 5, 1982, pp. 24–25.
5. These explanations are highlighted in Michael F. Lofchie and Stephen K. Commins, "Food Deficits and Agriculture Policies in Tropical Africa," *Journal of Modern African Studies* 20, no. 1 (March 1982): 1–25.
6. Robert E. Clute, "The Role of Agriculture in African Development," *African Studies Review* 25, no. 4 (1982): 1–21.
7. *IDS Bulletin* 14, no. 1 (1983) contains a special issue on Food in Africa, which covers many of these topics.
8. For one example, see Thomas J. Sloan, "The Politics of Hunger," *Peace Research Review* 8, no. 6 (1981): 1–65.
9. Amartya Sen, "The Food Problem: Theory and Policy," *Third World Quarterly* 4, no. 3 (1982): 459. For a U.S. counterpart, see Physician Task Force on Hunger in America, *Hunger in America: The Growing Epidemic* (Middletown, Conn.: Wesleyan University Press, 1985).
10. For a recent scathing indictment of the political factor in food insecurity see "People Are to Blame," p. 2491. This point is made repeatedly, and perhaps most effectively, by Robert Bates, *Markets and States in Tropical Africa* (Berkeley and Los Angeles: University of California Press, 1981). Also see Nick Eberstadt, "Hunger and Ideology," *Commentary* 72, no. 1 (1981): 40–49, and "Beyond Politics: Hunger and Thirst in the Horn," *Horn of Africa* 4, no. 1 (1982): 4–61.
11. Raymond F. Hopkins and Donald J. Puchala, eds., Special Issue, *International Organization* 32, no. 3 (1978) deals extensively with the global political economy of food. See esp., Raymond F. Hopkins and Donald J. Puchala, "Perspectives on the International Relations of Food," pp. 581–616; and Robert L. Paarlberg, "Shifting and Sharing Adjustment Burdens: The Role of the Industrial Food Importing Nations," pp. 655–678.
12. For an overview, see Paul Streeten, "Food Prices as a Reflection of Political Power, *Ceres* 16, no. 2 (1983): 16–22.
13. Sen, "The Food Problem," esp. p. 459. Also see Carl K. Eicher, "Facing up to Africa's Food Crisis," *Foreign Affairs* 9, no. 1 (1982): 153–174, passim.
14. For a general discussion of this question, see Donald Rothchild and Michael Foley, "The Implications of Scarcity for Governance in Africa," *International Political Science Review* 4, no. 3 (1983): 314 and passim.
15. In Ghana in 1980, for example, with the minimum wage set at twelve cedis a day, the price of a loaf of bread was frequently two to three times that amount. See *Daily Graphic*, July 10, 1980.
16. For a good review of the literature on multinational firms in this sphere, see Gerard Ghersi and Jean-Louis Rastoin, *Multinational Firms and Agro-Food Systems in*

Developing Countries: A Bibliographic Review (Paris: Development Centre of the Organization for Economic Cooperation and Development, 1981) Also see the excellent analysis in Jonathan Barker, ed., *The Politics of Agriculture in Tropical Africa* (Beverly Hills: Sage Publications, 1984). For a specific case, see Françoise Berthoud, "Objectifs et résultats d'une publicité alimentaire en Afrique: Le Problème du lait en poudre en marge du procès Nestlé," *Présence Africaine*, no. 113 (1980): 45–65.

17. W. David Hopper, *The Politics of Food* (Ottawa: International Development Research Center, 1977).

18. Rolf Hanisch and Rainer Tetzlaff, "Agricultural Policy, Foreign Aid, and the Rural Poor in the Third World," *Law and State* 23, (1982): 124–125.

19. On the Zambian perspective on this problem, see *Food Policy Issues in Low Income Countries*, World Bank Staff Working Paper, 473 (1981).

20. A good analysis of facets of this issue may be found in Gerald K. Helleiner, "The IMF and Africa in the 1980s," *Canadian Journal of African Studies* 17, no. 1 (1983): 17–34. Ghana's recent experience in devaluation furnishes a good example of some of the ramifications of acceding to IMF demands.

21. The urban aspects of poverty are covered well in Richard Sandbrook, *The Politics of Basic Needs: Urban Aspects of Assailing Poverty in Africa* (London: Heinemann, 1982).

22. Assefa Bequele, "Stagnation and Inequality in Ghana," in Dharam Ghai and Samir Radwan, eds., *Agrarian Policies and Rural Poverty in Africa* (Geneva: ILO, 1983), pp. 240–245.

23. For example, in Gambia groundnut production dropped from 132,000 metric tons in 1973 to 75,000 metric tons in 1981. *Africa Research Bulletin* 18, no. 8 (August 1–31, 1981): 6139.

24. John de St. Jorre, "Africa: Crisis of Confidence," *Foreign Affairs* 60, no. 3 (1983): 681. Also see *Africa Research Bulletin* 19, no. 1 (January 1–31, 1982).

25. *Africa Research Bulletin* 18, no. 1 (January 1–31, 1981): 5938–5939. In the spring of 1987 a similar rash of strikes was noted in Zambia.

26. *Africa Research Bulletin* 19, no. 4 (April 1–30, 1982): 6422.

27. The student uprisings and government reaction in Côte d'Ivoire are covered in *West Africa* in the Spring 1983 issues.

28. The terminology used for classifying types of conflict is taken from Donald G. Morrison and Hugh M. Stevenson, "Integration and Instability: Patterns of African Political Development," *American Political Science Review* 66, no. 3 (1972): 902–927.

29. John Ravenhill suggests that the two go together. See his introduction in John Ravenhill, ed., *Africa in Economic Crisis* (New York: Columbia University Press, 1986). For one critical assessment of the PNDC's (Provisional National Defense Council) attempt to bring about a voluntary reduction in the price of cocoa, see Elizabeth Ohene, "Words, Deeds and Cocoa," *West Africa*, August 19, 1982, pp. 2103–2105.

30. Streeten, "Food Prices as a Reflection of Political Power."

31. Frances Moore Lappé and Joseph Collins, "While Hunger Is Real, Scarcity Is Not," *Internationale Entwicklung*, no. 4 (1980): 24–27 and passim.

32. This is demonstrated in some detail in Cyril Koffie Daddieh, "The State, Land and Peasantry and the Crisis in Ghanaian Agriculture: Lessons from the Rice and Coconut Industries in the Western Region" (Centre for African Studies, Dalhousie University, Halifax, 28 October 1982), esp. p. 38.

33. Christopher Green and Colin Kirkpatrick, "A Cross Section Analysis of Food Insecurity in Developing Countries: Its Magnitude and Sources," *Journal of Development Studies* 18, no. 2 (1982): esp. 192–194. Also see F. Chidoze Ogene, *The Politics of Scarcity: African Resources and International Politics* (Lagos: Nigerian Institute of International Affairs, Seminar Series, no. 4, n.d.).

34. René Dumont and Marie-France Mottin, *Stranglehold on Africa* (London: André Deutsch, 1983).

35. For a general discussion, see W. Crawford Young, *Ideology and Development in Africa* (New Haven: Yale University Press, 1982). This general problem is demonstrated specifically in Timothy M. Shaw and Malcolm J. Grieve, "Africa and the Environment: The Political Economy of Resources," *The African Review* 9, no. 1 (1982): 104–124.

36. Graham Watts, "Drought and Apartheid: Partners in Death," *African Business*, no. 61 (September 1983): . 19–20.

37. Norman K. Nicholson and John D. Esseks, "The Politics of Food Scarcities in Developing Countries," *International Organization* 32, no. 3 (1978): 679–692.

38. For a general overview, see Donald Rothchild and Naomi Chazan, eds., *The Precarious Balance: State and Society in Africa* (Boulder, Colo.: Westview Press, 1987). For some detailed examples, see Naomi Chazan, *An Anatomy of Ghanaian Politics: Managing Political Recession, 1969–1982* (Boulder, Colo.: Westview Press, 1983).

39. See Nelson Kasfir, "State Magendo and Class Formation in Uganda," in Nelson Kasfir, ed., *State and Class in Africa* (London: Frank Cass, 1985). See Donald Rothchild and John W. Harbeson, "Rehabilitation in Uganda," *Current History* 80, no. 463 (1981): 115–119; and also Thomas Turner, "Mobutu's Zaire: Permanently on the Verge of Collapse," in ibid., pp. 124–128.

40. John Howell and Christopher Stevens, "Agriculture: Why Africa Cannot Feed Itself," *African Business*, no. 24 (August 1980): 55–64.

41. Official malfeasance of this sort has been documented for virtually every African country. For recent examples, see Dumont and Mottin, *Stranglehold on Africa*, and Thomas Callaghy, *The State-Society Struggle: Zaire in Comparative Perspective* (New York: Columbia University Press, 1984).

42. Deborah Pellow and Naomi Chazan, *Ghana: Coping with Uncertainty* (Boulder, Colo.: Westview Press, 1986).

43. Richard L. Sklar, "Democracy in Africa" (African Studies Center, University of California at Los Angeles, 1983), discusses some of these issues.

44. This has been documented in one case by Fred M. Hayward, "Perceptions of Well-Being in Ghana: 1970 and 1975," *African Studies Review* 22, no. 1 (1979): esp. 117.

45. *Africa Research Bulletin*, March 1–31, 1980, p. 5612A.

46. The problem of nonparticipation in elections has become fairly acute in recent years. Participation rates in the Nigerian and Kenyan elections of 1983 were exceptionally low. For discussion of participation in elections, see Fred M. Hayward, ed., *Elections in Independent Africa* (Boulder, Colo.: Westview Press, 1986).

47. This point is made convincingly by Diddy R. M. Hitchins, "Towards Political Stability in Ghana: A Rejoinder in the Union Government Debate," *African Studies Review* 20, no. 1 (1979): 171–176.

48. *Africa Research Bulletin*, March 1–31, 1983, p. 6779.

49. *Amnesty International Report 1985* (London: Amnesty International Publications, 1985).

50. All these techniques have been used, at one point or another, in Uganda, Zaire, and Ghana in recent years. See, for example, Claire Robertson, "The Death of Makola and Other Tragedies," *Canadian Journal of African Studies* 17, no. 3 (1983): 469–495.

51. Howell and Stevens, "Why Africa Cannot Feed Itself."

52. This problem revives the importance of ideology and common political values in the analysis of the authority of African states in the 1980s.

53. Cheryl Christensen, "World Hunger: A Structural Approach," *International*

Organization 32, no. 3 (1978):745–774.

54. In the debate on the question of food uncertainty in the Third World, there are many analysts who insist that the problem of scarcity is more mythical than real (Eberstadt, "Hunger and Ideology"). Nevertheless, in the mid-1980s there were more and more places in Africa where food was simply unavailable, and an absolute scarcity did exist.

55. For one example, see Michael Bratton, *The Local Politics of Rural Development: Peasant and Party State in Zambia* (Hanover, N.H.: University Press of New England, 1980).

56. This cycle is well documented in Bequele, "Stagnation and Inequality in Ghana."

57. Piet Konings, "Riziculteurs capitalistes et petits paysans: La naissance d'un conflit de classe au Ghana," *Politique Africaine* 2 (1983): 77–94, documents one example in some detail.

58. Some cases are reviewed in Robert Bates, "People in Villages: Micro Level Studies in Political Economy," *World Politics* 31 (1978): 129–149.

59. Roy Prieswerk, "Self-Reliance in Unexpected Places," *Genève-Afrique* 20, no. 2 (1982): 64.

60. Ibid., p. 62. Also see Johan Galtung, Peter O'Brien, and Roy Prieswerk, eds., *Self-Reliance: A Strategy for Development* (London: Bogle l'Ouverture, 1980).

61. Helmut Kloos, "Development, Drought and Famine in the Awash Valley of Ethiopia," *African Studies Review* 25, no. 4 (1982): 21–48.

62. John-Pierre Gontard, "When the Cat's Away the Rats will Play: The Kornaka Trap in Niger," in Galtung, O'Brien, and Prieswerk, pp. 330–336.

63. Prieswerk, "Self-Reliance in Unexpected Places," pp. 58–59.

64. Merrick Posnansky, "How Ghana's Crisis Affects a Village," *West Africa*, no. 3306 (December 1, 1980): 2418–2420.

65. Geoffrey Lean, "Three Disasters Hit Africa," *Africa Now*, October 1983, pp. 128–129.

66. Konings, "Riziculteurs capitalistes," pp. 84–88.

67. David Brokensha, "Review Essay: Rural Development and Inequality in Zambia," *Journal of African Studies* 10, no. 1 (1983): 24–29. Robert Bates, *Rural Responses to Industrialization: A Study of Village Zambia* (New Haven: Yale University Press, 1976): Geoff Lamb, *Peasant Politics: Conflict and Development in Mureng* (London: Julian Friedmann, 1974): and Harry Silver, "Going for Brokers: Political Innovation and Structural Integration in Changing Ashanti Community," *Comparative Political Studies* 14, no. 2 (1981): 233–263.

68. This point is highlighted by Richard Rathbone, "Ghana," in John Dunn, ed., *West African States* (London: Cambridge University Press, 1978), esp. pp. 34–36.

69. Frank Holmquist, "Class Structure, Peasant Participation and Rural Self-Help," in J. D. Barkan and J. J. Okumo, eds., *Politics and Public Policy in Kenya and Tanzania* (New York: Praeger, 1979), pp. 129–153. Also see Donald Rothchild, "Comparative Public Demand and Expectation Patterns," *African Studies Review* 22, no. 1 (1979): 127–147, and Victor Azarya and Naomi Chazan, "Disengagement from the State in Africa: Reflections on the Experience of Ghana and Guinea," *Comparative Studies in Society and History* 29, no. 1 (1987): 106–131.

70. Naomi Chazan, "The New Politics of Participation in Tropical Africa," *Comparative Politics* 14, no. 2 (1982): 169–189.

71. Rothchild and Foley, "The Implications of Scarcity for Governance in Africa," p. 315.

72. This technique has become commonplace. The latest instance is the Nigerian expulsion of aliens in January 1983 and then again in October 1983.

73. Prieswerk, "Self-Reliance in Unexpected Places," pp. 60–62. Also see Donald Rothchild and Robert L. Curry, Jr., *Scarcity, Choice and Public Policy in Middle Africa* (Berkeley and Los Angeles: University of California Press, 1978), and Hanisch and Tetzlaff, "Agricultural Policy, Foreign Aid, and the Rural Poor," p. 126.

74. Daphne Miller, "Food: The Obstacles in Feeding the Hungry," *Development Issue Paper*, no. 11 (1980).

75. Prieswerk, "Self-Reliance in Unexpected Places," p. 63.

76. I. William Zartman, "Issues of African Diplomacy in the 1980s," *Orbis* 25, no. 4 (1982): esp. 1029–1032.

77. For a discussion of some of the background factors involved, see Richard L. Sklar, "The Nature of Class Domination in Africa," *Journal of Modern Africa Studies* 27, no. 4 (1979): 531–552.

78. Rothchild and Foley, "The Implications of Scarcity for Governance in Africa," p. 319.

79. Dennis A. Rondinelli, "Administration of Integrated Rural Development Policy," *World Politics* 31, no. 3 (1979): 416.

80. Timothy M. Shaw, "Debates About Africa's Future: The Brandt, World Bank and Lagos Plan Blueprints," *Third World Quarterly* 5, no. 2 (1983): 330–344. Also see Timothy M. Shaw, ed., *Alternative Futures for Africa* (Boulder, Colo.: Westview Press, 1981), and Adebayo Adedeji and Timothy M. Shaw, eds., *Economic Crisis in Africa: African Perspectives on Development Problems and Potentials* (Boulder, Colo.: Lynne Rienner Publishers, 1985).

81. A defense of food aid may be found in Frank Shefrin, "Food Aid as a Target: The Critic's Choice," *Ceres* 16, no. 2 (1983): 44–46. The case for the need for increased participation is made well by Mark W. Delancey, "Cameroon National Food Policies and Organizations: The Green Revolution and Structural Proliferation," *Journal of African Studies* 7, no. 2 (1980): 109–122.

82. On issues of good government, see John Dunn, "The Politics of Representation and Government in Post-Colonial Africa," in Patrick Chabal, ed., *Political Domination in Africa: Reflections on the Limits of Power* (London: Cambridge University Press, 1986), pp. 158–174, and Eduardo Crawley, "The Politics of Food," *South*, no. 3 (1980): 22–27. This point is made repeatedly in the literature. For a specific example, see Jack Sheperd, "Feed Ethiopia Fast," *New York Times*, August 28, 1983.

83. Thomas O. Haglin, "Scarcity and Centralization: The Concept of European Integration," *International Political Science Review* 4, no. 3 (1983): 345–360. See also Naomi Casswell, "Death Wish in West African Economies?" *Africa Now*, October 1983, pp. 70–71.

84. For one example of such a possibility, see Thierry Lemarsquier, "Beyond Infant Feeding: The Case for Another Relationship between NGOs and the United Nations System," *Development Dialogue*, no. 1 (1980): 120–126.

85. Perhaps the most constructive approach to linking development with true participation is suggested by Richard Sklar in his innovative essay, "Democracy in Africa," and his later paper "Developmental Democracy" (presented at the annual meeting of the American Political Science Association, New Orleans, August 1985).

86. OAU, *Lagos Plan of Action*, p. 8.

·2·

Aid Debates and Food Needs

CAROL LANCASTER

As farmers in Sub-Saharan Africa have faced increased difficulties in meeting their countries' food needs since the late 1970s, African officials and development experts from abroad have become concerned about Africa's lagging agricultural growth and have begun to examine ways of accelerating that growth. Perhaps more than in any other region of the developing world, foreign-aid donors—bilateral governments as well as international institutions such as the World Bank—play a major role in the direction of development on the continent. Foreign aid is a source of foreign exchange for governments desperately in need of imports, as are many governments in Africa today. Aid supports a substantial proportion of national investment in African countries, especially the poorest. And aid donors provide much of the technical assistance that African governments require if they are to plan and implement their development projects. It is not surprising that donor viewpoints on agricultural development may have an important influence on investment priorities, macroeconomic policies, and individual development projects. When future analysts look back on African development of the next quarter-century, to about the year 2010, it is likely that even more so than in the past, foreign-aid donors will be credited (or blamed) for the success (or failure) of African farmers in meeting their countries' food needs. This chapter concerns the role of foreign aid in addressing those food needs.

· AFRICA'S FOOD NEEDS ·

Africa's food needs are growing rapidly. This growth is a consequence of expanding population, rapid urbanization, growth in incomes, and the pressing need by most countries to expand exports, which tend often to include agricultural products and thus may compete with the production of agricultural goods for domestic consumption.

Although the need for food in Sub-Saharan Africa is growing rapidly, African food production has been sluggish over the past several decades.

Agricultural production, including production for consumption and export, increased by 2.9 percent between 1965 and 1973, but the rate slowed to .7 percent between 1973 and 1984.[1] In some countries, between 1973 and 1984 agricultural production dropped, including Guinea-Bissau, Uganda, Gambia, Madagascar, and Nigeria. Without the major droughts in the mid-1970s and early 1980s, these figures would look somewhat better but would still show a slowing in the growth rate of African agriculture and be a cause for serious concern.

A number of factors account for the poor performance of African agriculture since the early 1970s. One derives from the same source as the rapidly increasing food needs on the continent: accelerating population growth. African agriculture remains primarily resource-based: that is, African farmers typically rely largely on their own and their families, labor plus hand tools, such as the machete and hoe, to produce their crops. Fertilizers, pesticides, herbicides, tractors, irrigation systems, and improved plant varieties are rarely used. Farmers clear, burn, and cultivate fields for several years until yields begin to decline. These fields are left to return to the bush for a period of time to restore soil fertility as the farmer clears, burns, and cultivates other fields. Agricultural growth in Africa has thus far been based largely on bringing additional land into cultivation. However, with accelerating population growth, cultivatable land is beginning to become scarce in a number of countries. What African farmers need are packages of inputs and technologies that will allow them to farm their lands more intensively without reducing productivity. Unfortunately, such packages are not at present available. Improved plant varieties that will perform well in farmers' fields have not been developed; fertilizer is often expensive and unavailable; irrigation is rare and also expensive to construct. In short, the Green Revolution has by and large passed Africa by. Moreover, scientists are only just beginning to learn about the farming systems that African farmers have developed to deal with an unpredictable and hostile environment. Despite the current emphasis in the research community on farming systems, the impact of such research is as yet modest. The variety of environments, soils, and other agricultural conditions on the African continent is great. What works in one country or region is often not easily translatable to other regions.

Population growth has put pressure on other regions of the world to move to more intensive, scientifically based agricultural production systems. But in the case of Africa, the time in which an adjustment to more intensive farming must take place is considerably shorter because of rapid population growth,[2] and these population pressures threaten to force a transition to more intensive farming before the technology is available. If such an adjustment does not take place quickly enough, and there is no guarantee that it will, one could expect to observe the continuation and spread of falling agricultural yields, declining productivity of labor, deteriorating environmental conditions, and possibly an acceleration in the rate of urbanization.

A second major factor in the slowing of agricultural production in Africa is the policy and institutional frameworks in which most African farmers must produce and sell. It is a commonplace now that government policies and institutions throughout much of the continent have discouraged agricultural production. They have set procurement prices low for agricultural exports, required farmers to sell to government marketing boards, and then have resold these products on world markets for higher prices and kept the differences as government revenues. Governments have also sought to keep domestic food prices low by prohibiting farmers from selling directly to consumers—instead, farmers must sell their products to government institutions for resale at home—and have manipulated in other ways to keep domestic prices low. Government monopolies on the sale of farm inputs or transportation to market have discouraged production when such monopolies have proven inefficient or unable to provide the services for which they were created.

Other economic policies have discouraged agricultural production, including overvalued exchange rates, which encourage food imports and discourage exports. Government investments emphasizing industrial development and ignoring agriculture have resulted in agricultural sectors that typically lack the research, education, and extension services common in other parts of the developing world. Inadequacies of government policies and institutions have been exacerbated by the serious foreign-exchange crisis many African countries have experienced since the start of the 1980s. During the latter part of the 1970s in particular, the prices of manufactured goods, which most African countries must import, rose rapidly because of inflation in the West. Petroleum prices sextupled during the 1970s, providing a windfall for oil-exporting countries but adding to the import costs of the large number of oil-importing African countries. Meanwhile, the prices of primary products on which most African countries depend for export earnings remained unstable during much of the 1970s, then collapsed in the beginning of the 1980s, and have remained largely depressed since then. At the same time, foreign-aid levels stagnated and commercial lending dried up, bringing on a foreign-exchange squeeze of unprecedented severity for many countries. Imports were sharply compressed, to the extent that in the case of Zambia, World Bank staff have wondered whether that country's modern sector could continue to function. Not only were imported agricultural inputs cut back, but roads were left to deteriorate and spare parts for transport vehicles were in short supply, making it increasingly difficult for African farmers to get their goods to market or to find the incentive goods—textiles, consumer durables, or imported goods—to purchase with their earnings.

Finally, droughts in the Sahel, the Horn of Africa and Southern Africa sharply reduced food production during the early 1980s. Civil strife in Angola and Mozambique and in Ethiopia, Uganda, Chad, and Sudan further added to problems of food production in those unfortunate countries.

African farmers have taken these problems into account in making their decisions on what and how much to produce. In countries where government policies have been especially exploitative of farmers or have been overly restrictive or inefficient, farmers have retreated from the market and sought to produce for their own needs. In addition to shifting production from cash crops to food crops and retreating into production for subsistence, a number of farmers have marketed their products through parallel markets, including smuggling them abroad, when this alternative was feasible. African farmers have proven that although they tend to be weak or voiceless politically, they are not without weapons in the struggle for resources and growth: They can withdraw from the market and survive. In most of Africa, where a substantial proportion of gross domestic product (GDP) and exports are produced by farmers, governments and urban dwellers cannot easily protect their standards of living in the face of food shortages.

There have been several consequences of the rapid increase in food needs in Africa and the growing inability of Africans to meet those needs through their own production. Food imports have increased dramatically over the past decade.[3] Despite the growing volume of food imports in many countries, food in urban areas is often scarce. As a result, real food prices have increased substantially (despite efforts by a number of African governments to enforce low fixed prices.) For low-income wage earners, rising food prices has meant that an ever larger percentage of their incomes must be spent on food. Judging from the increasing incidence of malnutrition in urban areas, there has also likely been a shift by some consumers away from higher-priced, more-nutritious foods (such as rice, bread, legumes) toward cheaper but less-nutritious foods (above all, cassava).

Finally, lagging growth in agricultural production can act as a drag on overall economic growth. As population and incomes increase, the demand for food accelerates. If farmers cannot meet that demand, either food prices will rise (and with them, labor costs and the general rate of inflation)[4] or governments will have to spend scarce foreign exchange on food imports. In either case, growth is likely to be restrained.

· AID DEBATES ·

Concessional assistance is the principal means by which foreign governments can influence Africa's ability to meet its immediate as well as long-term food needs. Foreign governments assist Africans to meet short-term food needs arising from natural or man-made disasters through the provision of food aid. This usually involves direct transfers of food products, normally in surplus in donor countries, to food-deficit countries to supplement what governments buy to meet a sudden drop in their own food production. Occasionally, cash loans or grants are also provided to needy governments to purchase food. But as the United States, the European Economic Community (EEC), and Japan (in the case of rice) all have burdensome surpluses of grain, oilseeds, and other commodities, these countries prefer to rely primarily on food aid for emergency relief.

The debates that arise in providing emergency food aid are seldom ones of substantive policy, and they typically have little to do with long-range problems of raising food production in recipient countries. On these longer-run problems, there are significant differences of opinion among experts and government officials both over the nature of Africa's food problems and the appropriate role of aid in helping to solve those problems. These differences often go to the heart of the development process and the ability of aid to influence that process. It is to the several fundamental differences among experts and officials regarding African agricultural development that we now turn.

Although most observers of African agricultural problems share a common position on the range of factors leading to Africa's agricultural decline, they differ considerably in the emphasis they place on the various causes of this decline. Two basic approaches are apparent. One, which we will call the "free market" approach, emphasizes the role of price distortions and market and institutional inefficiencies as major sources of Africa's inability to feed itself. A second approach focuses on a variety of "structural" obstacles (such as a scarcity of labor at critical periods, a scarcity of cultivatable land, or social and political structures) to more rapid agricultural development and, indeed, development in general on the continent. The proposed solutions to Africa's food problems offered by these two approaches and the implications for foreign aid in those solutions also differ considerably.

The Free-Marketeers

The free-marketeers point to the policy and institutional failures of African governments as the major causes of agricultural problems. Emphasis on these factors is characteristic in many of the publications of the World Bank and, above all, in statements by U.S. government officials. They are also reflected in the conditions with which African governments must comply to receive foreign-aid loans and grants from these aid donors.

African governments are advised that if more rapid agricultural production is to take place on the continent, African farmers must be able to produce, sell and invest in a supportive, efficient, and nonexploitative policy framework. Governments must undertake a range of policy reforms—including adjusting food prices to reflect relative costs and scarcities or freeing prices from government control altogether—in order to devalue currencies, to liberalize trade controls, and to streamline or even eliminate inefficient government agencies involved in agriculture.

This approach is essentially within the school of "neoclassical economics."[5] Implicit in it is that free-market-oriented prescriptions will over time have roughly similar effects wherever they are applied, regardless of social or political differences. It rests on the assumption that most people share similar objectives, that economically rational human beings will react in similar ways to economic incentives, and that societies and individuals are flexible enough over time to respond to such incentives. This approach is universalistic and essentially optimistic in its view that with adequate resources and efficient policies economic development will occur. President Reagan has emphasized the "magic" of the marketplace as the key to economic development.

There are several ways in which foreign aid may be linked to policy reform by recipients. First, there is the "policy dialogue" approach in which aid donors and recipient governments discuss economic conditions and needed reforms, inform and educate one another, and come to an agreement on what reforms will be undertaken. Aid is provided to ease the potentially painful impact or to enhance the effectiveness of such reforms through funding the import of key commodities (for example, fertilizer in support of agricultural price increases).

A second approach involves bargaining between donors, who have a preferred list of reforms and are willing to provide aid if those reforms are adopted, and recipient government officials, who agree to implement reforms, whether they are in accord with them or not, because they need the foreign exchange provided through aid. A variation of this approach occurs when the donor's preferred reforms coincide with the views of a faction in the recipient government. The coincidence of views between the foreign donor (plus the availability of aid in support of reforms) and the local faction strengthens the role of the faction in influencing government policies, and the government agrees to implement the reforms. A final approach is the ex post facto tie between reforms and foreign aid: Foreign aid (or commercial loans) is provided to governments that have already adopted economically efficient policies.

In reality, donors follow a mix of practices in conditioning their aid on policy reform. They tend to emphasize the need for a policy dialogue with recipients if reforms are to be faithfully implemented. It is clear, however, that many reforms have been agreed to and implemented despite objections or misgivings on the part of recipients. Although the process of negotiations between donors and recipients on policy reforms is seldom public and case studies are rare, what can be said is that aid donors have come to play an increasingly prominent role in macroeconomic decisionmaking in African countries through persuasion, dialogue, and leveraging change with their aid. As agriculture occupies an important position in these economies, policies and institutions affecting agriculture have been an important element in discussions and negotiations on policy reform. One indicator of the extent of the activity of one major donor in this area—the World Bank—is the number of loans undertaken through its new Special Facility for Sub-Saharan Africa. All of these included conditions involving policy reform by recipient governments, and many directly or indirectly affected agriculture: In 1986, the facility made twenty-two loans to fifteen African countries—a total of $782 million.[6]

The Structuralists

A second group of analysts of African agriculture have given more emphasis to structural impediments to agricultural progress on the continent. They have not ignored the roles of prices, macroeconomic policies, and government institutions in depressing economic growth. But they have argued that although policy reforms may be necessary, they are seldom sufficient on their own to stimulate long-term agricultural expansion in Africa. Other obstacles to growth must be removed as well.

The structuralists divide when it comes to identifying these obstacles. One group emphasizes the limitations on expanded agricultural production posed by scarce labor, especially at peak demand periods such as harvest time.[7] Because African farmers tend to use hand tools only (few utilize animal traction; fewer still have access to farm machinery), the area that an individual farmer can plant, weed, and harvest is limited. Even with a more favorable policy environment, existing technologies would still limit the degree to which farmers could expand their production. It is also argued that the supply of labor to agriculture is relatively inelastic. Even with substantially higher prices for agricultural products, it would be hard to attract labor out of urban areas and into agriculture, given the difficult living conditions in rural areas and the opportunities in the cities. Another group of analysts points to the inelastic supply of cultivatable land as an obstacle to agricultural growth.[8] Most of the increase in African agriculture in the past has been based on expanding the frontier of cultivatable land. With the recent surge in population growth throughout the continent, pressures on cultivatable land have grown with attendant problems of yield and productivity. Those who emphasize labor constraints and those who emphasize land constraints on agricultural growth both agree that poor infrastructure (roads, communications, educational facilities, input and output distribution systems) seriously exacerbates inelasticities in agricultural inputs and production in most African countries.

The implications for aid of this structuralist approach differ from the implications arising from the policy reform approach. The structuralists' priority is to relieve the constraints on agricultural expansion. Most experts agree that this must be done through funding agricultural research on improved crops, farming practices, and appropriate technologies. Important in this regard are the international agricultural research centers—such as the International Institute of Tropical Agriculture in Ibadan, Nigeria; the Center for Research on Maize and Wheat in Mexico; or the International Rice Research Institute in the Philippines—which engage in basic research on crops, farming systems and technologies, and agricultural implements and inputs. Also critical are national research institutions that can adapt the improvements developed in the international institutions to local conditions. It is these national institutions that tend to be especially weak or nonexistent in Africa. The strengthening of other national institutions involved in agricultural education and extension, together with the expansion of physical infrastructure, storage, marketing and other facilities necessary to support agricultural expansion are also important. The form of aid most appropriate to reducing these structural obstacles to agricultural expansion is project financing—the funding of specific activities—in contrast to aid for balance-of-payments support (that is, "program," or sector, aid), which usually accompanies donor efforts, to encourage policy reforms.[9]

Those analysts concerned with labor, land, and infrastructural obstacles to agricultural growth are not the only structuralists. Another group, primarily political scientists and political economists, emphasize a rather different obstacle to African agricultural development and development on the continent in general—the nature of the African state. Political theorists and historians have debated on this topic for some time: Is the African state an autonomous, modernizing institution? Is it instrumental, reflecting the interests of social classes, political elites, or ethnic groups? The recent deterioration in economic conditions on the continent has prompted a number of observers to examine the role of the state in Africa's economic decline. As a result, there are almost as many paradigms as there are analysts of the impact of the African state on economic development on the continent. But it is possible to perceive two general approaches.

The first, now somewhat discredited in the academy (but still widely held by African officials), is that of the "dependency" school. Dependency theorists argue that Africa's underdevelopment is a natural consequence of its peripheral position in the world capitalist system. African political leadership (a "comprador" class), these theorists say, has basically sold out national economic interests and resources to powerful capitalist multinational corporations in exchange for personal gain.[10] The solutions preferred by dependency advocates to Africa's development problems involve a withdrawal by African countries from the world capitalist system and state-led, "self-reliant" development. Although the implications for aid of this approach are not often made explicit, they would appear to involve the elimination of aid, at least from capitalist countries and from international institutions, such as the World Bank and IMF, which rely on Western contributions. Given the major role these institutions play in financing African imports and investment, eliminating aid would likely be extremely painful economically and unrealistic politically. Such a policy simply has not been seriously considered by African politicians.

The dependency approach to understanding African economic problems has received a decreasing amount of attention in the 1980s from scholars and practitioners alike, in part because available empirical material does not support the notion that African political leaders have "sold out" their national economic interests to foreigners. Rather, there is much evidence that many have exploited their national economic resources to advance their own personal and political interests, which are not necessarily consistent with those of multinational firms or foreign capitalist governments (or with the interests of their own people). Moreover, although dependency theory purports to explain Africa's state of underdevelopment, it has little to say about the deterioration in the 1980s in Africa's economic fortunes, the focus of much concern by economists, political scientists, and government officials in Africa and abroad.

A second group of political economists has taken a rather different approach to the role of the state in African development. Like the free-marketeers, these analysts have underscored the importance of African policies and institutions in inhibiting economic development and agricultural growth. But they have gone one step further and asked why these policies have been chosen as opposed to others that might have been more supportive of economic development, a stated goal of most African governments. Analysts have provided a variety of answers to these questions. Some have pointed to the economic structures and practices inherited from the colonial state and continued in the independence era as a major cause of economic decline;[11] others have sought to place the development of the African state in the broader historical context of state development in general and have concluded that African states, at early stages of development, are not all that different from European or Latin American states in their early decades.[12] A number of analysts have emphasized the instrumental nature of the African state—that is, that its policies and structures reflect the interests of major political groups as well as efforts by the members of the political leadership and bureaucracy to protect their own positions and advance their interests.[13] Those analysts who have looked at these questions specifically from the point of view of agriculture have concluded that the relative powerlessness of the mass of small farmers, compared to urban groups and political elites, provides much of the explanation for the often exploitative and inefficient agricultural policies typical of the continent.

By implication, political economists are in agreement with free-marketeers in that government policies must be reformed if agriculture and economies are to be developed in Sub-Saharan Africa. Where they diverge from free-marketeers is in what is required to reform policies. Because existing policies are a result of historical, social, and political phenomena (including the nature of the African state), political economists often argue that for reforms to be effective and sustained, these more basic phenomena must also change. However, political economists tend to be skeptical about the possibilities of such changes occurring quickly or easily. They view government policies as being embedded in particular social and political structures, often inherited from colonial days. Moreover, such structures differ substantially from country to country. In short, political economists tend to be particularistic and pessimistic in their approach to African development.

Political economists examining the African state seldom make recommendations on the use of aid based on their analyses. Where individuals have made such recommendations or where the implications of their analyses for aid are clear, there is little agreement among these analysts on how aid should be used to bring about change. One school of thought, shared by many on the political Right as well as the radical Left views foreign aid as in part responsible for the economic malaise in Africa.[14] Large amounts of aid, almost always channeled through the state, have in effect strengthened the role of the state in African economies, fueled its expansion, eased pressures on governments to deal with economic problems such as declining per capita food production, and possibly has inadvertently led to the corruption of political officials who find it difficult to resist appropriating portions of the large amounts of aid funds available. One recommendation based on this approach is to cut back or eliminate aid and so force a leaner state and remove opportunities for inefficiencies and corruption.

Another policy is often promoted by those concerned with the powerlessness of the poor. Recognizing the potential usefulness of aid in promoting growth, they recommend that, to whatever extent is possible, aid be channeled directly to the poor through nongovernmental, grass-roots organizations. This approach has much public appeal among those involved with or sympathetic to the work of private voluntary organizations, such as CARE, and has influenced recent foreign-aid proposals in the U.S. Congress. But there are serious limitations on how much aid can be channeled to African beneficiaries through local or foreign voluntary organizations, given the administrative and logistical costs of delivering relatively small amounts of resources directly to individuals or groups.

A rather different role for aid has been suggested by yet another group of political economists concerned with change in African countries. Like the free-marketeers, they would condition aid on policy reform, but specifically on political reforms aimed at protecting or expanding democratic and civil rights of African citizens.[15] This approach is, in effect, aimed at empowerment of the poor—using aid to force political changes that will ensure that those now effectively shut out of the political process, including the mass of small farmers, receive an influential voice. Calls for conditioning foreign aid on political reforms generally have been rejected by the development community. They are seen as impractical: Aid donors rarely have sufficient leverage to force political leaders to diminish their own power by transferring political power to others. Such an approach is also far more interventionist than are economic reforms tied to foreign aid and could endanger relations between donors (bilateral governments or international institutions)and the political leadership in recipient governments.

Judging from foreign aid provided by the United States, the World Bank, and other major donors to Africa, the free market approach has had the predominant influence on aid programs in the 1980s and is reflected in a rising percentage of loans and grants actually made to African countries. Project aid and aid for agricultural research has, of course, continued, but in the United States, at least, it has not increased proportionately, and under the Reagan administration it has decreased as a result of cuts in overall aid programs.[16]

· FOREIGN AID ·

The principal food problem we have examined in this chapter is the declining ability of African farmers to produce enough to meet the growing demand for food in their countries. Although this problem has both demand and supply aspects, most aid donors have emphasized the supply side—helping farmers expand their productivity and removing obstacles to a more rapid expansion in food supplies. Donors have focused their aid relatively little on the demand factors in this problem—rapid population growth and urbanization, the impact of rising incomes on the types of food demanded, and the need for African countries to expand their exports—probably because they recognize the great difficulties of making a significant impact on them. However, foreign-aid donors appear to have had an indirect influence on the rate of urbanization and the level of incomes in the cities. The austerity programs that many African governments have adopted in recent years, often with encouragement from aid donors as well as from the IMF, appear to have had the effect of reducing incomes and employment in urban areas and possibly reducing or reversing the rate of rural-urban migration. If this is true, there should be an increase in the amount of labor available for agricultural production. At the same time, donors have encouraged African governments to undertake measures—such as raising producer prices and providing expanded credit—to increase the volume of primary-product exports. When these products are agricultural commodities, they can in the short run compete with the production of foodstuffs for domestic consumption and so exacerbate the gap between food needs and food production.

Given the nature of Africa's food needs and foreign-aid programs, what impact have these programs had in the past, and what is their likely impact in the future in helping Africa meet its food needs? The worsening record of African agriculture underscores an obvious point: Foreign aid has not ensured agricultural progress in Sub-Saharan Africa. It is possible, through difficult to prove, that aid has indirectly contributed to the poor performance of agriculture by first (in the 1960s) promoting the development of industry. Many aid donors, development specialists, and government officials of that day shared a view that the fastest way of developing was to industrialize. Import-substituting industrialization was the conventional wisdom of the day. Agriculture was ignored, or worse, exploited for resources, to promote industrialization.

As development specialists began to emphasize the important role of agriculture in economic development in the 1970s, African agriculture remained relatively neglected. The monies provided in support of international agricultural research, which produced the Green Revolution crops (high-yielding varieties of rice and wheat), aimed at breakthroughs in the crops important to developing countries with large concentrations of populations—India and China. African crops (such as sorghum, millet, yams, and cassava) and African agriculture in general were regarded as having relatively low priority for international research. Moreover, during the period of the 1970s, the main thrust in foreign-aid giving tended to be to provide for the "basic human needs" of the poorer segments of developing-country populations through funding of such projects as primary health care and informal or primary education. Although these were potentially useful efforts, the emphasis was far less on expanding the productivity of agriculture in Africa.

Finally, aid for African agriculture has had some specific failures, now recognized by the donor community. A popular approach to aid in the late 1970s was "integrated rural development," usually large, complex projects involving the funding of a wide range of activities and services (the building of roads, provision of health, education, agricultural research and extension services, credit) designed to address the entire range of development problems associated with a particular region or area. Many of these projects proved too complicated to set up and operate in the difficult development environment of Africa. Another failure involved projects aimed at improving the quality and marketing of livestock. Such projects were rendered ineffective when cultural values and practices—the key element—were ignored. Also, technical problems have presented obstacles; for example, trypanosomiasis and other diseases have proven difficult to control or suppress.

These limitations on the past effectiveness of aid in promoting agricultural development in Africa should not obscure two important facts. First, there have been a large number of positive contributions made by aid to Africa's agriculture: the large number of farm to market roads constructed; the substantial number of Africans trained in agricultural sciences as a part of most agricultural projects; projects involving food marketing and storage; small perimeter irrigation projects, and so on. It is quite possible that many African farmers and consumers would be worse off in the absence of the aid provided to African agriculture since the 1970s.

Second, the problems for African agriculture—ineffective government policies, inefficient government institutions, the impact of accelerating population growth, civil conflict, and prolonged drought—have likely swamped the positive impact of aid. Aid can promote agriculture when the policy framework and physical environment are supportive; it cannot overcome obstacles of policy, environment, or population growth when these forces work against agricultural growth.

What of aid's future impact on African agriculture? The answer must be uncertain. Several factors promise a greater positive impact in the future; several point to a more limited impact. First, agricultural development in Africa has become a priority among aid givers. It is recognized as one of the major development tasks confronting the world community. African agriculture is now a focus of international agricultural research. Funds for agricultural projects are a major part of foreign-aid budgets for Africa. Aid donors have been giving particular emphasis to conditioning their aid on the removal of policy and institutional obstacles to agricultural growth in African countries. And, above all, African government officials themselves recognize the need to promote agricultural development in their countries.

On the other hand, a number of factors will limit the impact of aid on African agriculture in the future. The political element in bilateral aid giving—particularly in the United States—is unusually strong. Thus, the effectiveness of U.S. aid in promoting long-run agricultural development may be limited. The United States has always given aid for a variety of purposes; advancing political or strategic interests abroad has long been a key part. However, it is an especially strong element at present in determining which governments receive aid, at what levels, and over what period. Five countries of particular political importance to the United States—Sudan, Kenya, Somalia, Zaire, and Liberia—receive nearly half of all U.S. bilateral aid to Africa. Concentrating aid in this way is not necessarily a bad thing from a development point of view, especially if the recipient governments are seriously trying to deal with their development problems. In several cases, however, the major recipients of U.S. aid are among the most inefficient and corrupt governments on the continent. Aid programs to these countries likely represent wasted money from a development perspective, money not available to governments more serious about their development.

A second aspect about the politicization of U.S. aid is that it may be suddenly increased or reduced in the wake of government policies of which the United States disapproves. It is clear that the U.S. donors cannot continue aid programs (apart from humanitarian relief operations) with governments that are outspokenly hostile to it or to its interests. A difficult trade-off between development and politics may occur when a government is serious about its development, and not hostile to the United States, but occasionally criticizes U.S. policies or takes positions in international fora against those of the United States. The case of Zimbabwe is a good example. In 1984, U.S. aid to that country was reduced substantially in the wake of Zimbabwean votes against the United States on several UN resolutions. Aid in support for agricultural development is a long-run proposition if it is to be successful. Suddenly decreasing it or shifting it among countries because of votes in the UN or public criticism can be very disruptive of development efforts.

Another limitation on the contribution of U.S. aid to Africa's future agricultural development derives from domestic political issues within the United States. The record size of the federal budget deficit and the inability of the U.S. Congress and executive branch to agree on how to reduce it has resulted in deep cuts in foreign aid. However, in cutting aid, the Congress has sought to protect high aid levels for several countries of political importance for the United States—Israel, Egypt, and Pakistan. When aid levels for these countries are protected from cuts, then allocations to other programs must be cut even further. Africa is the region with the lowest priority in U.S. foreign policy, and expenditures for aid programs in African countries are likely to be slashed the most. (U.S. aid to Africa fell by one-quarter between 1986 and 1987.) In short, substantially less, rather than more, aid for agricultural development or for development in general in Africa could be available from the United States in the future (and possibly from other donors as well).

Finally, there is a problem already mentioned that will continue to confront aid donors in Africa. Even if adequate aid is available to help promote agricultural development and if aid donors are successful in persuading (or forcing) African government officials to raise food prices for African farm products and undertake other important policy reforms, there is still the problem of sustainability. This is in essence a matter of empowerment. Donors, in supporting policy reforms involving agriculture, are asking African government officials to shift income and resources from politically powerful groups to politically weak groups of small farmers. How likely are such shifts to remain once donor pressures ease? Without some means of assisting small farmers to enable them to protect their gains, it is likely that those gains will eventually be eroded one way or another. Yet, donors are reluctant to consider measures that would help empower small farmers. This is understandable in that such measures (for example, aid may be conditional on some sort of political organization or voice for farmers) would probably be strongly resisted by African politicians and could cause serious tensions in donor-recipient relationships. But there may be indirect ways of helping farmers to organize—such as by strengthening farmer organizations or including incentives in aid programs for farmers to organize. The difficulty of empowering farmers is little considered by donors, yet it may limit the long-run effectiveness of their aid to African agriculture.

Time will tell whether foreign aid is to realize its potential for helping African farmers to meet their countries' food needs. It appears that without effective foreign aid, the road to agricultural development on the continent will be long and painful. But without African involvement and commitment to effective agricultural development, African agriculture will likely continue to stagnate. Whatever the truth of aid debates or the realities of African agriculture, these two ingredients are essential for future progress.

· NOTES ·

1. Statistics used here are drawn from the World Bank, *Financing Adjustment with Growth in Sub-Saharan Africa* (Washington, D.C.: World Bank, 1986).

2. For an interesting discussion of this problem, see Teresa Ho, "Population Growth and Agricultural Productivity in Sub-Saharan Africa," in Ted Davis, ed., *Proceedings of the Fifth Agriculture Sector Symposium* (Washington, D.C.: World Bank, 1985).

3. World Bank, *Financing Adjustment with Growth*, p. 79.

4. Such price increases for agricultural products will likely call forth greater production from farmers, but the supply response could be slow and limited because of lack of infrastructure, inputs, or other rigidities. Meanwhile, inflation will have been given a boost.

5. For a discussion of this approach in terms of thinking on economic development in general, see I.M.D. Little, *Economic Development: Theory, Policy and International Relations* (New York: Basic Books, 1982).

6. World Bank, *Annual Report* (Washington, D.C.: World Bank, 1986), p. 23.

7. The best known proponent of this view is John W. Mellor. See his article, with Christopher L. Delgado, "A Structural View of Policy Issues in African Agricultural Development," *American Journal of Agricultural Economics* 66, no. 5 (December 1984): 665–670.

8. See, for example, Bruce Johnston, "Agricultural Development in Tropical Africa," in Robert J. Berg and Jennifer Seymour Whitaker, eds., *Strategies for African Development* (Berkeley and Los Angeles: University of California Press, 1986).

9. The distinction between project and program aid can be blurred. Policy reforms may be tied to project aid, and governments may promise to undertake specific investments as part of program or sectoral aid. However, policy reforms tend to be tied largely to program aid.

10. The best-known proponent of this approach for analyzing Africa's economic conditions is Samir Amin, *Accumulation on a World Scale* (Sussex: Harvester Press, 1974); another example of the extensive dependency literature is Colin Leys, *Underdevelopment in Kenya: The Political Economy of Neo-Colonialism* (Berkeley and Los Angeles: University of California Press, 1974).

11. See, for example, Crawford Young, "The African Colonial State and Its Developmental Legacy," in Berg and Whitaker, *Strategies for African Development*.

12. See, for example, Thomas Callaghy, "The Patrimonial Administrative State in Africa," in Zaki Ergas, ed., *The African State in Transition* (New York: Macmillan, 1987).

13. Robert Bates is the best-known proponent of this approach. See his *Markets and States in Tropical Africa* (Berkeley and Los Angeles: University of California Press, 1981).

14. For an example of the Right, see P. T. Bauer, *Equality, the Third World and Economic Delusion* (Cambridge: Harvard University Press, 1981). See Teresa Hayter and Catharine Watson, *Aid: Rhetoric and Reality* (London: Pluto Press, 1985).

15. See, for example, Claude Ake, "Coming to Grips with the Political Constraints of Development in Africa" (Washington, D.C.: Woodrow Wilson Center, Xerox, 1985).

16. For an analysis of the size and direction of recent U.S. aid programs, see Carol Lancaster, "Foreign Aid: Annual Budget Battle Resumes," *Focus*, no. 3 (Overseas Development Council, 1987); and by the same author, "The Budget and U.S. Foreign Aid: More Tough Choices," *Focus*, no. 2 (1986).

·PART 2·
Comparative Cases

·3·

Government Action, Government Inaction, and Food Production: Central Province, Cameroon

BARBARA LEWIS

In a continent of ailing agriculture and critical inadequacies of food supply, Cameroon stands as an apparent success story. Most striking are its extensive food exports to its oil-sick neighbors, Nigeria to the west and Gabon to the east. Food production for sale in urban markets in Cameroon has kept up with demand. The World Bank reports a 3.4 percent annual growth in agricultural production, with per capita food production up 2 percent from 1969–1971 to 1981–1982.[1] The contrast with 90 percent of Sub-Saharan African states, in which per capita food production has declined for the same period, compels further examination of the mix of the food-producing population and government agricultural policies in Cameroon.

Cameroon's agricultural policies are similar to those of other "liberal" African states with a strong emphasis on export agriculture.[2] Cocoa and coffee are peasant crops serviced by multifunctional marketing boards, whereas palm oil is produced by large-scale parastatal enterprises. The institutions linking producers and markets of these crops are little changed from original colonial structures. Despite strong government pronouncements in favor of food self-sufficiency and some efforts at policy innovation, the priorities of the colonial period remain. The export crops benefit from years of agronomic research and distribution of numerous inputs: insecticides, fertilizers, and fungicides. The food sector enjoys little investment. As many of the attempts to reverse downward trends in food supplies elsewhere in Africa have not lessened national shortages, the inaction of the Cameroonian government may be something of an asset.

The established orientation toward export crops both explains and constrains government policies with respect to food. The "revenue imperative," which has contributed to some governments' efforts to control food marketing and prices, thus taxing producers (compare Mali, Burkina Faso),[3] has been met in Cameroon by state taxation of export crops and, since the 1970s, by oil revenues. Cameroonian initiatives to increase food production appear to have been influenced by the kind of statist solutions adopted in the coffee and cocoa sectors. However, these latter exports have left the government "free" to exercise restraint and to back off when such policies proved ineffective in food production. Revenues from oil and export crops have provided a cushion, supplying revenues for the government bureaucracy and the regime's patronage needs.

Although Cameroonian food production has stayed ahead of population growth to date, some appraisals of future trends are pessimistic. Basing these appraisals on declining per capita productivity in agriculture, declining agricultural labor supplies, overcropping, and stagnating cultivation techniques, some see Cameroon joining other African states in inadequate food production. It is questionable whether the Cameroonian mix of state intervention in export crops and nonintervention in food crops should be continued in the future. The healthy 4.7 percent rates of growth in agricultural production in the 1960s have declined to 1.6 percent in 1983.[4] Although export-crop production has dropped more than food production, food yields per capita also appear to be declining. Urbanization was initially slow in Cameroon but climbed from 13 percent in 1965 to 41 percent in 1984.[5] As young men and women leave villages in large numbers, labor becomes an increasing constraint on agricultural production. The long-overdue road-building program being carried out may spur food production by giving rural enclaves access to urban markets. But, combined with the Paul Biya government's expansive investment posture and oil revenues, the extended road network may accelerate the rural exodus. And although Cameroon exports food, its cereal imports have grown from 81,000 metric tons in 1974 to 178,000 metric tons in 1983. If food production per capita is set equal to 100 in 1974–1976, it is down to 81 in 1982–1984—a significant drop.[6] Thus productivity gains are not compensating for rural outmigration.

Cameroonian policymakers are not complacent regarding past production and recognize the need to channel resources to the agricultural sector. But how production of both export crops and food crops can be increased is unclear. And increasing food production at the expense of export crops is unlikely to be politically acceptable. These questions are particularly relevant to the Yaounde area, where cocoa competes with food crops for land and, to some extent, labor. In addition, policies promoting food production will have to mesh with the existing export-crop policy apparatus (marketing boards, input subsidies, buying cooperatives). Because these structures serve political as well as economic ends, future agricultural policy will reflect accommodation to these entrenched interests. Government is thus extremely unlikely to promote food production at the expense of cocoa.

In this chapter I focus on the catchment area around Yaounde, the inland capital and second city in Cameroon. The problems and responses of local farming populations and the impact of policy institutions on local farmers' behavior provide only part of the total picture. Because the Yaounde area is the principal cocoa-producing area of the country and also is relatively accessible to food traders, how export farming and food production interact is a major question there. This question includes (1) the nature of trade-offs between food and cocoa production for government elites; (2) possible institutional carryovers from export crops to food farming in marketing, agricultural extension, and input supplies; and (3) allocational decisions among men and women in peasant households.

· KING COCOA IN CENTRAL PROVINCE ·

Cocoa production has dominated rural life since its rapid expansion during the 1940s and 1950s. The Cocoa Marketing Board has controlled sales and determined producer prices since the colonial period, keeping a margin between producer and international prices to support producer prices if international markets dropped. Since independence, the state has expanded its involvement beyond this price support structure to include purchasing in villages via a highly centralized network of cooperatives. As elsewhere in Africa, nationalist politicians attacked foreign buyers for cheating farmers when weighing, grading, and paying for produce.

The nationalists' remedy, cooperatives, have inflated operating costs, with patronage dispensed at every level. Local cooperatives oversee grading and sales of cocoa and provide inputs to members. Inputs for insect and disease control used to be sold on credit, but for the last decade, they have been supplied "free" to members through the cooperatives. The cost of inputs is in fact included in the differential between producer prices and international prices the marketing board receives. Input subsidization was intended to increase use of inputs by small farmers who might not have the cash or who might refuse to borrow, but the effect seems to have been to lessen inputs used by farmers. The shortfall between amounts purchased and budget allocations for these inputs suggests administrative irregularities. The inputs that do arrive at the local cooperatives are inequitably distributed: Formal allocation on the basis of outdated and nearly meaningless tree counts invites some farmers to sell their input allocations. In addition, cooperative authorities use them for patronage. Some farmers determined to use these inputs must buy them. Thus, they pay for the inputs twice—in the lower producer price and in their private market purchase. Although cocoa purchase and shipping is still done by private merchants in some areas, the chain that links cocoa producers with international purchasers is generally a cooptative political monopoly dispensing patronage through services and employment it controls.

The high cost of the cooptative system and the low morale it is believed to produce have resulted in a number of government efforts to reeducate users, to restructure personnel and input supplies, and to make the hierarchy more responsive to its local membership. One such project, National Center for the Development of Cooperative Enterprises (CENEDEC), has moved in and out of a number of regions in central Cameroon, producing apparently short-term improvements in cooperative functioning. But when its well-paid cadres move to a new locality, the old system of patronage reasserts itself.

The prices paid cocoa producers follow a trajectory much like that in other African cocoa-producing nations. The farmers' share of the F.O.B. price has declined from a mean of 65 percent for 1955–1959 before independence to a mean low of 30 percent for 1973–1977, regaining preindependence levels of over 60 percent in the 1980s. Although the government has reversed the decline, real producer prices based on the consumer price index have not attained the 1960 level.[7] The declining returns on cocoa over two decades combine with rising food prices to make cocoa less and less attractive. Cocoa production has in fact dropped considerably, with yields far lower than they were a decade ago. This is in part a reflection of the poor producer price: Farmers have had little incentive to maximize yields by extensive upkeep or to start new plantations. A second powerful factor is the increasing age of the plantation: Cocoa trees produce for about forty years, but yields decline as the trees age. Thus, plantations in Central Province planted in the 1950s are now in irreversible decline.

Losses in cocoa earnings to the farmers and in government revenues through the marketing board have resulted in much comment and analysis regarding how to revitalize the cocoa sector. Declining rural incomes are seen as having numerous effects: the rural exodus; the disinterest of farmers in maintaining or replanting cocoa trees; and, some claim, farmers cutting down cocoa trees to make way for food production. To improve cocoa revenues in Central Province, a parastatal, SODECAO (Cocoa Development Corporation) was formed in 1974 with World Bank funds. SODECAO extension workers have effectively displaced the Ministry of Agriculture's underfunded, poorly trained, and ineffectual extension services. Its personnel have inputs, equipment, good transportation, and high salaries; they are younger and far better trained than their Ministry of Agriculture counterparts.

SODECAO demonstrates the government's concern with cocoa production and its recognition of the poor performance of the Ministry of Agriculture's extension services. SODECAO is a parastatal, independent of the Ministry of Agriculture, well funded and staffed by technically superior extension workers. To international donors, its creation was preferable to attempting to reinvigorate the Ministry of Agriculture hierarchy by retraining extension workers and policing budget allocations and expenditures. To the political elite, such a new parastatal offers a new career structure for managerial cadres and young technicians and, ultimately, a new patronage structure for a new generation in the growing political family. Thus SODECAO, along with the numerous other new parastatals, represents an organizational innovation to serve the national interest by promoting economic growth, but also serving the political elite in promoting economic and social mobility of cadres while tying them to the state.[8]

In a further attempt to improve agricultural production, the National Plan of 1980 designates regional umbrella structures to coordinate planning and development projects. By moving decision making out of the capital, this plan seeks to overcome paralyzing overcentralization and to improve responsiveness to local conditions. It is neither democratization nor decentralization because the regional structures are highly technocratic; rather it is akin to the "deconcentration" favored in Gaullist France. The umbrella organization selected for the Central Province is SODECAO. Thus an organization set up to rejuvenate cocoa yields is now in charge of regional economic growth, including food production. Because food crops and cocoa both draw upon the same broad labor force and land, coordinated planning makes sense. But an organization like SODECAO, specialized in cocoa research and production, is unlikely to shake easily its established focus in favor of a much more complicated agenda in which it has little expertise and no experience. Because technical packages for cocoa farming are well established and feasible low-cost ways to improve food farming are as yet unclear, SODECAO's new mandate implies high risks and low payoffs to the organization.

By 1985, SODECAO's response to its mandate to promote food production had proved timorous and closely circumscribed by its efforts in cocoa farming. SODECAO's sole effort to promote food production was to advise farmers planting cocoa seedlings to intercrop the cocoa with plantain bananas. The plantains provide useful shade for the cocoa seedlings and provide a cash crop to tide the farmer over until the cocoa trees outgrow the plantains and then start to produce. Although SODECAO agents have some specific suggestions on plantain cultivation, plantains generally grow well on the rich soil required for cocoa plantations. Because farmers have been interplanting cocoa and plantains since the 1950s, the SODECAO innovation is unlikely to have significant impact on food production. Second, because relatively few farmers have the land to plant new cocoa plantations, the SODECAO approach reaches few farmers. The farmer who SODECAO advises on maintenance and disease control learns nothing to aid or urge him to supplement his income with food production. Nor does SODECAO promote food production by women, all of whom grow food crops, or by the young farmer who inherits an aged cocoa plantation or has no cocoa plantation—the farmer who needs an alternative to cocoa farming.

It may be argued that SODECAO awaits research findings that would provide its agents with a "viable package" before intervening vigorously in food production. SODECAO has not opted for approaches like on-farm mixed-cropping trials. Such approaches are tedious and unlikely to yield big breakthroughs in productivity, although they may ultimately have a very wide impact because they build on existing food cropping practices. SODECAO has fulfilled its food production mandate only with food crops compatible with cocoa farming. This compatibility is very limited: Food cultivation can last only through the seedling stage because the close planting of cocoa trees for shade precludes intercropping thereafter (unlike planting methods for coffee trees). Thus SODECAO has responded to its mandate to promote food production only when food cropping actually promotes cocoa. This strategy can work for export crops like cotton and even coffee, which lend themselves to intercropping. But in cocoa farming, this strategy will not promote food production.

The mandate that SODECAO promote food production in Central Province followed some bolder but unsuccessful government initiatives during the Green Revolution and the Yaounde Green Belt Campaign launched in 1972. These efforts involved a marketing parastatal intended to compete with and outperform private marketing structures, as well as large-scale state food farms and some cooperatives of small farmers provided with inputs, tools, and technical advice. The difficulties encountered by all these initiatives shed some light on SODECAO's very cautious and technocratic approach.

· FLIRTING WITH PARASTATAL FOOD MARKETING: MIDEVIV ·

Rising urban food prices in the late 1960s and early 1970s led to increasing dissatisfaction with the government's "hands-off" policy in this sector. Food price controls imposed on Yaounde markets in September 1972 led to retailers' refusal to sell. The government withdrew the food price controls. But the issue of high food prices, sharpened by the West African drought of the period and the short-term unavailability of imported rice in 1973, galvanized government determination to act. In important speeches at the national party congress and the national agricultural fair, President Ahmadou Ahidjo announced food self-sufficiency as the new national goal. A number of initiatives followed, but the most visible was Food Development Authority (MIDEVIV), founded in September 1973 in Yaounde with branches in other cities. MIDEVIV is a nonprofit parastatal mandated to tackle urban food supplies in three ways: (1) to provide producers with an alternative buyer to the existing private sector; (2) to sell food in cities at prices below those prevailing in the markets; and (3) to encourage production of food by state farms as well as by producer cooperatives. The MIDEVIV state farm, specializing in plantain production, is judged by MIDEVIV to be a failure. Factors include high production costs, resulting from an excessive number of employees; theft of inputs and tools; and low yields.[9]

MIDEVIV's marketing venture was based on the premise that existing private sector marketing was disorderly, unreliable, and unfair to the farmer. As such, it was seen as a constant disincentive to small producers. Farmers are said to produce food that rots on the ground for want of a buyer or that traders buy at prices affording huge profits. The view that producers are victimized by private traders is widespread in peasant economies, although the traders' great profits are not always self-evident. In the Yaounde area, most food trading is in the hands of buyam-sellams who reach rural markets in bush taxis; those with enough capital rent a truck or part of a truck. Some live in Yaounde, whereas others are village women who combine food farming with trading the goods they buy from their neighbors. They are extremely numerous, small-scale operators who seem to have none of the characteristics making collusion or monopolistic practices possible. But MIDEVIV's proponents stress the needs of the isolated peasant with no alternative access to market, who surely does exist, and the presumed inefficiency of the private buyers, whose high operating costs and profits deprive producers of profits that a just intermediary could give them.

MIDEVIV was intended to serve both producer and consumer by its highly efficient operations. It was to buy at stable public prices higher than those offered by buyam-sellams. By purchasing by the kilogram, rather than the variable units and negotiated prices used by the buyam-sellam, MIDEVIV was to educate producers and rationalize marketing. And MIDEVIV was to sell produce in several outlets throughout Yaounde at prices below current market prices—a feat made possible by operating more efficiently than private traders. The rationales for MIDEVIV's marketing operations were similar to those of the cocoa cooperatives and the marketing board: State purchasing would serve producers and the community better than would the private sector. But the very different characteristics of domestic food marketing—goods' perishability, the dispersion of producers, and the shifting availability of produce through the seasons—led to very different results.

MIDEVIV's marketing efforts in the Yaounde area still elicit strong, divergent responses from farmers and technocrats. MIDEVIV operates at a huge deficit and angers farmers when its purchasing trucks fail to appear on schedule or when its prices are judged to be no better than those of the buyam-sellam. Its sales operations, according to its detractors, provide good buys for its own personnel and their kin, to consume and to retail. Its defenders say that MIDEVIV was a good idea—that one can, on occasion, find good quality merchandise at fair prices—but concede that MIDEVIV's share of the market has been so small that it never significantly increased foods marketed nor depressed market prices.

MIDEVIV's management concedes that the organization has never been able to control its cash flows. MIDEVIV buyers who go into the villages and agents who retail at MIDEVIV outlets in Yaounde handle quantities of cash under conditions fostering abuse. It has been reported that MIDEVIV's buyers and retailers both disappear with large sums with some regularity.[10] Vehicle maintenance costs are unreasonably high, again implicating employees' lack of professionalism. In self-defense, MIDEVIV buyers say that they often arrive at a designated buying point to find that buyam-sellams have preceded them and picked over the assembled produce, leaving the second-rate goods for MIDEVIV. Because MIDEVIV buys by the kilogram at set rates, it then overpays for low-quality goods. Thus MIDEVIV labors under structural vulnerabilities that, in its management's view, it cannot overcome.

MIDEVIV stopped buying in the Yaounde periphery in the early 1980s, moving its operations to areas much farther from the city that are rarely frequented by buyam-sellams. It still runs the big deficits, but it may be argued that it serves the public good by providing (subsidized) transport to widely dispersed farmers who, some 200 to 300 kilometers from the capital, have difficulty finding a marketing outlet. In 1985 MIDEVIV also served some isolated villages in the Mbam region, settled by farmers from the overpopulated Lekie, as long as a villager took the initiative to travel to Yaounde to arrange each pickup.[11]

MIDEVIV's foray into food marketing has had no measurable impact on prices. The very small percent of all food sold in Yaounde handled by MIDEVIV is too slight to have forced private-sector prices downward. And its purchasing prices have been no better than those of the private sector. A paradox inherent in MIDEVIV's marketing activities during its second phase far from Yaounde is that when buyam-sellam start turning up at MIDEVIV's new buying points to undercut them, MIDEVIV has indeed encouraged production for sale, stimulated the assemblage of that produce, and prompted the linkage between producer and traders. But this is a slim reed by which to justify the parastatal's large deficits and necessary subsidization.

Seed multiplication has been added to MIDEVIV's activities. New varieties of corn (which the producer must purchase anew each year), sweet potatoes, grafted fruit seedlings, and pineapple shoots are some of the seeding material for which a demand has developed and which will certainly grow. Research, such as a project at the Nkolbisson Agricultural School to isolate a disease-resistant strain of cassava, will increase the need for an agency to supply seed materials that extension workers should be introducing to farmers.

In light of MIDEVIV's expanding role in seed multiplication, some of MIDEVIV's managers want to terminate the parastatal's marketing activities. Seed multiplication is an activity in which MIDEVIV has some experience, and by making this its sole business, the personnel and some of the physical investment could be maintained. But the governing council, which is directly attached to the national presidency, did not agree to change the parastatal's policy and drop food marketing. The presidency's desire to retain MIDEVIV's marketing activities despite its big subsidies begs for an explanation.

The occasions when MIDEVIV has been ordered to intervene in marketing suggest that, despite its deficits, MIDEVIV is seen as politically useful. Indeed, the government called upon MIDEVIV in 1983 when drought conditions touched the entire country, lowering production and causing food prices in Yaounde to double, triple, and quadruple. During the summer months, the price of one staple, plantain bananas, sometimes purchasable for CFAF1,500 reached the unprecedented price of CFAF8,000 (The Cameroonian unit of currency is the West African franc. The exchange rate in 1980 was $1 = CFAF206; in 1982 it was $1 = CFAF307; and in 1987 was $1 = CFAF302.)

At this time, MIDEVIV was ordered to make purchasing trips to the Western Province in order to bring food to Yaounde's population. MIDEVIV's purchases there were insignificant, even with the support of one subprefect, who attempted to outlaw purchases by private food buyers to force sales to MIDEVIV despite its low producer prices (a rare Cameroonian example of an attempt to impose effective price controls). Nonetheless, MIDEVIV buyers were unable to find sellers at the prices they were paying.

MIDEVIV was called into action during another commodity crisis in December 1983 when palm oil shortages caused considerable tension and some violence in Yaounde. Palm oil, produced largely by the Cameroon Development Corporation (CDC) in the southeast, is marketed at a fixed price. Shortages led to numerous accusations on the street and in the press that private traders were hoarding oil to drive prices up, as the black-market price climbed 300 percent over the published price. MIDEVIV was ordered to purchase palm oil directly from the CDC and sell at the official price, well below the black-market prices. MIDEVIV had difficulty acquiring supplies, given the great incentive for CDC personnel to sell on the black market. But with increased official support, MIDEVIV did acquire sufficient stock to attract great crowds before dawn at its stores, causing near riots as people broke queues. When the army was called in to keep order, angry buyers claimed that now soldiers' kin were enjoying privileged access and selling the oil at black-market prices on the side. Tension did not subside until the government flew peanut oil in from France.

MIDEVIV has proved unable to compete with the dense network of individual private retailers or to resolve the crises of runaway prices triggered by severe drought and reduced supplies. Its management, publicly attacked for its failures, requested that the presidency permit it to withdraw from food marketing—a request that was denied at that time. Acute shortages of staples, such as occurred in 1983, creates a public demand for an official remedy. Although ultimately the only solution was to increase supplies, in the short run MIDEVIV was cast as the lightning rod.

By 1986, MIDEVIV was indeed permitted to drop food marketing to specialize in seed multiplication.[12] Nonetheless, it seems likely that the government will feel compelled to attempt to regulate prices and even to control supplies through some public agency in the face of politically threatening shortages.

· SMALL-PRODUCER FOOD PROGRAMS ·

Proclamation of the Green Revolution spawned a number of initiatives to promote food farming by small producers. These efforts are of two kinds: those seeking to set up young men in commercial farming and those aimed at women farmers. Their lackluster record is variously interpreted. Some conclude that better planning and more investment are needed to reach small producers, whereas others believe that agricultural extension in food production must wait until agronomic research provides attractive, profitable technical packages for peasant producers.

The male-oriented younger farmers' programs have had variable outcomes. Some of these were peasant groups (Modern Agricultural Associations, or GAMs) under MIDEVIV, and they received loans from the agricultural credit bank (National Fund for Rural Development, or FODADER). Most of these dwindled out of existence when defaults on loans ended their access to credit. Truck farmers (growing lettuce, tomatoes, leeks, herbs) are the exception; these have survived the demise of the GAMs in Obala and some other localities. Obala, fifty kilometers north of Yaounde, benefited from Israeli trainers and managers ensuring a steady supply of inputs and expertise to become the truck farming "capital" of Central Province. The truck-farming GAMs in other areas have foundered from input shortages at critical junctures. Individual truck gardeners using modern inputs succeed where access to a stream or river makes irrigation, and thus dry-season production, possible. Today Yaounde's needs are supplied by established truck farmers who use meticulous and labor-intensive cultivation practices and capital inputs in profitable, commercial food production.[13]

Other programs for young farmers are run by the National Office for Rural Development (ONPR) and the Civic Service. These are justified as programs to retain youth on the farm in the face of the rural exodus and increase food supplies. These programs target young men who have no prospects of inheriting land and who lack capital. The projects have attempted to locate land for these youths, often in "pioneer" villages, to teach cultivation skills, and to provide credit for housing, basic tools, and inputs. In addition to instruction in agriculture, the Civic Service programs include civic education and military training.

The programs are small-budget pilot projects outside the Ministry of Agriculture, attached either to the Ministry of Youth and Sports or directly to the presidency. It has been reported that they suffer from inadequately trained extension personnel, an inability to provide good land that is free of competing claims of ownership, and failure to provide tools, credit, cash, or inputs as expected. The programs promised more than they delivered, and the participants have quickly become discouraged. Land available for pioneer villages tends to be very sparsely populated, distant from cities, and thus rarely frequented by private traders. Expectations of commercial food farming are dampened by the spartan reality of subsistence farming with no social services: pioneers find conditions far harder than life in their original villages. Where markets are accessible, loans from the agricultural credit bank or other inputs do not arrive on schedule. Successful projects in commercial production of crops not habitually farmed by men would require careful planning and political clout to ensure timely delivery of services from relevant government agencies. A weak ministry like the Ministry of Youth and Sports or small autonomous agencies lack the technical personnel themselves and lack the political leverage to mobilize them.

· SOCIAL AFFAIRS AND COMMUNITY DEVELOPMENT PROGRAMS FOR WOMEN FOOD FARMERS ·

Farm women in Central Province supply both domestic food needs and most of the produce marketed in Yaounde. This gender division of labor emerged as men specialized in cocoa farming. As Yaounde's demand for food has increased, women have expanded their work hours and altered their farming practices to increase food surpluses and sales. With the exception of specialized truck gardeners, men have participated little in this response to food demand except to release women from work in cocoa when this results in marked gain from food marketings.[14] Production and marketing patterns are highly responsive to market accessibility, so that women living near the few tarmac roads sell up to half of what they produce, whereas others, far from main roads, market much less. Men appear much less responsive to available markets at going rates than do women; men presumably demand a greater return on their labor.[15]

Despite women's dominant role in food production, only two government programs have attempted to reach women farmers. Both of these programs utilize voluntary women's labor on community fields to produce food. The one day a week women devote to these fields surely takes labor away from their own farms, while they teach women little about techniques for improving productivity.

The most widespread of these community field programs is under the auspices of the Community Development Department. This agency, now in the Ministry of Agriculture, has been something of an administrative orphan. Community Development originated in Cameroon's two English-speaking provinces, and since becoming a national program, it has been attached to the Ministry of Youth and Sports, then to the presidency, and since independence to the Ministry of Agriculture. The women's community fields that Community Development organized are intended to increase community spirit and earn money for community projects, such as safe water points. Despite its current ministerial affiliation, Community Development rarely has access to Ministry of Agriculture extension workers or improved techniques. Indeed, its director, in 1983–1985, did not favor increasing women's food sales, believing that women should concentrate on nourishing their families.[16]

The second program that addresses women farmers was initiated by the minister of social affairs, who was until 1984 also the head of the women's wing of the national party. Seeking to increase women's income, the minister obtained small grants from international and nongovernmental agencies to promote the familiar women's community fields. The minister, determined to get good technical support for these projects, obtained the assignment of young, better-trained extensionists to the three Ministry of Social Affairs projects. These extensionists provided advice and, more important, obtained the necessary inputs for attractive crops such as pineapples and high-yield varieties of corn. But village women's suspicions regarding the destination of future profits from community fields and the fact that the labor demands of community fields compete with those of women's own fields have resulted in irregular attendance and low yields.

Women farmers have received little attention as food producers and even less competent technical assistance. The Community Development fields serve to fund a community good, such as clean water, rather than to increase food yields. They too suffer from planners' inattention to the opportunity cost of women's labor and some women's preference for individual over collective goods. The fields under the party auspices, although claiming to promote cash earnings for individual members, have been more politicized than have the Community Development fields, raising members' skepticism about who will benefit from the projects. They have done no better, and probably less well, than the Community Development projects in gaining members' commitment.

Both of these efforts seem to have mired down in the problematic of the community field model and have thus never addressed the needs of women farmers. Even the party fields, which innovated in seeking the best technical assistance available, are not seen as demonstrating techniques that women can apply to their own fields. Both programs impose a big opportunity cost by taking women's labor off their farms rather than seeking to increase the productivity of their farms. The ways women have adapted the crop mix on their own farms to changing markets—without agricultural extension—suggests that they will incorporate change on their individual farms far more than is generally believed.

Good extension, on-farm trials, and work groups (which exist, though they are subsets of village women) that rotate from one member's field to another's are possible alternatives by which agricultural extension could begin to serve women more directly. These would not conflict with women's primary and necessary attention to their own farms.

· POLICY PATTERNS IN FOOD AND COCOA PRODUCTION ·

Although food prices have outstripped cocoa prices in Central Province, food supplies have been sufficient to keep prices from rising precipitously. Yaounde is not supplied solely by Central Province, but production around Yaounde has expanded to meet much of the growing demand. With the exception of men's garden cropping with equipment and purchased inputs, rural women have been the principal source of this local growth in production.

These women have innovated and expanded production, largely without agricultural extension or research, by expanding the time they farm. The irrelevance of existing extension is confirmed by women and by extension workers, as the latter see themselves as knowing nothing applicable to women's farming. The extension workers are convinced that monocropping is "progressive," "modern," and "scientific," whereas women's mixed-cropping methods are "archaic." Food crop research is little advanced, although an improved sweet potato is in wide use, and high-yield corn is beginning to be used. Research on improved cassava may be ready for extension in the near future. But currently extension does not, and perhaps cannot, serve women or the crops they produce.

Food extension efforts aimed at men are hampered by the same weaknesses in project planning, research, and extension. Like the women's community fields, projects targeting young men have been touted as community and character-building. But the rewards of virtue are surely enhanced by persuasive material incentives, which are often absent. Good land with good access to markets is not likely to be unoccupied and available for such projects. Growth in food production rests more on private efforts in favorable localities than on distant pioneer villages.

MIDEVIV's marketing initiative represents a very different kind of policy initiative in food production: By tackling the uncertainty and risk in food marketing, its premise was that farmers would and could produce much more food if sales and good prices were ensured. Although the policy solution proved faulty, the problem it addressed is real: Except on the main roads, buyam-sellams do not reliably appear. More isolated farmers feel powerless, because if they refuse to sell at the price the passing buyam-sellam offers, they may indeed find themselves with spoiling produce on their hands. In the case of perishables like fresh corn, plantains, and other vegetables, refusal may mean a total loss for the labor expended.

In addition the buyam-sellam extends her purchasing area only as prices in Yaounde permit, as she must rent her own transport. In a year of favorable weather and high production, many farmers in the periphery will be unable to sell crops that would earn well for them in a poorer year when Yaounde prices are higher. Thus farmers feel the need for a certain purchaser. But the perishable nature of these food crops means that at time of peak production in a good year, such a buyer will be unable to sell or to store the produce. Until some processing innovations permit storage of local crops, or until farmers shift to crops that can be stored (corn is one candidate, though it is not yet dried and used as a year-round staple in this area), either farmers or traders will absorb the loss of food surpluses. As long as marketing is handled by the private sector, the farmers will do their best to adjust planting to demand and win or lose depending on yields and their access to market.

It is not certain whether Cameroonian authorities interpret MIDEVIV's failure in marketing as a function of the structure of food markets (perishables plus local buyers and consumers) or the result of an unprofessional staff. Pressures from urban consumers have led some governments to apply the export-crop marketing-board formula to domestic food markets, thereby creating vigorous black markets. What explains the prudent restraint of Cameroonian authorities—their willingness to let MIDEVIV withdraw from the grand marketing agenda that had been proclaimed for it, rather than attempting to impose an official monopoly to end the "disloyal competition" of the private traders?

The answer is not clear. Wisdom and right-minded liberalism are possible explanations. In addition, other factors may be noted that might predispose government to assure a monopoly for such a faltering parastatal. MIDEVIV was not set up as a means of recuperating funds loaned to farmers to purchase inputs, as was Integrated Zones of Priority Action (ZAPI de l'est), the development parastatal in eastern Cameroon. ZAPI de l'est used the familiar and logical device of advancing agricultural inputs to farmers, to be paid back through crop sales to the parastatal. This failed because farmers sold their crops elsewhere and thus evaded their credit obligations. Having made no loans to farmers, MIDEVIV had no moral or legal claim on farmers to sell to MIDEVIV.

Further, the interests of political pressure groups may have been decisive. Consumers, presumed to favor government controls, especially when food costs are rising, have indeed faced a steady increase in food prices, though not as severe as in some African cities. Food producers, largely women and some young men, looked for alternatives to the private sector, but they surely did not favor a monopoly. It is possible, but seems improbable, that these peasant producers' policy preferences prevailed over those of consumers.[17] The traders themselves constitute a smaller group with at least some influential members who speak unambiguously in favor of free market solutions. At the national level, the private sector has been relatively strong in Cameroon, offering groups like the Bamileke, who have been little favored politically but are economically extremely effective, an avenue of upward mobility. Some of these bigger traders are purchasers in the greater Yaounde area, though most of the food moves along the marketing chain to Yaounde markets in the hands of local women, part-time or full-time traders handling little more than a couple of headloads. Finally, MIDEVIV was never intended to generate revenues (as cereal boards have been in Mali), so the government did not have this stake in making it work. The structure of the cocoa market makes it a sector far more easily taxed to meet the state's revenue needs. Thus, Cameroonian prudence with regard to state intervention in food marketing may derive from this far more viable alternative to the "revenue imperative."

The policy instruments in food production and in cocoa production contrast sharply. The differences in institutions and scientific knowledge have conditioned the development of differing political functions. From an established research base and heavy involvement in marketing and extension in the colonial period, the Cameroonian government has extended state intervention to include highly centralized cooperatives that have taken over produce purchasing, and later, all input supply and its payment. With the important exception of private-sector exporters, who purchase from cooperatives and sell to the marketing boards, the system is entirely public (see Table 3.1).

The difference between the state's role in these two sectors parallels the differences in each sector's existing technical expertise and in the structure of the markets. But the heavy involvement of the state in cocoa certainly conditions the other sector, food marketing. The liberal critics argue that if cocoa marketing and particularly input supplies were handled by the private sector, cocoa farmers and food farmers would benefit from the increased volume of traders' business. Private-sector handling of cocoa inputs would hasten the diffusion and adoption of food inputs: Currently such inputs are only occasionally available in rural markets. Farmers' expectations learned from the steady prices and total input subsidy program in cocoa farming must make food farming appear very risky indeed. A farmer unable to absorb a big loss might, as a food producer, expend considerable resources on production, including purchased inputs, for which her spouse markets, pays cash, or negotiates his own credit, all with no certainty of his ultimate sale price. Even at stagnating prices, cocoa farming offers a much more comfortable prospect.

Economic liberals, including the World Bank and USAID (U.S. Agency for International Development), argue that private marketing and the end of input subsidies would benefit cocoa and food farming. The inefficiency of the cocoa cooperatives and marketing board deprive cocoa farmers of a potentially much better producer price. The centralized and subsidized system of input supply is not only inefficient in cost terms, but it fails to distribute sufficient inputs to many, possibly most, producers.

Thus far, Cameroonian officials seem little inclined to cut back the state's role in cocoa marketing. Despite policy restraint in government action in food marketing—that is, through MIDEVIV—the government is unlikely to embrace the policy prescriptions of the liberals in the export sector, as the existing state structures handling agricultural exports serve rulers in ways that they could not easily forego and for which increased food production would be no substitute:

1. Cocoa provides the government with state revenue in precious foreign exchange. Increased food production is certainly a net gain for the government in averting urban discontent. But food production does not lend itself to government taxation, as does cocoa production.

2. The marketing board, the parastatals, and the cooperatives all provide the regime with vehicles for the selective distribution of these revenues. The revenues generated by cocoa sales are in turn used for political patronage, tying Cameroonians to the regime. The marketing board and cooperative structure

both provide political plums for chosen members of the elite. In addition, the cocoa cooperatives selectively distribute employment, inputs, and cash at the village level. This selective patronage is inherently individualizing; the cooperatives function as arenas for individual gain rather than as instruments for the collective good. Thus, they are a barrier to class action by the peasantry.

· PROSPECTS FOR FOOD PRODUCTION ·

Agricultural policy institutions in Cameroon bear witness to the privileged position of export-crop agriculture. The important position of these crops in the economy and the statism that characterizes the export sector will change only at considerable risk to the established political order. These export-oriented state structures probably retard modernization of food production, although in Cameroon governmental nonintervention in food production has resulted in sufficient food production to date.

Cameroonian agricultural policy research in Central Province warns that cocoa and commercial food production compete both for scarce land and scarce labor. Land pressure is increasing, particularly in the Lekie, so that women report fallow periods as short as two years for their food fields, with resultant declining yields. Women complain of soil impoverishment and are planting a poor-soil crop, cassava, extensively. Labor is also seen as a constraint on improved cocoa production as well as food cropping by some new methods. Students of cocoa production have concluded that without a decisive (30–50 percent) increase in producer prices for cocoa, farmers will turn from cocoa to food farming or migration. Some claim that cocoa's stagnating producer prices have already led some farmers to cut down cocoa trees illicitly in order to free the land for food crops.[18]

My research suggests, contrary to these arguments, that farmers are not ready to leave cocoa farming. Certainly farmers have released their wives from certain tasks in cocoa farming in localities where women can then capture key food markets.[19] Some men have become truck farmers, but they are not numerous. Some men also take over fertile land from their wives, such as the area around the house that benefits from food waste and goat manure, to grow plantain bananas. But in the Lekie, I have no evidence that men have cut down cocoa plantations for food farming. Most men leave food farming to the women, and the women have satisfied most of the increasing urban demand.

Migration since 1980 into what had been an enclave in Central Province provides a good test of farmers' interest in cocoa farming because, unlike men in the villages they have left, these migrants had no prior investment in cocoa. A spontaneous team of such migrants is using a bridge completed in 1980 to leave the overcrowded Lekie for Mbam, where they clear land to plant cocoa plantations as well as to cultivate large amounts of food crops. The food crops are not only for subsistence, but to provide cash revenue until the cocoa trees begin to yield. Among these migrants, men and women work in both food and cocoa plantations; the settler situation brings a departure from the strong gender division of labor in the Lekie as well as much longer hours for men and women. Cocoa is, the male migrants say, an investment for the long term and something to leave to their sons—despite low prices. These men are not yet sure how much of their labor they will invest in food farming once the cocoa comes into production; they will see how prices and marketing conditions are when the time comes.

These settlers take advantage of the abundance of virgin land to farm both food and cocoa. Their evaluation of cocoa and food crops is not based simply on food and cocoa prices. Cocoa offers long-term income with less labor once the plantation is established, whereas food crops, because they are generally not perennials, require a continuous outlay of labor. Second, state structures offer services that assist the cocoa farmer, including marketing outlets. Third, cocoa is recognized proof of landownership, whereas food crops support no claim to land. Such proof of ownership is valued by peasants, as population growth and the 1972 private land registration act have combined to increase land pressure and, thus, disputes and litigation over land.[20]

These observations suggest that peasants make allocational decisions based on more than prices. Food prices have risen largely without government interference; farmers have responded by diversifying production for market within the household. Thus far, food markets have been supplied by women selling the surplus over what they use for household consumption, with men remaining largely specialized in cocoa, the areas's earliest and ongoing cash crop. Women's "surplus" food production has increased in response to rising demand. And some men grow bananas for sale even when their cocoa fields are well established. Evidence from the Mbam settlers and scattered cases in the Lekie suggest that a decline in the gender division of labor between cocoa and food crops is occurring; both men and women are producing food crops. But to conclude that men will turn away from cocoa is to ignore the advantages of cocoa. They are more likely to pursue a strategy of diversification, which preserves flexibility and income from both food and cocoa. Cocoa is far less risky than most food crops because of its stable price, its relatively slight perishability, and its easy marketing through the extensive purchasing structure sponsored by a keenly and directly interested state. Because of variable market access, payoffs from food farming are more sensitive to location; for most farmers perishability and price variability make food farming risky. Thus, a cocoa plantation remains a happy complement, even when men move into those food crops that have been women's domain.

The public sector is unlikely to become involved in food marketing or price fixing, given the MIDEVIV experience and the present impossibility of stocking food crops grown in central Cameroon. The legal question of landownership is one area of government action that might affect farmers' production strategies: When land titles are clearly established, cocoa will cease to function as proof of ownership. But registration of landownership is moving very slowly, as cash and political influence are needed to activate the bureaucracy and cut through the morass of competing claims.

Government noninterference has served food production relatively well in the past, but government efforts to promote food production are now oriented toward research and extension rather than marketing. The public sector's greatest contribution to food production will surely be research and testing improved varieties, retraining of extension personnel, and meeting farmers' demand through seed multiplication centers. These efforts will not greatly alter the risk of food farming and marketing, but can improve productivity and the quality of yields. The extent of the farming population that such public policies reach depends directly on the strategies of research and extension recycling adopted. An emphasis on varieties that do not require extensive investment in inputs, emphasis on farm trials where mixed cropping is practiced, and attention to labor calendars for cocoa and food crops to maximize compatibility are strategies consistent with the farmers' strategy of risk aversion, diversification, and increasing income through market sales.

This scenario requires no grand reversal of the political and economic functions currently filled by structures associated with export crops: The Cameroonian regime's restraint regarding MIDEVIV's food-marketing foray is not presumed to presage a similar liberalization in the cocoa sector. But this type of food crop research and extension—targeting small farmers unlikely to specialize or make big investments in inputs—will require a new kind of organization. Such an organization will have no powerful clientele to ensure that it receives the resources necessary to operate effectively. International donors appear ready to use their leverage to support such an enterprise. But appropriately defined research goals are not sufficient; achieving a corps of extensionists with both the necessary expertise and motivation to reach out to small producers will mark an innovation of considerable proportions.

TABLE 3.1 State Action in Cocoa and Food Crop Production and Marketing

	Cocoa	Food crop
Input supply	marketing board (payment) cooperatives (delivery)	none[a]
Extension	Ministry of Agriculture SODECAO	none[b]
Purchasing	cooperatives	MIDEVIV[c]
Sales	marketing board	MIDEVIV

[a]FONADER has given credit to few small farmers, though it has funded some truck gardeners.
[b]Although the Ministry of Agriculture extension workers profess little knowledge of food cropping, in 1985 SODECAO took over all cocoa extension, leaving ministry extension workers with nothing but food crops.
[c]MIDEVIV was active in marketing for only a few years around Yaounde.

• NOTES •

The field research on which this chapter is based was made possible by a Fulbright Lectureship to the Department of Law and Economic Sciences at the University of Yaounde. The research project was conducted under the auspices of the Direction Générale de Recherche Scientifique and Technique during 1983 and the spring of 1985.

1. World Bank, *World Development Report 1984* (New York: Oxford University Press, 1984), pp. 222, 228. The 1985 and 1986 *World Development Reports* use 1974–1976 rather than 1969–1971 as the baseline and report declines of 17 percent and 16 percent in per capita food production for 1981–1983 and 1982–1984, respectively. These may reflect higher production in the later baseline period, the drought of 1983, and/or a long-term decline in per capita agricultural production. The view that Cameroon is joining other states in declining food production is elaborated below.

2. Kenya and Côte d'Ivoire are the obvious examples.

3. Both of these very poor states have attempted to impose food marketing through state agencies at controlled prices. These efforts have created extensive black markets and discouraged food production. See, for example, Elliot Berg, *Marketing , Price Policy and Storage of Food Grains in the Sahel* (Washington, D.C.: USAID, 1978, for Club du Sahel/CILSS), and my monograph *Political Variables and Food Price Policy in West Africa* (Washington, D.C.: USAID, 1981).

4. World Bank, *World Development Report 1986* (New York: Oxford University Press, 1986), p. 182.

5. Ibid., p. 240.

6. Ibid., p. 190

7. *Bilan diagnostique au secteur agricole de 1960–1980* (Yaounde: Ministry of Agriculture, 1980), pp. 145, 160, and also Michael McLindon, Anthony Wawa Ngenge, and Timothée Ayssi, "Cocoa in Cameroon: Policy and the Economics of Production (Yaounde: Ministry of Agriculture, 1983), p. 58a. For analysis of cocoa production in Cameroon, see ibid. and Jean Assoumou. *L'Economie du cacao: l'Agriculture d'exportation et bataille du développement en Afrique Tropicale* (Paris: Editions Universitaires, Jean-Pierre Delarge, 1977).

8. See Goren Hyden, *No Short Cuts to Progress* (Los Angeles: University of California Press, 1983), ch. 3, "Decentralization and Parastatals," for a general discussion of widespread African use of parastatals as an antidote to overcentralized, mediocre administration. In Cameroon, several agricultural parastatals have been placed directly under the Ministry of Economy, Finance and Planning in order to circumvent the Ministry of Agriculture.

9. Jane Guyer, "Feeding Yaounde" (1983 ms.), gives an excellent analysis of this initiative. She describes the official hostility toward petty traders that led to the short-lived price controls of 1972. MIDEVIV's marketing activities marked a retreat from this coercive statism, but its proponents continue to talk about the "disloyal competition" of the petty traders (ibid., p. 48). Guyer also provides valuable historical depth on state policy and food production in this article, some of which is also available in Jane Guyer, "The Food Economy and French Colonial Rule in Central Cameroon," *Journal of African History* 19, no. 4 (1978): 577–597; idem., "The Administration and the Depression in South Central Cameroon," *African Economic History*, no. 10 (1981): 67–79; and idem., *The Provident Societies in the Rural Economy of Yaounde, 1945–1960* (Boston University, African Studies Series, Working Paper No. 37, 1980).

10. Interviews at MIDEVIV were conducted in the fall of 1983.

11. Interviews, Sa'a and Mbam, 1965. I do not know how widely MIDEVIV was playing this "angel" role for isolated food producers at this time.

12. Personal communication, Professor Joseph Ntangsi, Department of Economics, University of Yaounde, September 1986. Professor Ntangsi's comments and observations on this chapter are gratefully acknowledged.

13. In 1983 and 1985 Lekie truck farmers were facing increasingly stiff competition from Western Province producers. Completion of road construction from Yaounde to Bafoussam will make Western Province farmers still more competitive, forcing major adjustments among Yaounde-area truck farmers and other food producers.

14. Jane Guyer, *Family and Farm in Southern Cameroon* (Boston: Boston University African Studies Center, African Research Studies #15, 1984).

15. Jeanne Henn, "Intra-Household Dynamics and State Policies on Food Production: Results of a 1985 Agro-Economic Survey in Cameroon" (Conference on Gender Issues in Farming Systems, Research and Extension, February 1986, at the University of Florida, Gainesville).

16. Interview, 1983.

17. Robert Bates, *Markets and States in Tropical Africa* (Los Angeles: University of California Press, 1981), notes that wealthy farmers may promote policies serving themselves and small, less politically effective farmers as well. FONADER, the agricultural credit bank, has loaned widely to the aspiring landed bourgeoisie, especially to functionaries. Some of these have set up food farms. But I am not certain that these farmers have played a significant role in protecting the small traders and food farmers from price controls.

18. Ministry of Agriculture interviews, 1963. No one at my research site, Sa'a, confirmed that anyone had cut down cocoa trees to this end. However, this could conceivably have occurred closer to Yaounde.

19. See Guyer, *Family and Farm.*

20. Cocoa farming undermined the customary system of usufruct, because, as a perennial crop, it created long-term interests in land. Tree crops have come to indicate a legitimate claim, a step toward ownership. An old woman will even plant a couple of cocoa or avocado trees to firm up her son's claim to certain land. Migrants pay for land on which they will plant cocoa: the payment and the cocoa trees are evidence of their permanent claim.

·4·

The Political Economy
of Food in Ghana

JON KRAUS

Ghana has experienced wrenching and prolonged food and agricultural crises in the last fifteen to twenty years, provoking impoverishment, social turmoil, class conflict, political upheaval, and the degeneration of public institutions and political capacities. The crises in food have involved, first, sharply rising prices; then, significant nonavailability to poorer parts of the population; and, during severe drought years, absolute shortages. In early 1977, Ghanaian university students demonstrated over poor and insufficient food, protests that escalated into a widespread confrontation with the military government and demands that it withdraw and restore civilian rule. A government-appointed ad hoc committee on union government held public hearings on possible forms of government and found that "a subject which came up at many public sittings was the shortage of such food items as rice, flour, and maize. [The chairman's admonitions to address the constitutional topic] often drew the response that food was the primary need of many Ghanaians." Many Ghanaians spoke of the "moral degeneration of Ghanaian society and the scarcity of food."[1] Popular outrage at escalating food prices and extreme shortages of essential commodities drove successive governments in the 1970s and 1980s to devise ad hoc and destructive distribution systems—attacks upon the market women and traders who run the retail distributive system—and to launch forays into the countryside in search of food for the cities.

To explore the political economy of food, and necessarily of agriculture, in Ghana, I will first delineate the dimensions and character of Ghana's agrarian crisis. We will then pursue questions regarding three major aspects of the political economy of food. First, what major internal and external structural relationships and government policies have shaped Ghana's pattern of agricultural production and accumulation in the last thirty years, and what has been their impact? Second, how have Ghanaians responded to the agrarian crisis over time? Have there emerged distinctive patterns of response and protest among the differentially affected groups and social classes? Third, how has the political economy of food affected the processes of distribution, in terms of patterns of commodity distribution, public attitudes, and government policies toward distributive mechanisms, and the distribution of wealth, poverty, and malnutrition?

These questions will be examined in successive regimes in Ghana: Kwame Nkrumah's Convention People's Party (CPP) government, before independence (1951–1957) and after (1957–1966); the military National Liberation Council (NLC) regime (1966–1969) and its civilian successor, K. A. Busia's Progress Party (PP) government (1969–1972); the Supreme Military Council (SMC) government (1972–1979) and the brief radical populist Armed Forces Revolutionary Council (AFRC); the civilian People's National Party regime (1979–1981); and the current military-civilian Provisional National Defense Council (PNDC) government (1981–), led by Flight Lieutenant Jerry Rawlings.

· ASPECTS OF GHANA'S AGRARIAN CRISIS AND AGRARIAN ECONOMY ·

Ghana enjoyed fairly rapid economic growth in the 1950s, partly buoyed by rising cocoa production and relatively high world cocoa prices. Despite a much more concerted development effort and high levels of gross investment in 1960–1965, however, the economy stagnated during 1960–1970, with per capita GDP declining by .6–.8 percent per year. The economy experienced a drastic decline in the 1970s, with per capita GDP falling by about 3.2 percent per year in 1970–1981, which understates the collapse of productive capacities and infrastructure.[2] The Nkrumah regime's attempt to pursue a state-led import-substitution industrialization in 1960–1965 was expensive, poorly planned and implemented, and highly dependent upon imported inputs. Continuous foreign-exchange shortages in the 1960s and 1970s permitted inadequate inputs and spares for factories and infrastructure, drastically reducing production activity and marketing.[3]

A key to Ghana's economic development has been cocoa production, whose export has regularly constituted 60 percent or more of Ghana's foreign-exchange earnings. Stimulated by rising and stable cocoa prices and increased disease-control measures instituted by the Nkrumah government, cocoa production rose from 220,000 metric tons in 1954/55 to 317,000 metric tons in 1959/60 to a peak of 557,000 metric tons in 1964/65. Since then cocoa production has declined systematically. Falling production in gold, timber, and diamonds also have combined to create permanent foreign-exchange constraints, which have affected all sectors of the economy, including cocoa, food, and other crop output, and the infrastructure, especially transportation, necessary for production. Cocoa production averaged 380,000 metric tons in the three crop years 1968/69–1970/71 and dropped to an average 285,000 metric tons in the three years 1976/77–1978/79 (Table 4.1). In the midst of

Ghana's economic and political collapse, it plummeted to 225,000 metric tons in 1981/82 and 158,000 metric tons in 1983/84 before starting to recover.

The most dramatic expression of Ghana's agrarian crisis has been in local food production. The extent of the crisis may be gauged in terms of local food prices and acreage and production estimates. In some areas of Ghana with low and erratic rainfall, poor soil, and dense population, such as in the northeast, traditionally there have been "months of hunger" before a new harvest. But escalating food prices and shortages have often flowed from external price changes, severe import shortages, droughts, and, especially, government policies. Food prices rose 152 percent from November 1945 to April 1952, fueled by rising urban demand and import shortages, prompting protests, strikes, union formation, and nationalism. Food prices rose slowly during 1954–1962, 4.25 percent per year, when budget deficits were small and food imports rising. Food prices increased rapidly in 1963/64 (28 percent) and then by 29 percent in January–June 1965, given strong money demand and falling food imports,[4] contributing to popular dismay with the Nkrumah regime and to the 1966 coup. Under the military NLC, with government spending (demand) low and food imports increased, local food costs were somewhat lower but high enough to generate a growing wave of strikes in 1968/69 (Table 4.2). Under the civilian Progress party regime, a sharp contraction in imports in 1971 helped generate a 12.4 percent food inflation, one justification for the SMC military coup in 1972. Under the SMC, droughts, reduced output, enormous deficit spending, and exacerbating disruptions of the distribution system created an average food inflation of 52.3 percent per year during 1972–1979. The successor PNP government experienced 52.3 percent and 111.2 percent food inflation per year over the two years 1980/81, which led to popular outrage, malnutrition, and to the Rawlings coup and PNDC regime in 1982. Terrible drought years in 1982/83 and populist attacks upon the distributive system generated food inflation of 35.8 percent (at least) in 1982 and 145 percent in 1983. However, economic policies that restored market confidence, as well as good weather and bumper crops in 1984/85, led to an 11 percent price decline in 1984 and an 11 percent increase in 1985, the lowest since 1972.[5]

To what extent did stagnant or declining food production play a crucial role in local food costs in addition to external inflation and massive government deficits from 1972 on? Poor and inconsistent Ghana government estimates indicate significant increases in major grain (maize, millet, rice) and tuber crops (cassava, yams, cocoyams) during 1964–1969, but U.S. estimates suggest that Ghana's per capita production of all crops in 1970 and 1971 declined by 1 percent and 7 percent, respectively, from average production during 1960–1965.[6] If one excludes the decline in cocoa production, this could mean there was stagnant food production per capita. The Food and Agriculture Organization's (FAO) index of production indicates that both total agricultural and food production increased by 15 percent during 1969–1980 but declined by 15 percent on a per capita basis.[7] The World Bank estimates that Ghana's total food output declined by .1 percent per year, or 3.1 percent per capita, between the years 1967–1969 and 1977–1979, or a total of over 30 percent per capita decline.[8] Acreage and production estimates, based initially on a 1970 agricultural census, are shown for 1970–1986 in Table 4.3. The military SMC government in 1972 proclaimed an Operation Feed Yourself (OFY) campaign, making agriculture its major focus of development. In 1974, it announced that OFY was a success. A comparison of acreage planted and production for crop years 1972–1974 with those of the average in 1970/71 shows a *decline* in acreage and production in most major food crops (maize, yams, millet, guinea corn) but significant increases in cassava (30 percent), plantain (17 percent), groundnuts (22 percent), and rice (31 percent); rice received highly subsidized credits and inputs. There were also significant increases in production in some key industrial crops; oil palm, cotton, sugarcane, rubber, and tobacco. There followed three years of fairly severe drought, 1975–1977. Comparing average 1978/79 production with the 1970/71 average indicates severe declines in all major food crops partly related to size of landholding; for example, 73 percent of those producing for subsistence only had less than 1.6 hectares, but 43 percent of those producing mainly for sale also had less than 1.6 hectares.[9] There appears to be a significant degree of land inequality, but it is unclear how great is the inequality and if it constitutes a restraint on production, as some have suggested.[10] The 1970 agricultural census lumped together food holdings (typically small) and cocoa holdings (12.3 acres, average) and counted only land cultivated or cleared for cultivation, not fallow and uncleared land. Because peasant food farmers practice shifting cultivation, the land cultivated is no indication of the land available, either uncleared or fallow. Of land cultivated or cleared in 1970 (excluding fallow or uncleared), 30.5 percent of the holders used less than 2 acres, 24 percent used 2–2.9 acres (or, 54.7 percent used less than 4 acres); 27.2 percent used 4–9.9 acres; 10.7 percent used 10–19.9 acres; and 7.4 percent used 20 or more acres.[11] However, there is a strong direct relationship between size of cultivated land and family size (meaning family workers available), which strongly suggests that a major constraint on expansion of cultivated acreage among peasant farmers is labor availability during peak labor seasons.[12] Last, capitalist development in cocoa has created great inequalities in land and cocoa income among farmers. Various surveys in the 1950s and 1960s suggest that there is a small class of relatively well-to-do cocoa farmers: The top 20–25 percent gain 40–50 percent of net income, a middle 30–40 percent make 25–35 percent of net income, and the smallest 40–50 percent make only 15–25 percent of the cocoa income.[13] These characteristics suggest that government policies that failed to support small- and medium-sized peasant food farmers would be unlikely to increase significantly local food production.

A number of explanations for Africa's agrarian crises will be examined briefly to suggest their possible relevance to Ghana.

1. *Ecological/climatic explanations*. Many analyses stress the impact upon production of African soil infertility and fragility, insufficient fallow periods, and inadequate rainfall.[14] Comparing rainfall with local food and cocoa output is inadequate, except for severe drought periods, as rainfall timeliness and humidity levels have often been as important as inadequate rain in affecting output and marketing, such as in 1968.[15] Many studies depreciate the impact of climate as a determinant of food output, presenting it as one factor among many. However, drought or untimely rains certainly greatly reduced food output in four of five crop years in 1972/73–1976/77 in Ghana's northern regions, created famine conditions in 1976/77, and pushed many workers out of agriculture, which reduced later production.[16] The 1982/83 droughts were the worst in fifty years.[17]

2. *Demographic and employment factors*. All African states since the 1950s have experienced rapid population growth, urbanization, and significant changes in the size and composition of the agricultural labor force (for example, reduction in child labor as a result of compulsory education; the aging and feminization of the peasant farmer population). These constraints on production do not appear to have been greater in Ghana than in other African states and hence do not explain (or do so marginally) Ghana's much lower than average agricultural growth. Ghana's population growth during 1960–1980 was only slightly more rapid than the African average. Although it had a larger urban population in 1960 and 1980 than the African average, the rate of urbanization in 1960–1980 was much lower than average. Primary-school attendance as a percentage of the age group in Ghana was only marginally above the African average in 1960 and 1980, though attendance was far above the average for secondary school. Although Ghana had a much smaller agricultural population than the African average in 1960 and 1979, the difference was constant (17 percent).[18] We lack comparative data on feminization of the farming population. But its rapid occurrence in Ghana may be important for Ghana's production, because males are needed for land clearing and have much greater access to modern inputs and credit. Women were 45 percent of food farmers in 1960, 51 percent in 1970; the total number of male cocoa farmers fell by 1.5 percent during 1960–1970 (and undoubtedly further in 1970–1980), whereas the number of women farmers increased by 37.8 percent.[19]

3. *Neo-Marxist versions of dependency theory*. Briefly, these analyses stress the incorporation of peripheral capitalist countries into the world capitalist system on unequal terms (in trade, production, finance), a state policy stress on cash-crop exports to the detriment of food farming, destructive capitalist penetration of peasant subsistence production, the development in postcolonial states of class forces and statist policies based on the extraction of peasant surpluses to enhance elite consumption, urban-biased and import-substitution development, and capital accumulation by foreign capital (sometimes) and by a new merchant-professional-bureaucratic bourgeoisie, in tandem with

political leaders, using legal and illegal means. Some argue that a major cause of Ghana's food crisis has been the diversion of land and labor from food farming to cash-crop production for export (cocoa, oil palm).[20] This has occurred in some areas, and male preferences for cash-crop farming is clear. However, evidence suggests its nonsalience in Ghana's declining per capita food production. Historically, the great expansion of cocoa farms involved not a substitution for food farming, but a massive expansion of labor and land employed.[21] An enormous amount of new cocoa planting in the 1950s coincided with food expansion and stable prices. And falling food production in the 1970s and early 1980s coincided with the huge decline in cocoa production (Tables 4.1, 4.3).[22] There is no doubt that the postcolonial state in Ghana greatly increased extraction of cocoa farmer surpluses through low state-set prices and monopoly purchases, in part to create a less dependent, industrial base. Heavy statist expenditures required extractions that robbed the cocoa export economy of incentives to produce.[23] But food prices were not taxed or controlled (until the abortive attempts in the late 1970s and thereafter). Food farmer incomes rose in the 1960s and greatly in the 1970s and 1980s relative to other incomes.[24] Analysis has demonstrated the dominant impact of external influences upon African economic performance in 1960–1980, including developed-country demand and policies and terms of trade, which produced import strangulation.[25]

Bates employs a non-Marxist variant to explain state extractions of export-crop surpluses and persistent preferences for failing direct state projects over market incentives to increase production. State rulers gain economic surpluses to invest, (hoped-for) cheap food to feed potentially disruptive urban social forces, and political-economic resources to deflect opposition and selectively reward regime supporters.[26] Although surely correct in part, this rational choice model oversimplifies the decisional context, emphasizes the most cynical of several motives,and ignores that some interventions reflected elite perceptions of the failure of market incentives to increase peasant output.[27] Bates discounts wholly the ideology of state activism in developmentalist thinking in Ghana and elsewhere.

4. *Declining terms of trade.* Leaving aside debates on the sources of the problem,the thesis is that Ghana has faced throughout the postindependence period relatively low or declining terms of trade.In consequence, its economy has been intensely constrained by scarce foreign exchange and starved of imports, including inputs to farmers—for maintenance of roads and good vehicles to ensure marketing efficiency—and wage-incentive consumer goods. Low terms of trade contributed to state tendencies to keep producer prices low, creating production disincentives, and discouraged pursuit of a comparative-advantage development strategy. Table 4.4 shows that Ghana's terms of trade declined from the 1954–1956 average level to 1960; sank 20–23 percent during 1961–1966; rose back to the 1960 and 1954–1956 levels only for two years, 1969/70; then was relatively depressed (by 20–25 percent) from

1971–1976; then rose to new heights for three years, 1977–1979 (by which time disincentives had reduced production); and collapsed thereafter, with 1982 being only 60 percent of the 1960 level.[28] Ghana's massive increase in cocoa production after 1959 meant that its export purchasing power (export volume times terms of trade) could barely stay near the 1960 level during 1961–1964, and exceeded it again only in 1970. It remained decent while exports were high in 1972/73, then shrank quickly again. This is a favorable terms-of-trade series, showing an increase between 1970 and 1977 of 30 percent and by 1978 of 71 percent; other series indicate declines.[29]

5. *Market Efficiency.* A widely voiced explanation for the failures in African export and food crops is the unwillingness of African governments to permit the market to allocate resources "freely and efficiently" for production and distribution. The model argues that African governments failed to pursue their natural comparative advantage in export crops by imposing state-mandated low export prices, overvalued exchange rates, and misallocations of scarce investment resources and agricultural inputs to inefficient state-sector enterprises.[30] It assumes that capitalist relationships and markets invariably serve the general good. Ghana's low prices (high taxes) to cocoa producers in the 1970s (though not the 1960s) was one major cause for the collapse of cocoa production. However, the Ivory Coast has taxed export crops highly—though less so than has Ghana—but production continued to grow rapidly. It is clear that Ghana's overvalued exchange rate (which animated smuggling), spiraling inflation, and the collapse of the transport system—leaving considerable cocoa unmarketed and unsold—may have been as (or more) important as disincentives to production as the cocoa price itself. Moreover, the market did set prices for local foods yet failed to elicit higher levels of production. It was Ghana's major macroeconomic policies—especially enormous budget deficits, poorly conceived price controls, and highly overvalued exchange rates from the mid-1970s on—that completely distorted prices and incentives to produce and punished exports. These policies created a quasi-legal and illegal "parallel economy," encompassing an estimated 5–25 percent of Ghana's GDP during 1977–1980, over which the state lost all control.[31] The market-efficiency thesis is unreasonable in arguing that all state economic management ignores economic for short-term political considerations and is incompetent and chaotic.

6. *Disruptive Political Change.* Extreme economic deterioration is often inexplicable without regard to the political order that sustains normal economic expectations and relationships. First, frequent, coercive changes of government and of political elites tend to bring policy disruptions,often policy incoherence, and balking or listless implementation. Second, leaders who ascend to power by coercion may enjoy meager legitimacy and have many enemies. In Ghana there has been a tendency to seek legitimacy through populist policy measures that stress consumption over production, through repeated efforts to contain food and other prices by direct action, such as in distribution by means that

have severely disrupted without controlling the market—for example, coercing women traders and farmers to sell more cheaply. Third, rapid changes and incoherence in authority relations, as occurred under I. K. Acheampong and successor governments among patrons, brokers, and intermediaries,[32] tend to generate reliance upon personal loyalties, crass opportunism, no authoritative attention to real problems, mass-appeal policies (such as massive spending), and endemic corruption. These and the dominance of coercive elites manifestly contributed to the phenomenal disintegration of the political and economic order in Ghana after 1974.

These six factors provide partial explanations for Ghana's agrarian crisis. Notable were ecological/climatic factors in several periods, poor terms of trade that terribly reduced resources available to state and society, and highly disruptive political changes. The market-efficiency thesis helps explain the cocoa production decline and the massive pricing distortions that helped wreck the economy, but these were also partly the effects, not the causes, of food production failures, which fueled inflation.[33] Neo-Marxist theory can help explain policy choices, resource allocations, and the dynamics of accumulation by focusing on the weakness and contradiction of a colonial export economy in the world capitalist system, the class dimensions and inequalities in state accumulation or development policies, and the critical character of state-peasant relationships.

• THE POLITICAL ECONOMY OF FOOD •

For each Ghanaian regime, we will examine the political-economic forces that shaped economic and agricultural policies, the response of Ghanaians to these, and the distributive consequences.

The Nkrumah–Convention People's Party Government

The CPP was a populist movement of anticolonialism and economic nationalism, initially with diverse group and social class support, led by an aspiring, nonpropertied petite bourgeoisie (in education), with urban and rural roots. After independence and intraparty struggles, CPP leaders' economic nationalism and development strategies assumed state socialist forms. The CPP's rise to power (1947–1951) had been driven by broad economic protests against cocoa disease control methods and the rising prices of imported goods and local foods (152 percent from November 1945 to April 1952). This animated worker protests and union formation and agitation.[34] On attaining power in 1951/52, the CPP increased minimum wages. Thereafter, until 1960, low levels of food inflation reduced government attention to food production policies, though food output was promoted by government policies, the growing extension services, and intermittent wage pressures.[35]

During 1951–1959, the CPP government's major concerns with agriculture were threefold and reflected a preference for a capitalist mode of accumulation, increased government revenues for development spending, and the need to develop political support. First, cocoa farmer resistance to the cutting out of diseased cocoa trees was met with an educational campaign, renewed cutting, replanting subsidies, and a heavy investment in subsidized spraying machines and Gammalin to reduce capsid disease. These measures and higher cocoa prices (1951–1954) led to greatly increased cocoa planting and production. Second, the CPP taxed for development spending some of the gains from high world prices; the Cocoa Marketing Board (CMB) set producer prices well below the world market. Resistance to this pricing policy led to a strong, ethnic-based protest movement, the Ashanti National Liberation Movement (Ashanti NLM). Third, the government formed a Cocoa Purchasing Company (CPC), linked to the CPP's United Ghana Farmers' Council (UGFC) in response to pervasive problems of peasant cocoa farmer indebtedness, a desire to challenge British "middlemen" cocoa-buying firms, and the need to mobilize rural support for the CPP. The CPC purchased cocoa and lent funds to farmers until it was liquidated as a result of a political scandal in 1956/57, when the CPP's UGFC replaced it as a cocoa buyer.[36]

As a result of internal policy and power conflicts and low foreign investment, the CPP government in 1959–1961 altered its economic policies to emphasize import-substitution industrialization in manufacturing, mechanization in agriculture, and direct state participation in production and marketing in agriculture and industry. These policies were to be accomplished rapidly in large, job-generating projects, financed by state retention of a larger portion of cocoa earnings. The program shifted resources sharply from consumption to capital formation (16 percent of GDP in 1958/59, 23 percent in 1964/65); consumer and food imports declined after 1962 (Table 4.4).

Important agricultural policies, many contested by CPP ministers and members of parliament (MPs), were initiated in 1960–1963; these attempted to modernize agriculture and increase output rapidly by bypassing (noncocoa) peasant farmers. In 1961 the CPP's UGFC was given monopoly rights to purchase cocoa for the CMB (which it carried out successfully), eliminating the European firms and independent marketing cooperatives. With the cocoa-trading profits, the UGFC undertook to develop peasant producer coops to raise food and industrial crops; to assist it, the Agriculture Ministry's growing extension division was diverted to working with the coops. In 1962 many thousands of Agriculture Ministry laborers were replaced by farmers in the task of cutting out diseased cocoa trees (but the farmers did not do it). The laborers were put to work on newly created state farms to develop food and industrial crops. Government policy was partly animated by the belief that small "traditional" food farmers (who produced most of Ghana's food) could not produce enough increased output to sustain rising urban food and food-processing-factory needs. This strong belief that only modern and scientific means—mechanized agriculture—could increase output rapidly was shared by Ministry of Agriculture officials.[37] The UGFC organized by 1966 some 900 cooperatives; 15,000 peasant farmer members worked these in addition to their own farms. The State Farms Corporation (SFC), with 22,000 workers, and the Workers Brigade (WB), with 10,000, had acquired vast acreages by 1966 (but much of it in 1965), only a small part of which was in production by 1966 (6.8 percent and 18.6 percent, respectively).[38] Consequently, scarce budget resources and trained personnel were diverted from peasant farms, though there was great "leakage" in seed, tractors, and personnel from public projects to private farms. Second, despite inadequate time to make state farms successful, the SFC and WB farms performed poorly in terms of production and generated enormous losses because of hasty efforts, labor employment over production goals, inadequate managerial staff, and no plantation agriculture experience.[39] Also, as food prices rose, the SFC and WB were required to sell their produce in the cities far below market prices.[40]

The state socialist pattern of accumulation under Nkrumah's CPP was substantially unsuccessful, despite major gains in education, health, infrastructure, and agricultural inputs. This was because (1) the rush to industrialize and mechanize let to incredible waste (such as: a huge percentage of tractors in disrepair, food-processing factories without inputs); (2) the industrialization was financed by heavy short- and medium-term borrowing, creating high external debt; (3) import-substitution industrialization increased dependence on scarce imports; and (4) declining world cocoa prices and heavy public expenditures required increasingly low prices to cocoa farmers. The real producer price index fell from 130 in 1960/61 to 48.6 in 1965/66 (-63 percent, Table 4.1), when huge crop sizes greatly increased producer costs. This drastically reduced future incentives to plant, maintain, or even harvest cocoa crops. Along with CPP authoritarianism, CPP leadership corruption was extensive and severely undermined public and farmer confidence in state policies and economic institutions, such as the UGFC.[41]

During 1963–1965, sharply higher food prices animated increasing levels of popular discontent and attracted growing criticisms of the UGFC and especially state farms among the public, which were voiced by CPP MPs. In the National Assembly, many of the regular MPs' criticisms of the UGFC, Agriculture Ministry, SFC, and CPP leadership and policies were scathing.[42] Local food prices rose by 28 percent in 1963/64 and by 29 percent in the first six months of 1965, a result of lower grain production, sharp declines in food imports (Table 4.4), rising urban demand, and perhaps one-third of goods vehicles in disrepair. Ghanaians were outraged. CPP MPs forced the setting up of a commission of enquiry into trade malpractices; the high prices of food, fish, and imported essentials animated suspicions of hoarding and price manipulations by wholesalers, Ghana National Trade Corporation (GNTC) and State Fisheries Corporation (SF) managers, and market women, who control much of the wholesale and almost all retail trade in local foods. The commission found widespread corruption among GNTC and SF managers, stating in its report that the high food prices could pose a "real threat to the morale of our society." It observed that "queen mothers" (market women leaders) in the foodstuff market "exert control over purchases, . . . arranging bulk or even monopoly purchases. . . . She next ensures that food is retailed at prices fixed on her authority," a finding confirmed in part by other observers.[43] Worker protests and strikes were muted by state controls over the trade unions.

Government efforts to rationalize distribution tended to give state bodies like GNTC and SF near monopolies in wholesaling, which fed corruption. Since 1964, the government supplemented private food trade by having SFC and WB market directly at below-market prices their meager food output and other food purchased locally. These efforts did not ease the impact of higher food prices. Efforts of the government reduced by 30–33 percent real minimum and average wages in 1963–1965 (Table 4.2) and redistributed income to food farmers and traders. Regime support was greatly weakened.

The National Liberation Council and Progress Party Regimes

The military police NLC (1966–1969) overthrew the Nkrumah government because of the government's dictatorship and corruption, the military's corporate interests, and the sharply declining economic conditions, notably "food shortages"and prices. Its military leaders had no strategy for economic accumulation or agriculture except a distaste for the clearly unproductive SFC and WB farms and the CPP's "socialism." The few military and police officers actively involved in NLC rule took the economic advice of senior civil servants and members of the merchant-professional-managerial bourgeoisie (among whom were many ex-opposition leaders), who were recruited into state offices and advisory councils. There was a clear policy and civilian leadership continuity (K. A. Busia, Nana Akufo-Addo, J. H. Mensah) between the NLC government and its civilian successor, the Progress Party (PP) government, elected in 1969.

Early NLC economic measures were aimed at eliciting public legitimacy (for example, cutting taxes, increasing food imports) and coping with real economic liabilities inherited from Nkrumah's regime: huge budget and balance-of-payments deficits, a pressing debt crisis, no external reserves, and many poorly managed, overstaffed state corporations with low productivity. A central thrust of NLC and then PP economic policy was to reduce the overextended state regulatory and direct production and marketing activities (pursued with some but limited success) and to revive and open new opportunities for Ghanaian and foreign private capital. This still left the state as dominant economic actor. In agriculture, the NLC and, with more energy, the PP governments sought to (1) increase prices and inputs to, and provide a new buying structure for, cocoa farmers; (2) reduce greatly the costly state farm sector; and (3) provide incentives and support to food and industrial-crop farmers, especially large "progressive" farmers using modern methods. Inherited economic constraints, IMF-inspired economic stabilization policies, low institutional capabilities, and low apparent commitment limited accomplishments. The NLC initially reduced and then contained budgetary expenditures. During 1966–1969 recurrent expenditures were only 52 percent greater on an average annual basis than during 1961–1965, but the NLC slashed capital expenditures, which were 43 percent in current cedis (still less in constant cedis) on an average annual basis in 1966–1969 of those in 1961–1965. (The Ghanaian unit of currency is the cedi, divided into 100 pesewas.) The largest part, capital expenditures in economic services, which included agriculture, averaged 67 percent less than in 1961–1965.[44] The agriculture budget declined (as a percent of the total) from the CPP's 10.8 percent to 7.1 percent and 6.9 percent in 1968 and 1969.[45] After a year of retrenchment in 1966 (real GDP, -4.3 percent), the economy grew haltingly in 1967–1969 (average 3 percent), buoyed by rising cocoa prices and imports.

Cocoa fared poorly under the NLC and PP governments. Although rising world cocoa prices permitted increased producer prices each year, restoring real prices to 75–80 percent of the 1963 value, the NLC gave cocoa farmers a smaller proportion of average export prices (40.6 percent) than did the CPP (55.5 percent, 1960/61–1965/66) or the PP (44 percent) (Table 4.1). Total real payments to cocoa farmers were only 47 percent of their 1960/61 level, sharply reducing incentives for new planting or maintenance. Production in the 1966–1969 crop years at an average 337,000 metric tons was markedly lower than in 1960/61–1965/66 (average 438,000 metric tons); very good weather revived production under the PP (average 433,000 metric tons) (Table 4.1). Under the NLC there was a great decline in the number of sprayer sales and over 40 percent fall in average Gammalin 20 sales to cocoa farmers fighting capsid disease, which can reduce production by 20 percent. Given falling world cocoa prices by 1970 (-26 percent), the PP government declined to raise cocoa prices. Although the government sharply increased the volume and distribution channels of Gammalin 20 sales in 1970 and promised massive free spraying, Gammalin use fell by 67 percent in 1971. The PP government's aliens expulsion order in 1969 badly hurt cocoa and other farmers, causing 50–60 percent of alien agricultural workers to leave Ghana; previous labor shortages were accentuated, with 20–50 percent of labor needs unfulfilled and rural wages increased.[46]

Despite the NLC's initial concern over food shortages and high prices, its efforts were relatively meager. It reduced the number of state farms from 105 in 1966 to 66 in 1967 (they fell to 33 in 1971 under the PP). Extension services were strengthened. A USAID pilot "focus and concentrate" program was devised to encourage progressive farmers who were oriented to market production by allocating to these farmers seeds, fertilizers, credit, and advice. Several crop-specific programs were organized, which were later successful: in 1968, a Cotton Development Board to give assistance to small farmers; in 1969, a reorganized state-private Ghana Tobacco Company that provided close extension support to smallholder growers and purchased their crops. The belief of NLC advisers that increased food production depended on capital-intensive commercial farming was expressed in the Agricultural Development Bank (ADB) and extension support for large-scale rice farming in Ghana's north in 1968/69.

The support for more capitalized commercial farming became more clear with the PP's election to office in 1969. PP leaders were drawn largely from Ghana's commercial-professional-managerial bourgeoisie (55 percent of PP MPs were university graduates, almost one-quarter lawyers, as were one-third of the cabinet). The NLC had been unable to contain rising food costs, except in 1967 (-15 percent); food costs rose by 15.7 percent in 1966 and 8.7 percent in 1968 and 1969, despite large increases in food imports and purported gains in production (Tables 4.2, 4.4).[47] Alarmed by this, PP policies emphasized that agriculture was a priority and rural development necessary to promote agriculture, stem urban migration, and reduce urban-rural inequality; the private sector would be emphasized and supported with government assistance and credit to nurture scientific commercial farming. J. H. Mensah, finance minister, was the most articulate proponent of Ghanaian private capital and the need to involve the educated stratum in farming. Noting the large food price increases in 1967–1969 (maize 103 percent, cassava 41 percent), Mensah argued that the failure of farmers to respond to higher prices reflected Ghana's "predominantly traditional low productivity agriculture."[48]

Peasant mixed-crop plantings made unfeasible maximum yields and proper fertilizer use. PP policies emphasized reducing further unprofitable state production, turning state tractors over to a private firm, expanding to new districts the "focus and concentrate" program that focused on the most market-oriented farmers, increasing credit, subsidizing fertilizer by 50 percent, expanding high-yield seed use, building feeder roads, clearing land for prospective educated farmers, and allowing foreign firms to farm in Ghana. Key imported crops—sugar, kenaf, cotton, and rice—as well as maize were aided through quasi-government boards.[49] These programs were promoted by a large expansion in agricultural credit during 1969–1971 from commercial banks (+62 percent), the National Investment Bank (+346 percent) (all to large private and joint state-private firms), and the ADB (+181 percent).[50] Most of these programs ignored small peasant farmers (over 50 percent of them women) and focused on medium to large farmers and educated nonfarmers, many of whom, like Mensah himself, were often quick to take advantage of subsidized services and free land but were uninvolved in and uncommitted to agriculture.[51] During 1969–1971 various Ghanaians came forward with plans for vast farms—for example, a civil servant who took retirement and announced a ¢2-million scheme for ten commercial farms on 4,100 hectares in northern Ghana, to be financed by himself and U.S. investors.[52] (In 1974, the exchange rate was $1 = ¢1.1; $1 was equivalent to ¢2.7 in 1982 and to ¢175 in 1987). Last, the PP considered the traditional food-marketing and storage systems (which permit high wastage) grossly inadequate. Though nothing was done to halt the decline in goods vehicles, a PP cabinet committee decided to launch an Emergency Task Force for Food Distribution to supplement private networks, initially using private traders as buying and selling agents at fixed prices to direct food to urban areas (little came of this).

Ghanian responses to NLC food policies were initially muted by NLC popularity in overthrowing Nkrumah and restoring some freedoms. But strong pressures on the NLC emerged in 1967 from the newly elected trade union leaders and the relatively large group of unionized workers for increases in minimum and other wages to offset real wage losses in 1963–1966. The Trade Union Congress (TUC) requested a rise in minimum wages to ¢1 from ¢.65, but the NLC-appointed Salary Review Commission raised the minimum to only ¢.75, leaving the real minimum wage in 1968 at 68 percent of its 1963 level, with roughly similar results for other grades, but with the gap between lowest- and highest-paid more unequal (1:39).[53] According to government-set standards for minimum nutritional requirements, 88 percent of the employed labor force had an inadequate diet, even if they were single and spent all their wages on food.[54] The unions also fiercely resisted an NLC Prices and Incomes Board mandated to approve collective-bargaining agreements with wage increases of 5 percent or less.

Strong NLC pressures had kept down strikes in 1966–1967, but in 1968 and thereafter the number of strikes and workers involved escalated rapidly; virtually all were wildcat strikes by rank-and-file workers. The NLC used harshly repressive measures on strikers, with arrests, trials, and shootings. As government hostility and nonresponsiveness to union claims grew, and food prices rose, union leaders drew closer to rank-and-file sentiment, threatening strikes and then supporting them.[55]

Initially, relations between the PP and the unions were friendly. With worker support, PP candidates for the National Assembly won in all major cities except the capital, Accra, where voting was split. TUC delegates' conferences demanded an increase in minimum wage to ¢1 in 1968 and to ¢1.50 in the 1970 conference. Relations between unions and the PP government soured quickly, fed by the PP leadership's arrogance and indifference to union claims, a rising strike movement, and extraordinarily slow government responses in investigating wage claims and implementing collective agreements. Although defensive wage claims were the most frequent issue in strikes during 1966–1969 (34.8 percent), in 1970–1971 aggressive wage and collective-bargaining claims were an issue in 60 percent of the strikes (versus 36 percent in 1966–1969), with strikes increasingly aimed at the central government (21 percent) and state corporations (25 percent).[56] Local food prices rose less rapidly (4.4 percent) in 1970 than in 1969, but food prices climbed in 1971 by 12.4 percent (Table 4.2), escalating demands for increased wages and subsidized lunches. The agitation over food prices, moreover, affected all Ghanaians. In 1971 there was a spate of protests and riots by secondary (boarding) school students, largely over food quality (degraded by rising prices).[57] The *Spokesman*, an opposition newspaper, headlined: "FOOD: WE ARE STARVING" and observed: "Ghanaians are starving. This is the truth pure and simple." It noted the rise of yam, maize, and cassava prices, marital conflicts over food budgets, and the disappearance from the streets of the "saviour of the ordinary worker, 'Kofi Broke-man' [roasted plantain]."[58] PP ministers in late 1970 and 1971 found themselves coping almost daily with union ultimatums or actual strikes. On March 31, 1971, Busia appointed a salary review commission on wage levels and, in a populist act, increased direct state food production activity (hence employment) by the Food Production Corporation (FPC, formerly WB) and the National Service Corps.[59] Equally statist was the agriculture minister's proposal that the state acquire all uncultivated land in Ghana for direct leasing to farmers.[60] The TUC calculated a minimum wage for a family of four at ¢4.93 daily but only requested a ¢2 minimum wage.[61]

In July, with the real minimum wage index at 56 (1963=100), Finance Minister Mensah rejected any wage increase. He announced instead austerity measures to cope with a looming trade and budget deficit and a new Development Levy of 1 percent on all incomes. The TUC and individual unions vigorously opposed in rallies and speeches the Development Levy and wage decision. In September 1971, the PP government suddenly legislated the abolition of the TUC and froze TUC and union assets and the check-off, which created an indelible union hostility to segments of Ghana's bourgeoisie. An attempted general strike by rank and file died.[62]

Economic growth under the PP of 7 percent in 1970 and 5.2 percent in 1971 in real GDP was based, apart from good weather and harvests, upon an unsustainable inflow of imports, financed by gains from rising cocoa prices in 1968/69 and vast new short-term credits. With the cocoa-price collapse in 1970/71 (down 44 percent from 1969 average prices), the government faced severe budget and balance-of-payments deficits and a debt crisis. The austerity measures and large devaluation sapped the real earnings of key Ghanaian groups and hence PP legitimacy. The economic crisis reignited an antagonism to external debt (Busia's) and reinspired a populist economic nationalism, initially focused on food. The PP government was overthrown by a military coup in January 1972.

The Supreme Military Council and Successors, SMC II and AFRC

Despite enormous early efforts to raise agricultural production, Ghana's economy as a whole, its agricultural sector, and its public institutions regressed and withered under the SMC rule of Colonel I. K. Acheampong (1972–1978) and his military successors.[63] Several interrelated factors structured SMC economic and agrarian policies and performance: the impact of international trade-financial linkages: the SMC power structure, political-economic beliefs, and institutional capabilities; agrarian inequality; and severe drought during the mid-1970s. Ghana experienced very poor terms of trade for its major exports during 1971–1976 (Table 4.4, column 1); the economy was as starved of imported intermediate and consumer goods and spare parts in 1972–1975 as it was in 1966–1968, despite higher export volumes in 1970–1973. Imports were unavailable to maintain its productive and infrastructural capacities—roads, railways, vehicles. Export capacity had eroded drastically by the time Ghana's terms of trade rose (1977–1979). Low world cocoa prices also constrained the PP and SMC in prices they paid cocoa producers. Acheampong's unilateral repudiation of some loans and rescheduling of others greatly reduced foreign-capital inflows in 1972–1976 that could have eased import contractions.[64]

The SMC's major macroeconomic policies were dictated by the SMC leadership's political legitimacy needs and beliefs in populism ("one man, one bread"), economic nationalism, and state activism. These beliefs and legitimacy needs were reflected in the highly popular debt repudiation and rescheduling, the Operation Feed Yourself (OFY) agricultural campaign for self-reliance, seizure of majority equity ownership in key foreign enterprises, partial reversal of the 1971 devaluation (reducing import prices), subsidies on some essential consumer imports, and favorable responses to the grievances of key groups: unions, entrepreneurs, civil servants, military, students, and cocoa farmers.[65] Poor, and poorly managed, macroeconomics policies inflicted major damage. First, sharp expenditure increases after 1972 rose 28–54 percent annually to 1977/78, creating colossal budget deficits of 30 to 136 percent of expenditures.[66] Initially, these stimulated economic activity and employment, rewarded specific groups, and kept public services cheap. However, the deficits contributed to a devastating inflation (10–18 percent in 1972–1974, then 30–116 percent in 1975–1977), which had destructive effects on social and institutional behavior and fostered black markets and corruption. Producers lost, traders gained. Local food-price increases were high in 1972–1974 (15.5 percent average) and immisserating thereafter—31 percent, 70 percent, 153 percent, and 59 percent in 1975–1978 (Table 4.2). Droughts during 1974–1978 were only one factor in local food scarcities. Second, inflation made Ghana's currency overvalued. Thus, exporters with rising costs were paid too few cedis to cover production costs, hence reducing production incentives and encouraging smuggling, of cocoa, for example. Production of cocoa, gold, timber, and diamonds fell drastically, further reducing import capacity. Exports in 1977 were half the 1968–1970 average, 40 percent of the 1972 level. As a result of these policies, inflation, and scarcities, market and urban-rural linkages unraveled in 1977/78.

Cocoa production deteriorated drastically under SMC rule. Prices to cocoa farmers were increased each year (as world prices rose), restoring the real producer price in 1972–1974 to an average of 84.5 percent of its 1963 value. But by 1977/78, inflation had driven down real prices to producers to 58 percent and then 49 percent of 1963 prices; hampered by drought, production fell 31 percent in the two crop years to 1977/78 (Table 4.1). During 1974–1978, the SMC paid the smallest percent of average export prices that cocoa producers have received (Table 4.1). Cocoa farmer complaints regarding inadequate labor supplies and insecticides were ignored.[67] Incidences of smuggling cocoa to Togo or the Ivory Coast for higher prices rose; smuggled cocoa was estimated at 30,000–50,000 metric tons. Many farmers neglected cocoa for food production, whose unfixed prices soared relative to cocoa, especially in 1976–1978.[68]

The extraordinary food-price inflation reflected the failure of the SMC's OFY. Acreages cultivated and production in many food crops fell from the beginning, 1972–1974 and in 1972–1979 as a whole (Table 4.3), despite drastically higher prices, which should increase output, and the SMC's political and budgetary support, which reached 8.8 percent and 11.7 percent in 1976 and 1977. Agricultural loans increased by 445 percent during 1972–1976 and in 1975 exceeded the agricultural budget. But ADB loans rose less than inflation (513 percent versus 571 percent during 1971–1977).[69]

Several major factors were responsible for decreased production. First, drought was significant in four of the five years 1972/73 to 1977/78, affecting primarily northern Ghana but other regions as well. This explains some of the reduced acreage and production in grains and root crops in 1975–1977 (Table 4.3). Back-to-back drought years led to farm abandonment, male migration to towns, and high increases in malnutrition in the Upper Region.[70]

Second, and more important, the major beliefs and interests of leaders of the SMC and Ghana's agrarian bureaucracies yielded policies that wasted scarce resources and added little production. SMC leaders believed in direct action, massive "campaigns," which served politically to symbolize their determination. The SFC, the FPC the Food Distribution Corporation (FDC), the CMB, and Ministry of Agriculture all sought to enhance their roles and resources. They shared the belief that rapid increases in production must involve modern inputs and efficient uses of scarce labor, management, credit, and inputs that were concentrated on SFC or FPC farms or large private or corporate farms. However, these institutions systematically drained scarce resources. SFC and FPC grew less than 1 percent of food in 1974, except rice (2 percent) and maize (1 percent).

In 1974/75 the FPC used .5 percent of agricultural labor on .18 percent of land planted, with 27 percent of Ministry of Agriculture planting materials and 28 percent of the Ministry of Agriculture's extension staff. Yet its yields were no better then those of private farmers, but at greater costs.[71] In 1978 the FPC produced and sold food worth ¢432,000 and cost the government ¢19.2 million. Acheampong created in 1977 a Ghana National Reconstruction Corporation (the GNRC); its purposes were to prevent urban migration by youth by placing them on "settlement" farms and to obtain former CPP political support. In 1977–1979, with 21,000 young workers on 426 farms, the GNRC cost Ghana ¢60 million and produced ¢1 million of food.[72] Distressed by declining cocoa production, the SMC ordered the CMB in 1976 to develop plantations of 40,000 acres in cocoa and 25,000 in coffee, which diverted it from its major tasks of distributing inputs and purchasing and hauling out cocoa. In 1975/76 and again in 1977 the military had to mobilize "Operation Haulout" to evacuate to ports cocoa that the overstaffed CMB could not market. All large-scale capital-intensive farms in 1976/77 cultivated less than 3 percent of noncocoa land, produced 1–2 percent of total foods (except rice), received 80 percent of low-cost bank credit and most of the extension assistance and highly subsidized fertilizer. In 1976 less than 10 percent of all farmers received bank credit; of these, only 20 percent were farmers with less than 4 hectares. The heralded northern rice farming involved preferred access to land, capital, inputs, and an agricultural proletariat (which had to be created). The largely nonfarmer "stranger" farmers in the Upper Region acquired enormous areas from chiefs, invested in tractors and hybrid seeds, maintained fields poorly, and achieved low yields at great public (subsidized) expense. Often they abandoned the farms, confronted by problems with labor, bank debt, and tractor-part shortages. The scale of threatened land alienation provoked local farmers to burn rice fields and engage in other protests.[73] Whereas rice output rose quickly in the early 1970s, in the late 1970s it stagnated.

Third, these heavy investments diverted the government from key tasks of maintaining marketing infrastructure—feeder roads, railways, goods vehicles, spare-parts availability— and supplementing existing marketing and storage networks. But feeder and main roads deteriorated massively. In 1977 it was estimated that 70 percent of farmers had to headload produce from their farms, that 38 percent of feeder-road movement was by headloading, which clearly limited the quantities of food that could be marketed, thus discouraging production. Estimated vehicle spare parts in 1975 were 60 percent of 1970 levels; estimated goods vehicles available in 1975 in proportion to population were 29 percent less than in 1960, which fails to note those hobbled by lack of spares, such as 80 percent of FDC trucks in Ashanti.[74]

Fourth, inequality in the agrarian structure meant smallholders had much less access to land, capital, increasingly scarce labor, and inputs that the SMC supplied, however erratically. Inequality foreclosed many opportunities to small farmers to which they had earlier responded.[75] Nor were SMC authorities responsive to smallholder protests where improved and irrigated land was allocated overwhelmingly to "progressive" farmers, entrepreneurs, civil servants, and state farms—protests that were successful only with Acheampong's overthrow.[76] Parastatals that worked closely with smallholders did succeed in inducing new and increased production.[77] It was primarily foreign-aid agencies that pushed for extension services and input outlets for small farmers; examples are the German-Ghanaian project, the USAID MIDAS project, and the World Bank's Upper Region Agricultural Development Project (URADEP). The ADB's Commodity Credit Scheme, which lent to groups of smallholders (organized by extension staff and farming a minimum of 6 acres in one crop), did expand its small-farmer lending, from 10,000 loans in 1972 to 74,278 in 1976, involving 61 percent of total loans in 1978.[78] Repayment rates were 90 percent.

Fifth, the combination of collapsing infrastructure, consumer goods nonavailability in rural areas, and unequal access strongly suggests a market contraction, farmer withdrawal from market production, to explain declining food production despite rising prices. There is evidence that smallholders actually did benefit from the drastic food-price increases, that farmers even in some remote areas could sell their food on the farms to traders.[79] Nonetheless, the evidence of progressive breakdown in farm-market linkages is impressive for many areas and suggested by acreage/production declines and the political and economic conflicts of 1977–1979.

Ghanaians responded to the soaring food prices and scarcities with political protests and attempts to remove the SMC government, a huge increase in worker strikes, and many legal and illegal means of coping in a society that threatened their ability to secure food and survive. The large number of malnourished included 69 percent of children aged 1–5 in six villages studied in southern Ghana in 1974.[80] In 1976 the Ghana Bar Association (GBA) condemned SMC economic incompetence and authoritarianism and demanded civilian rule. In October, Acheampong countered with a proposal for union government that would involve civilians but was essentially a disguise for prolonged military-police rule.[81] In January 1977 he appointed an ad hoc committee to inquire into "Unigov" and opened up a lively public debate. As food prices shot up in the early months of 1977—30 percent by March, 82 percent by May—and food became more scarce, protests escalated. In March, students at Ghana's three universities protested against poor food, high prices, and Unigov. The SMC promptly closed the universities, prompting a medical school doctors' strike. The universities were reopened, then closed two more times as new student protests occurred. The SMC "retired" some doctors, the chief justice, and the governor of the Bank of Ghana. Led by Ghana's Bar Association, on June 24 the Association of Recognized Professional Bodies (ARPB) gave the SMC until July 1 to resign and permit a civilian government to be formed or it would strike— which it did.[82] Acheampong then announced a referendum for March 1978 on Unigov proposals and a return to civilian rule in 1979—under his control, he assumed.

These political events occurred in the throes of widespread turmoil over food scarcities and the increasingly desperate and erratic SMC measures to control inflation. In February 1976 the SMC pinned responsibility for the rising prices and scarcities on the tens of thousands of Ghanaian market women who dominate retail sales and some wholesale trade. The SMC banned them from trading essential goods or fish, which henceforth would be sold only by designated supermarkets. This led to long queues, "queue contractors," and the disappearance of many commodities.[83] Price controls were intermittently enforced at factory or government depot gates but were enforceable only on exemplary occasions at retail levels. In May 1977, amidst the political challenges, the SMC ordered a *reduction* in the prices of most domestic food staples and their sale at fixed prices. The military and regional organizations (headed by military leaders) were to enforce this first attempt to control domestic food prices.[84] Market women were being told to sell the food below their cost. Kenkey (a West African "fast food") traders in one Central Region area briefly withdrew their products, as did large numbers of food traders in Accra and Koforidua, Eastern Region capital. Local food in Koforidua was quickly exhausted. The military regional commissioner (RC) tried to enforce the price controls, sending military troops into the surrounding rural areas to obtain food, selling it from trucks in town or delivering it to civil servants at district offices. There was a high level of tension, many military threats, and a chief and a prominent ex-politician were asked to mediate. Essentially, the RC here, and the SMC in general, quickly backed away from the decree; market women set the prices.[85] But the government, through military task forces, remained determined to obtain more food directly from farmers.

A new finance minister in 1978 ended the system of designated stores for distributing essential commodities, but the state persisted in attempts to manage distribution, for most of which it had no capacity: The agriculture minister ordered the Rice Mills Unit to reduce its price for milled rice, although this price reflected the higher prices the SMC offered to farmers; a new Special Marketing Unit was set up at SMC headquarters to organize farm-to-market sales of food directly to market women. One reasonable, TUC-initiated effort involved TUC registration of genuine kenkey producers and a TUC-monitored distribution of maize directly from FDC warehouses to kenkey makers at fifteen points in Accra in order to eliminate maize diversion to intermediate sellers and subsequent markups, especially in imported maize; maize supplies were seldom adequate to contain prices.[86] In 1978 the minister for consumer affairs organized a system of direct deliveries of 10 percent of various food and other commodities to consumer cooperatives, of which some 300 sprang up in Accra, allegedly with 250,000 members.[87]

Wage-salary earners were impoverished by inflation, as were those on paltry wages in the informal bazaar sector, unless they were traders or artisans producing goods. Real minimum and other wages fell by roughly 55 percent during 1974–1977 and 65 percent by 1978. Hence, the unions strongly supported price controls and direct distributions, however haphazard. Workers and civil servants absented themselves for second jobs. Factory and farm workers insisted on the right to acquire free or at control prices commodities they produced, which were sold on the black market for food money; for example, the fifty-six workers and three managers at the Komenda Sugar Factory appropriated 4,000 1-kilogram sachets of refined sugar.[88] Managers and workers in state corporations distributing goods (such as GNTC) diverted goods to traders in the black market. Incomes were massively redistributed from wage-salary earners and producers (where prices were controlled) to importers, traders, and food farmers, from none of whom could taxes be collected.

Following the fraudulent 1978 referendum on Unigov, repression of the leaders of the major opposition groups,[89] and continuing strikes and protests, senior military leaders removed General Acheampong in July 1978 and set up SMC II, under Brigadier Fred Akuffo. The reduction of coercive constraints upon protest activity and of price controls unleashed an incredible range of protests by aggrieved groups. Akuffo's effort to shield senior officers and Acheampong from punishment or investigation led to a June 1979 military mutiny-coup, led by a furious Flight Lieutenant Jerry Rawlings and other ranks.

The Armed Forces Revolutionary Council, composed of Rawlings, junior officers, and noncommissioned officers, was a short-lived regime with several key characteristics. First, there was a complete breakdown in the military and police hierarchies; AFRC leaders and other officers were subject to the direct, threatening pressures of other ranks. Second, AFRC's radical populist impulses, expressed peremptorily and coercively, had two foci. AFRC sought to arrest and punish rapidly military and civilian leaders who had destroyed the economy and enriched themselves. Hence, it conducted quick "trials" (without legal procedures) of key military-civilian leaders—executing seven and giving twenty- to fifty-year sentences to others—and launched sweeping investigations into Ghana's many corrupt, deteriorating public institutions, which led to administrators fleeing and further enfeeblement. Second, it sought to impose through controls on food and other commodities "just prices" that Ghanaians could afford and an adequate food supply. This passion for justice had harsh repercussions for Ghana's traders and created disincentives for farmers. AFRC's immediate demands that all businesses, traders, and food retailers sell at controlled prices led to the withdrawal of many traders from the market.

AFRC military-police investigations went after the wholesalers who defrauded the government on imports (such as "Kojo Sardine," who received life imprisonment for rice-maize frauds)[90] and the large shopkeepers and hoarders (mostly men). But the most popular animus was directed at market women in the large food markets in Accra, who were the source of more than 70 percent of Accra's food, as well as at market women elsewhere. AFRC set up maize-buying centers for kenkey producers in Accra, but insisted all kenkey be sold at approved prices. Price controls on all items were enforced with vigor and coercion in the main cities and towns. Those caught selling at higher prices and "queue contractors" were summarily flogged or caned, made to lie in the streets, and otherwise humiliated.[91] Despite a decent harvest in 1979, very real food shortages and high prices incensed many Ghanaians, who cheered the assaults on women and the impotent AFRC decision to establish feeding centers in Accra where food sellers would provide food at control prices.[92] Artisans in Accra, auto mechanics among them, were told to reduce prices by 40 percent and admonished that "some of you artisans are the basic cause of food shortages in the country. You charge exorbitant fees while in fact making vehicles less roadworthy."[93] In blind frustration with climbing prices and with the practices of market women, and to symbolize AFRC determination for an avidly misogynistic public that believed in market women's price-gouging and hoarding out of all proportion to the reality,[94] AFRC destroyed Makola Market No. 1, the key wholesale and retail market for foodstuffs in Accra.[95] AFRC thus further disrupted a system both neglected and assaulted in recent years.

Some disruption in agricultural production, or at least marketing, was caused by AFRC teams of soldiers who forced farmers to sell their produce at control or low prices.[96] The fear thus created undoubtedly reduced readiness to sell or maintain the same level of cultivation in 1980. Moreover, the most prosperous market women, the wholesaler/collectors who went to the rural areas to make food purchases and arrange shipments, were deterred by AFRC's harshly imposed controls. Severe food shortages in July–August 1979 were also caused by Nigeria's cutoff of oil shipments to Ghana as a consequence of Ghana's execution of SMC military leaders; in many rural areas, goods trucks were idled for long periods by lack of fuel. Food scarcities occurred despite a better harvest in 1979 than in 1978 (maize, +74 percent; cassava, +51 percent; yams, +11 percent; plantain, -13 percent (See Table 4.3). AFRC recognized the need for increased incentives in cocoa (it raised prices 50 percent) but only occasionally recognized the need for incentives in food production. Last, the legacy of AFRC's price controls meant that the successor civilian government was constrained to support vigilante teams in their surveillance of market prices.

People's National Party–Limann Government

The People's National Party (PNP) government, a presidential regime with a PNP National Assembly majority, had been built on ex-CPP leader networks and was headed by a weak, indecisive president, Hilla Limann.[97] The PNP's incomparable incompetence in economic and agricultural policy and performance was partly mitigated by its disastrous institutional, economic, and political inheritance. Economically, Ghana had large debt arrears, no foreign-exchange reserves, and poor credit; it saw a disastrous 44 percent drop in world cocoa prices in 1978–1981, to a postwar low in real terms. Terms of trade fell 50 percent in 1979–1981. The infrastructure was literally collapsing. Shortages of spare parts, factory inputs, and consumer goods were debilitating. In 1980/81 Ghana imported no more by volume than in 1954–1956 (Table 4.4, column 4)—in per capita terms, 60 percent less. Major PNP economic policies compounded the disaster: The budget deficit exceeded revenues by 58 percent in 1979/80 and by well over 100 percent in 1981/82, contributing to inflation of 50 percent in 1980, 116.5 percent in 1981. The PNP's political inheritance and its lack of autonomy from major social class factions and groups led to weak and incoherent policies and little government control over production or distribution.[98] Despite a great cynicism about, and detachment from, state policies, many aggrieved individuals and groups looked to the PNP to relieve the dispiriting economic conditions and scarcities.[99] Civil servants and the unions insistently pushed for raising wages and salaries, containing prices, and ensuring food supplies. The number of strikes and strikers surged in late 1979, 1980, and 1981 to record levels. Former AFRC leaders and supporters monitored PNP fidelity to AFRC's populist ethos. With union pressures, this made difficult a lifting of counterproductive price controls. PNP MPs acted as vigorous patrons for their constituents. These reinforced PNP instincts to focus on distributive policies of the grossest sort. So insistent were the pressures for imports and the fair distribution of commodities that the government—when successfully threatened by a TUC general strike in April 1981—gyrated between getting commodities into Ghana, regardless of price (thus recreating the just-vanquished black market), and reemphasizing price controls and direct goods distribution to specific groups.[100] A progressive, public PNP disintegration in factional conflicts undermined its legitimacy and tenuous elite support for imperative economic reforms.

PNP agricultural policies were wholly ineffectual.[101] Agricultural production levels were not disastrous, comparatively, with small declines from 1979 in grains and starchy staples, except cassava (Table 4.3). But the level of food inflation—52.3 percent in 1980, 111.2 percent in 1981—and the frequent food scarcities indicate the genuine impoverishment that afflicted Ghanaians, especially urban, but the rural poor as well. In early 1981 Eastern Region hospitals discharged most patients for lack of food or the funds to buy it. Secondary boarding schools sent students home, unable to feed them, their budgets exhausted by raging inflation.[102] Food imports as a percent of total imports were down sharply in 1980 and 1981 and down in volume also, in part a reflection of scarce foreign exchange (Table 4.4).

PNP food and agricultural policies imitated and exceeded—by politicizing—the most wasteful SMC policies. A large portion of scarce budget, managerial, input, and credit resources were allocated to the wholly unproductive GNRC, FPC, and state farms, plus an estimated ¢8 million a month in 1980 to the FDC. Small farmers were largely ignored. The FPC, beset by land disputes by local farmers, disabled vehicles and tractors, and an often absent labor force, was "a colossal failure," producing ¢4 million in food with a government subsidy of ¢56.5 million in 1981.[103] The GNRC "settlement" farms, often deserted by the daily-wage "settlers," produced little in 1977–1979, were allotted ¢36 million in 1980 and spent ¢80 million.[104] The failed armed services farms were financed to raise food specially for the military. The PNP recognized a pro-PNP Ghana National Farmers' Council (modeled on the CPP's UGFC) as the sole representative of farmers and made it a major allocator of agricultural inputs. The PNP also made MPs the distributors of 140,000 cutlasses. While farmers decried the scarcity of cutlasses, many MPs failed to collect their consignments.[105]

Cocoa production declined precipitately under the PNP, from 296,000 metric tons in 1979/80 to 258,000 metric tons in 1980/81 and 225,000 metric tons in 1981/82. Plummeting world prices made the PNP extremely reluctant to raise producer prices in 1980 and 1981, so inflation eroded real prices in 1980/81 to 36.5 percent of 1963 prices, a one-year drop of 33 percent. An incredibly indecisive Limann government delayed by more than a month opening the 1981/82 buying season until it finally decided to raise prices by 200 percent, a painful dilemma because the decision involved shifting huge resources to producers and compounding the budget deficit.[106] Increasingly, cocoa could not be transported to the ports. Probably 130,000 metric tons, or over half a year's production, remained unevacuated in 1980/81.[107] Severe transport problems in getting cocoa to CMB depots quickened farmer moves out of cocoa into more profitable and marketable food crops.

Rawlings and the Provisional National Defense Council

Food scarcities and hyperinflation in 1980–1981, PNP corruption and incompetence, and especially the reborn *kalabule* (excessively priced) black market[108] created a firestorm of class conflict. Rawlings returned to power in a mutiny/coup on December 31, 1981, this time organizing lower-class political support and unleashing class conflict. Within a year, however, with PNDC institutions in factional and mutinous turmoil, and realizing economic recovery required vast capital infusions to restore production, Rawlings had initiated a quasi-orthodox economic recovery program. He survived major protests against this program as well as Ghana's worst droughts in 1982–1983 and obtained large IMF, World Bank, and Western loans and grants. With neocolonial capital and the rain gods' blessings, agricultural and economic growth resumed in 1984–1987.

In its radical phase, the PNDC encouraged thousands of grass-roots People's/Workers' Defense Committees (PDCs/WDCs) in neighborhoods and workplaces to mobilize lower-class support behind collective efforts and to uncover corrupt, incompetent state management. With the military, they organized food and commodity distributions and coercively enforced price reductions and controls. PDCs pushed for rent reductions and harassed nonsupportive judges, attacked the professionals' associations, and in their zeal removed managers (even in Accra's mental hospital); they took over some factories and inadvertently brought many state institutions to a standstill, such as the Ghana National Trading Corporation and its distributive activities.[109] Where PDCs were well organized and militant, supported by the National Defense Committee and Regional Defense Secretariats, as in some areas of Tema, Accra, Kumasi, and Sekondi-Takoradi, they presented themselves as the true avatars of popular power, a second structure of power, contesting government regional and district secretaries, even cabinet secretaries, whose resignations they demanded on occasion. When the PNDC reversed its economic policies and reined in PDC aggressiveness, PDC leaders and the radical intelligentsia insistently criticized the PNDC and the infiltration of the bourgeoisie for "betraying the revolution."

Citizen Vetting Committees investigated the assets and tax compliance of large traders, businesspeople, and professionals. National and regional public tribunals, ignoring "legal technicalities" for "natural justice," tried persons accused of corruption, coup attempts, and other crimes. These have remained active as populist institutions.

The regime's initial class enemies included: members of the merchant-professional-managerial bourgeoisie, especially traders and lawyers; market women, attacked for price-control violations; trade union leaders, who were coercively evicted from office by dissident local union leaders in Accra-Tema; and, to some extent, even food and cocoa farmers. In February 1982 the PNDC's secretary, P.B.D. Asamoah, told the Ghana National Farmers' Council that the Limann government's 200 percent cocoa price increase could not be paid. "Most farmers were part of the demoralizing process of the former administration and should change for the better. The revolution has no room for evil and selfish practices."[110] Rawlings wanted a voluntary cocoa price reduction by the farmers but refused to impose one.[111] The PNDC, through the military and PDCs, tried to control local food prices in the market; thus, of necessity it attempted to restrict prices farmers received, often requiring market women and farmers to sell at losses. Numerous measures were taken to control traders, including registration and continual forays by PDCs and the military. In May 1982 soldiers seized large amounts of commodities at Kumasi Central Market following "reports of trade malpractices"; in June, soldiers beat up and arrested yam sellers in Accra's market and confiscated the yams.[112] Teams of soldiers and PDCs went to villages and used forced sales at PNDC-set prices to acquire foodstuffs, demoralizing farmers who reduced food-crop harvesting.[113] As occurred elsewhere, the central WDC in Nkwanta in 1983 resolved to seize one-third of food items bought by middlemen locally and sell them to workers cheaply.[114]

The PNDC's and Rawlings's initial class bases of support were among portions of the working class (despite the PNDC's antiunion actions), the urban poor in general, some university students, the radical intelligentsia in parties, press, and academia, and the military's lower ranks. Military personnel employed violence so frequently—slappings, canings, beatings, and, on some occasions, murder and rampage—that by mid-1982 many Ghanaians feared and intensely loathed the PNDC and the military. Only after the May 1983 protests against the PNDC budget and policy changes—that is, price increases—did Rawlings perhaps appreciate the depth of popular hostility and work to reestablish controls over military personnel. Protests by workers, students, professionals, entrepreneurs, and church leaders in mid-1983 turned into pressures for the PNDC's resignation, which some PDCs and WDCs countered with rallies and coercion.[115]

Several factors made Rawlings back away from his populist-mobilization approach to Ghana's economic and food problems. The populist assaults on institutions were highly disruptive to production and PNDC administration. The disintegrating infrastructure enfeebled many production and marketing efforts in agriculture: Railway tonnage in 1983 was one-half that in 1981, 22 percent that in 1970; an estimated 500,000 tires plus spare parts were needed, with an estimated 85 percent of private transport vehicles idled in March 1983.[116] Factory utilization was about 10 percent. By late 1982 the PNDC's radical institutions were in tumultuous, intermittent revolt, riven by contentious factions and leaders. The PNDC itself had lost five of its seven members to resignation, expulsion, revolt, and arrest (for the murder of four judges in June 1982). The scale of the drought that hit Ghana in 1982 drastically reduced output and by early 1983 required massive food aid from abroad to avert widespread starvation.[117] The sudden expulsion of 1.1 million Ghanaians from Nigeria greatly compounded the crisis. Moreover, Rawlings's economic advisers knew that PNDC efforts to control market and farmer food prices, whatever the justifications, reduced food flows to market and probably planting and harvesting by farmers.

In the intensely dry period in early 1983, caused by extensive harmattan winds, bush fires raged out of control, with estimates indicating that perhaps 35–40 percent of standing food and other cash-crop output was destroyed.[118] The 1982 and 1983 droughts and bush fires pushed cocoa to the disastrous lows of 178,000 and 158,000 metric tons, respectively. Prices of food staples soared; increases from January 1982 to January 1983 and then April 1983 were, respectively: maize, 100 percent and 800 percent; kenkey, 400 percent, 1000 percent; cassava, 50 percent, 250 percent; gari (poor man's food), 500 percent, 1165 percent; yams, 78 percent, 256 percent; plantain, 56 percent, 525 percent.[119] Food relief came and reduced prices, but drought was worse in 1983 than in 1982, killing seeds and plants in the ground. Production declines between 1981 and 1983 were: maize 54 percent, rice 59 percent, millet 66 percent, cassava 17 percent, plantain 59 percent (Table 4.3). Malnutrition and disease were widespread; food aid did not reach distant villages; parents sent young daughters away with migrant builders and as house servants.[120] Average food price increases in 1982 over 1981 were—officially but unbelievably—35.8 percent and in 1983 over 1982, 144.8 percent. But during some months local foods were up 250–1,000 percent or were wholly unavailable. Some called the prominent collarbones of the emaciated "Rawlings's chains."

In April 1983, the PNDC, guided by Finance Secretary Kwesi Botchwey, launched major economic reforms intended to lower inflation (deficit spending was sharply reduced), encourage rather than discourage production for export (90 percent cedi devaluation, increased cocoa prices), promote savings (increased interest rates), and increase rewards to producers by raising control prices and gradually eliminating them. The price controls on domestic manufactured goods and imports had been counterproductive, controlling prices at factory gate only; products were diverted to black markets, where customers paid full prices. Botchwey's policies were designed to correct Ghana's massive price distortions, which misallocated scarce resources. These are harsh, valid criticisms of the assumptions, effectiveness, and consequences of IMF programs, but most of these measures clearly fit Ghana's need for some economic rationality and fiscal prudence. Also only these measures brought the massive foreign loans and grants desperately required for economic rehabilitation and investment. Within eighteen months, most price controls had been lifted. Further cedi devaluations occurred during 1983–1986, with a relatively slight impact on domestic inflation during September 1985 to mid-1986, when the cedi value of a U.S. dollar fell from ¢52 to ¢150 (a lower rate applied to state imports until early 1987). In 1983–1986 Ghana received $600 million in IMF loans; in 1984–1986, $550 million in soft World Bank loans, with 1984–1986 loan commitments of $1.5 billion. IMF loan renewals and a three-year $250-million Extended Fund Facility in 1987, as well as massive new aid commitments of $818 million in 1987, have kept the debt repayment burden down.

The PNDC's agricultural priorities have been self-sufficiency in cereals, starchy staples, and animal protein; development of buffer stocks of maize and rice to smooth seasonal fluctuations; industrial-crop sufficiency; and improved storage, processing, and distribution systems. Rapid turnover in secretaries of agriculture—five between 1982 and 1987—suggests PNDC frustration with agricultural leadership and the danger of policy or implementation incoherence. But the wilder ideas of 1982/83—that bakers, hotels, factories, and teachers should all produce their own food—have been put aside. Excellent weather and rains in 1984 yielded bumper crops of key staple foods, including maize (a surplus), rice, millet, cassava, and yams, which led to sharp declines in food prices in 1985. Crop output in 1985 showed some expected reductions from the high 1984 levels, in cassava and maize, whose price dropped by 94 percent between August 1983 and September 1984; farmers greatly reduced acreage planted to maize in 1985, as the FDC had been unable to purchase maize at the government minimum price. Overall, average food costs increased 11 percent in 1984 and fell by 11 percent in 1985 (Table 4.1). Food prices rose 20 percent in 1986 over 1985, despite generally rising agricultural output in 1986, especially in maize and cassava (near historical highs), guinea corn, and millet (Table 4.3). Yam, plantain, and rice production remained very low. Good rainfall in 1984–1986 has been a key factor in reviving output. The inflow of tires and spares has resurrected Ghana's aging truck fleet, restoring the farm-market linkage. Despite prior poor performance, the FDC has been given large amounts of credit and equipment to support the guaranteed minimum maize price, which has been regularly raised, in order to sustain farmer incentives and to build stocks for off-season sales; reducing high off-season prices protects low-income earners. Despite new and rehabilitated silos, storage capacity remains slight.

Despite Agriculture Ministry decentralization, and the appointment of agricultural under secretaries for each region, there remain large problems in getting inputs to small farmers, who have been frustrated by inadequate availability of seeds, seedlings, and cutlasses. A major World Bank project to develop Agriculture Ministry extension services began in 1987. Farm service centers in the Upper and Volta regions, part of World Bank programs, have been increasingly effective in providing inputs. Labor remains in short supply and costs three times the urban minimum wage. Credit is being made somewhat more available to small farmers through the ADB, the development of privately subscribed rural banks (ninety-six by 1984), and the Ghana Commercial Bank's Commerbank Farmers Associations. The latter lent to 40,400 small farmers in 1978, 80,000 in 1981, and ¢1 billion to 250,000 farmers in 1983/84; it also channeled inputs to farmers.[121]

Cocoa exports remain the crucial multiplier in Ghana's economy, indispensible for financing imports and government revenue. The 200 percent price increase to cocoa farmers in 1981/82, 67 percent in 1983, and 50 percent in 1984 failed to offset inflation, left 1984 real producer prices at 33 percent of the 1963 level, and provided little incentive for exploiting existing holdings. But the 67 percent increase in 1985 reduced smuggling incentives; the 52 percent hike in 1986 restored real prices to 85 percent of the 1963 level. Output has responded slowly from the 1983/84 low, reaching 210,000 metric tons in 1985/86 and 230,000 metric tons in 1986/87. This very low production level relative to the 1970s reflects a roughly one-third loss in Ghana's cocoa-tree stock since the early 1970s and the declining productivity of roughly half the trees, which are close to or over thirty years old. The 52 percent price hike in 1986 to ¢85,000 per metric ton reflected a determination to provide incentives for new planting, which had to be double the 7,000 hectares planted in 1985 if production is to reach 250,000 metric tons. In 1987 cocoa producer prices were raised 65 percent, yielding the highest real price since 1963, to compensate for 1986/87 inflation. The Cocoa Marketing Board reported some 30,000 hectares of new cocoa planted in 1986, the replanting of 150,000 hectares destroyed in the 1983 fires, and extremely high demand for cocoa pods and seedlings by farmers. Ghana hopes to reach 300,000 metric tons in output by the 1990s, not a return to the 400,000–450,00 metric tons of the early 1970s. Given high world market supplies, world cocoa prices are expected to fall in the next five years.[122]

In the fall of 1982 the PNDC began to pay cocoa farmers by "Akuafo" checks (IOUs) rather than cash in order to reduce theft by CMB buying agents and to increase the small proportion of the money supply in the liquidity-starved banking system (13 percent in 1982). Although the Akuafo check scheme was initially greeted with suspicion and required mobile banks sent to cocoa areas, it has apparently worked. In 1983/84 farmers were paid for all cocoa purchased for the first time since 1974.[123] Other efforts to revive cocoa include replanting cocoa farms rehabilitated from swollen shoot disease, mass spraying against capsid, clearing areas of swollen-shoot-diseased trees, and direct supplying by the CMB of incentive consumer goods to farmers. The PNDC has made large reductions in CMB staff—roughly half by 1986, with another 20,000 of the remaining 66,000 to be dismissed in 1987—in order to reduce its large operating costs. To confine CMB activities to purchasing, marketing, extension, and research, the CMB in 1987 sold fifty-two of its ninety-two cocoa/coffee plantations.[124]

In 1984–1986 economic growth revived reasonably (average GDP increases of 6.1 percent per year), inflation slowed, and major production investments were under way in mining, timber, and infrastructure, though exports of gold, diamonds, and timber were still extremely low in 1986. Much of the 1984–1986 growth had been funded by the IMF, World Bank, and by loans and grants from other foreign institutions to create the rehabilitation and investment for future growth. Agricultural output started to recover, though production of some staples was below 1970–1973 averages. However, wage and salary earners continued to have painfully depressed living conditions, for which many erroneously held the IMF-inspired recovery program responsible. For virtually all wage-salary earners and the urban poor, the prices of food, key services (education, health), and employment were paramount in assessing PNDC performance, especially as food prices rose again in 1986 and 1987.

The 1983 policy changes led during 1983–1985 to a major realignment of the social-class forces supporting and opposing the PNDC and its recovery program. Farmers, businesspeople, market women, chiefs, and many professionals and managers—whatever their aversion to PNDC authoritarianism—supported PNDC policies and benefited from them. Urban wage-salary labor and the rural poor have lost massive portions of their incomes, roughly 80 percent, since 1974. PNDC policies of channeling resources into investment instead of consumption has meant slow gains to these sectors.

Hence, the TUC and its national unions have been the major dissenters against PNDC economic policies. The interim TUC and national union executives installed after the takeover by the PNDC and dissident locals in 1982 protested mildly the 1983 budget and had union headquarters and leaders attacked by Accra-Tema militants in consequence. Union leaders protested all the new taxes and successfully fought for a somewhat higher daily minimum wage than that offered (¢25 versus ¢21.19), under which someone would have to work 9.4 days for a tin of maize, 1.9 days for three plantain pieces (prices later fell).[125] The scale of the wage increases required to compensate for the inflation in 1981–1984 was such as to once again make the government the wage leader. Finance Secretary Kwesi Botchwey, with Rawlings's confidence, was constrained by IMF guidelines to limit wage increases in order to reduce budget deficits and inflation. He limited private and state corporate-sector increases to those of the civil service in order to reduce state corporate subsidy needs and to reduce the massive civil service–parastatal wage inequities.[126]

During 1983, new national union leaders were freely elected. In the face of PNDC opposition, Augustus K. Yankey, an old guard union general secretary, was elected TUC secretary-general. The new union leadership included some ousted in 1982 and some dissident leaders; they were strongly united in behalf of protecting union rights, collective bargaining, and government's obligation to consult union leaders on wages through the tripartite bargaining committee. Botchwey resisted such consultation and announced new wage levels unilaterally, sought to limit additional increases negotiated by collective bargaining, attempted to contain, reduce, or make taxable large allowances, and, by 1985, started to reduce the overstaffed bureaucracies (though high termination benefits were paid).

During 1982 and 1983, real government minimum wages (and others in proximate proportion) fell to 12.6 percent and 10.2 percent, respectively, of the 1963 level, or about 17.6 percent and 14.3 percent, including roughly 40 percent in allowances won in the 1970s (Table 4.2). Many of the private and state corporate workers had real wages/salaries of roughly 150–200 percent more when cash allowances are included.

In late 1983 the newly elected TUC leadership protested state price increases of 92–254 percent on maize, rice, sugar, and soap, with a muted strike threat; the government lowered the food price increases somewhat.[127] In January 1984 the TUC issued a proposal that minimum wages be raised from ¢35 to ¢300, based on food costs. Its unpublished proposal was publicly denounced by Rawlings on TV as "rubbish" and unwarranted. TUC statements were generally unreported and received no government response but were publicly criticized. PNDC resistance to increasing wages in 1984, when food prices remained high through August, provoked a harsh TUC denunciation. Ghana's "grave economic situation" flowed from the PNDC's "submission to the dictates" of the IMF and World Bank, creating "unbearable conditions of life," inflation, rising unemployment, and crime.[128] The PNDC then announced a 50 percent across-the-board wage increase for all employees for December and a flat ¢17.5-increase in January 1985, hence doubling the minimum wage, giving the largest percent increases to the many poorest workers. But by reducing the lowest-to-highest government pay gap to 1:1.8, it left impoverished all senior government employees, teachers, and others.

In February 1985, the TUC executive board scathingly denounced PNDC economic policies and accused it of betraying the revolution and failing to implement the progressive parts of the Economic Recovery Program (such as People's Stores).[129] The TUC leadership "cannot justify the present economic, social, and political situation . . . to our mass membership." It criticized collective-bargaining rights violations, the refusal to consult unions on policies, the loss of union power in parastatal management boards, the change in name, roles, and subordination to the state of the PDCs/WDCs. the rising direct costs of previously free health and education services, the prospective sale of state enterprises to the private sector, and major layoffs in the private and state sectors.[130] These views resembled the radical intelligentsia's charges of PNDC betrayal.[131]

Despite good organizational capacities and internal autonomy, unions were highly constrained in their protest behavior by the government. Police surveillance of union meetings was regular. Strike actions were extremely curtailed. The outbreak of demonstrations and protests in Accra-Tema, and Sekondi-Takoradi in early 1986, when the government unilaterally announced an end to leave allowances (10–25 percent of annual wages), led the government to withdraw the measure. But it also arrested without charges some radicals and union militants for allegedly instigating the demonstrations.[132] Protests regarding regime brutality and PNDC economic policies in 1985 and 1987 were met by harassments and intimidating threats of wholesale arrests. Union leaders are not unmindful of Ghana's weak economy and have curtailed high wage-benefit demands. But miserable living standards made workers and unions highly sensitive to signs of inequality; for example, many worker demonstrations (the substitute for strikes) broke out in January 1986, when the PNDC's announced wage-salary increases widened the tiny 1:1.8 gap between lowest- and highest-paid government workers. Union leaders reject angrily PNDC suggestions that worker claims impede economic recovery and suspect that PNDC measures involved an effort to "undermine, weaken, and eventually destroy the trade union movement and its class representation."[133]

• CONCLUSION •

In the 1970s and 1980s lagging agricultural production, poor policies, and terrible state economic management put food prices and scarcities at the center of the crises in Ghana's political life and economy. Quasi-populist responses (under the SMC) and populist ones (AFRC, early PNDC) involved attempts to maintain consumption in the face of falling or stagnant domestic production and declining international commodity prices and terms of trade. Given Ghana's limited management capacities, incentives for corruption, and porous borders, this only compounded and deepened rather than relieved the crises. In the face of the limited competence and unwillingness of state institutions and managers to organize production efficiently and the largely counterproductive consequences of efforts to control prices, the PNDC has permitted greater space for market forces and the private sector without surrendering the state's overall role in economic management. The government is just beginning the long road to modernizing agriculture. The government does seem more attentive to small peasant farmers than were past regimes. The period 1969–1983 was one in which the vast proportion of the population lost much of their real income, much of it because of the massive real fall in the production of goods and services. Ghana's estimated per capita decline in GDP of 1.3 percent per annum during 1960–1982 probably underestimates the loss.[134] The current recovery is sharply increasing prolonged unemployment.

In its modern political life Ghana possesses two powerful strains of political culture—one liberal and capitalist, the other populist with statist and socialist strains. If Ghanaian agricultural output falters again, bringing more hunger and food scarcities, populist outrage will again tear at the political fabric. If the resurgence of the private sector hastens conspicuous inequalities amidst the widespread impoverishment, the class consciousness and anger so palpable in 1982–1984 and now articulated by the trade unions will delegitimize the regime and its policies.

TABLE 4.1 Nominal and Real Cocoa Prices to Producers and World Cocoa Prices

Crop year	Cocoa producer price (¢ per metric ton)	Real producer price index (1963=100)[a]	Total cocoa production (thousands of metric tons)	Average cocoa spot price (£ per metric ton) (calendar year)	Percentage change average cocoa price	Producer price as percentage of average f.o.b. export price
1960/61	219.9	130.0	432	222	−21.0	56.3
1961/62	198.0	114.2	410	177	−20.3	54.0
1962/63	198.0	104.3	422	167	−5.6	52.9
1963/64	198.0	100.0	428	205[b]	+22.8	56.9
1964/65	198.0	83.4	538–557	188	−8.3	61.1
1965/66	145.37	48.6	401	138	−26.6	51.0
1966/67	197.56	58.3	368	193	+39.9	46.9
1967/68	237.81	76.7	415	238	+23.3	41.6
1968/69	256.10	76.3	323	320	+34.5	38.2
1969/70	292.69	81.5	403	415	+29.7	35.8
1970/71	292.69	78.6	413	306	−26.3	45.5
1971/72	292.69	71.9	454	232	−24.2	42.5
1972/73	365.86	81.9	407	270	+16.4	44.4
1973/74	439.04	83.4	340	585	+116.7	33.9
1974/75	548.80	88.1	376	990	+69.2	32.5
1975/76	585.38	72.4	396	723	−27.0	38.3
1976/77	731.72	58.0	320	1,399	+93.5	28.2
1977/78	1,333.33	48.8	271	2,994	+114.0	33.8
1978/79	2,666.67	56.4	265	2,006	−33.0	25.7
1979/80	4,000.00	54.8	296	1,727	−13.9	
1980/81	4,000.00	36.5	258	1,270	−26.5	85.5
1981/82	12,000.00	50.7	225	1,114	−12.3	
1982/83	12,000.00	41.3	178			45.0[c]
1983/84	20,000.00	30.9	158			27.0[c]
1984/85	30,000.00	33.2	172			34.0[c]
1985/86	56,000.00	56.1	210			50.0[c]
1986/87	85,000.00	68.1	230			
1987/88	140,000.00	E93.5				

[a]Cocoa producer price deflated by the national consumer price index and as a percentage of base year producer price. This index overstates the price decline to farmers who produced their own food, the key factor in inflation.
[b]Calendar year data on line 1963/64 crop year is 1963.
[c]Declines in producer prices as percentage of average export price from 1982/83 and after reflect several extremely sharp devaluations of the Ghana currency exchange rate. Prior percentage figures overstated because of overvalued exchange rate.

Sources: World Bank data: Gill and Duffus, *Cocoa Market Report*, no. 298 (November 1981), p. 27; Ghana, Central Bureau of Statistics, *Statistical Newsletter*, monthly issues, 1976–84.

TABLE 4.2 National Consumer and Local Food Price Indexes, Rates of Inflation (official), and Nominal and Real Government Minimum Wage[a]

Year	Average national consumer price index (1963=100)	Rate of inflation (percent)	Local food prices index[b] (1963=100)	Local food inflation (percent)	Nominal government minimum wage[a] (¢)	Real minimum wage index[e] (1963=100)	Estimated union real minimum wage index[d,e]
1965	151.3	26.2	172.0	37.0	.65	66.4	
1966	171.4	13.5	199.0	15.7	.65	58.3	
1967	156.9	−8.5	169.5	−14.8	.70	68.6	
1968	169.7	8.2	184.3	8.7	.75	67.9	
1969	181.8	7.1	200.1	8.6	.75	63.5	
1970	188.5	3.7	210.0	4.4	.75	61.2	
1971	206.0	9.3	236.1	12.4	.75	56.0	
1972	226.7	10.0	259.4	9.9	1.00	68.1	
1973	266.4	17.5	313.4	20.8	1.00	57.1	
1974	315.3	18.4	362.7	15.7	1.50c	73.2	
1975	408.9	29.7	473.6	30.6	2.00	75.2	
1976	639.3	53.3	805.6	70.1	2.00	48.1	98
1977	1,382.5	116.3	2,033.8	152.5	3.00c	33.4	67
1978	2,401.4	73.7	3,241.9	59.4	4.00	25.6	51
1979	3,695.4	53.9	5,241.1	61.7	4.00	16.7	33
1980	5,546.5	50.1	7,982.7	52.3	6.00c	16.6	33
1981	12,009.6	116.5	16,856.1	111.2	12.00	15.4	31
1982	14,687.5	22.3	22,888.4	35.8	12.00	12.6	25
1983	32,728.8	122.8	56,023.1	144.8	21.75c	10.2	20d
1984	45,679.9	39.6	62,203.8	11.0	32.50c	11.5	22+d
1985		10.4		−11.1	70.00	21.0	30–35+
1986		25.0		20.0	90.00		

[a]Nominal government minimum wage after 1968 was for the first year; it was supposed to rise 2 percent per year for each year a worker was employed. Wages of unionized minimum wage workers were a little higher than government minimum wage during the 1960s and, from 1974 on, were substantially higher, in some instances double the government minimum.

[b]Up to 1978, a local food price index was kept separately from imported food and had a weight of about 50 percent in the national consumer price index, whereas imported foods had a weight of 4.4 percent in the urban areas, 2.5 percent rural. Data for 1978–1980 is total food. Imported food had an inflation rate less than half that for local food.

[c]Figures for nominal government minimum wage represent the average over twelve months for 1974, 1977, 1980, 1983, and 1984 when there were changes during the year.

[d]From the mid-1970s on, trade unions in state enterprises and private firms often won minimum wages two times the government minimum plus large, nontaxed allowances.

[e]Does not include large untaxed allowances, in government adding 30–50 percent of base, in private and state corporate sector often two or three times larger than wage.

Sources: Ghana, Economic Survey, 1969–71 (1976), p. 106; Ghana, Central Bureau of Statistics, Statistical Newsletter, monthly issues, 1976–1986.

TABLE 4.3 Agricultural Production in Ghana, 1970–1986

	1970	1971	1972	1973	1974	1975	1976	1977	1978	1979	1980	1981	1982	1983	1984	1985	1986	1972/74 Average as percent of 1970/71 average	1974/75 Average as percent of 1970/71 average	1978/79 Average as percent of 1970/71 average
Area (1,000 ha)																				
Maize	453	433	389	406	425	320	273	256	205	358	355	372	373	a				-8	-14	-26
Rice	55	61	70	66	67	79	77	129	123	105	99	116	61					17	26	93
Millet	249	230	176	192	222	199	243	208	157	250	139	157	172					-18	-12	-11
Guinea corn	243	233	200	221	216	208	249	175	160	211	261	198	216					-11	-11	-22
Cassava	351	351	380	373	389	285	250	232	235	219	315	308	339					9	-4	-23
Yam	172	172	134	130	133	117	100	89	95	105	113	116	111					-23	-27	-37
Plantain	288	288	306	336	343	230	211	168	161	139	123	128	141					14	0	-46
Groundnuts	98	98	92	79	111	102												-4	9	-7
Oil palm	111	111	113	125	146	144	144	108	149	157								15	31	40
Cotton	0.8	1.9	3.7	4.4	4.5	12.9	24.8											211	544	
Rubber	10.1	10.1	10.5	10.9	10.9	11.3	5.6	7.0	7.5	7.5								7	10	
Sugarcane	4.0	4.0	5.3	4.7	5.3	5.8												28	39	87
Tobacco	1.6	2.2	2.5	3.2	4.0	3.1												70	87	
Production (1,000 tonnes)																				
Maize	482	465	402	427	486	343	286	274	218	380	382	378	346	173	574	395	495	-9	-13	-26
Rice	49	55	70	62	73	71	70	109	108	93	78	97	36	40	66	80	80	31	39	93
Millet	141	130	99	109	154	122	144	125	93	149	82	119	76	40	139	120	140	-11	2	-11
Guinea corn	186	173	152	167	177	135	189	131	121	158	132	131	85	56	176	185	190	-8	-14	-22
Cassava	2388	2388	2840	2865	3606	2398	1818	1811	1895	1759	2322	2063	2470	1721	4083	3075	3040	30	26	-23
Yam	909	909	679	686	850	709	575	535	544	602	650	591	588	866	725	560	660	-19	-14	-37
Plantain	1641	1641	1670	2071	2024	1246	1256	927	940	817	734	829	745	342	760	676		17	0	-46
Groundnuts	102	102	89	127	157	111	81	83	107					91	90	128		22	31	-7
Oil palm	696	696	711	782	917	901	901	739	935	1012								15	31	40
Cotton	0.4	1.2	1.9	1.7	2.2									6	6	6		232	31[b]	
Rubber	9.1	9.1	9.6	10.3	9.9	10.3												9	11	
Sugarcane	112	112	145	161	171	205	190	258	272	272								42	68	143
Tobacco	0.9	1.5	1.8	2.7	3.4	2.3								2	2	3		119	138	

aBlank space indicates data not available.

bDashes indicate that the calculation is not possible.

Sources: Ghana, Ministry of Agriculture; World Bank, Ghana: Policies and Program for Adjustment (1984), p. 93; FAO, Production Yearbook, 1985 (1986), pp. 120, 130–133, 143; West Africa, January 12, 1987, p. 72.

TABLE 4.4 Ghana: Terms of Trade, Import and Export Volumes, and Food Imports

Year	Terms of trade	Purchasing power of exports	Export volume index	Import volume index	Merchandise import volume index	Food volume import index	Food imports as percent of total[a]
1954–56	107	91	85	99			15.6
1960	100	115	115	168			16.2
1961	87	114	132	183			18.3
1962	80	114	142	155			19.1
1963	81	105	130	167			14.2
1964	82	111	135	153			16.4
1965	68	108	158	196			11.0
1966	68	90	133	154			15.6
1967	81	100	124	133	174.3	96.0	16.5
1968	84	111	132	133	148.0	107.5	16.2
1969	100	108	108	148	159.2	103.4	15.6
1970	109	161	147	172	180.5	154.7	19.0
1971	82	115	140	170	169.7	109.7	14.1
1972	72	130	180	106	100.0	100.0	18.4
1973	78	152	194	130	130.1	119.0	21.2
1974	91	124	137	166	183.7	106.8	14.9
1975	95	129	136	150	161.5	96.0	11.5
1976	89	126	141	159	161.0	81.0	12.0
1977	142	145	102	194	175.0	61.4	8.5
1978	186	143	77	160			8.5
1979	136	108	80	109			11.7
1980	100	100	100	100			7.8
1981	68	81	119	100			7.1
1982	60	70	115	67			

[a]Includes food and live animals; excludes beverages and tobacco, which were on average .86 percent of total imports during 1970–79.

Sources: Columns 1–4, UNCTAD data; columns 5–6, IBRD data, *Ghana Economic Memorandum, 1979*; column 7, Ghana, *1961 Statistical Yearbook*, p. 94, Ghana, *Economic Survey(s), 1965*, p. 33, *1968*, p. 43, *1972–74*, p. 33 (Accra: Government Printer), World Bank, *Ghana: Policies and Program for Adjustment* (1984), p. 116.

• NOTES •

1. Ghana, *Report of the Ad Hoc Committee on Union Government* (Accra: Government Printer, 1977), pp. 4, 51.

2. World Bank, *World Development Report 1983* (New York: Oxford University Press, 1983), p. 150; Tony Killick, *Development Economics in Action* (New York: St. Martin's Press, 1978), p. 90.

3. Killick, *Development Economics*, pp. 185–188, 195–208.

4. Rowena Lawson, "The Distributive System in Ghana," *Journal of Development Studies* 3, no. 2 (January 1967): 196–197.

5. Calculated from Ghana, Central Bureau of Statistics, *Statistical Newsletter*, June 14, 1985.

6. U.S. Department of Agriculture (USDA), *Food Problems and Prospects in Sub-Saharan Africa* (Washington, D.C.: Government Printing Office, 1981), p. 3; Ghana, *Economic Survey 1969* (Accra: Government Printer, 1970), p. 64.

7. Robert Clute, "The Role of Agriculture in African Development," *African Studies Review* 25, no. 4 (December 1982): 4.

8. World Bank, *Accelerated Development in Sub-Saharan Africa: An Agenda for Action* (Washington, D.C.: IBRD, 1981), p. 167.

9. Ghana, *Ghana Sample Census of Agriculture 1970*, vol. 1 (1972), pp. 46–47.

10. Assefa Bequele, "Stagnation and Inequality in Ghana," in Dharam Ghai and Samir Radwan, eds., *Agrarian Policies and Rural Poverty in Africa* (Geneva: International Labour Office, 1983), pp. 228–230.

11. Ghana, *Ghana Sample Census of Agriculture 1970*, pp. 40–44.

12. Ibid., p. 45.

13. See Ghana, *Survey of Population and Budgets of Cocoa Producing Families in the Oda-Swedru-Asamankese Area, 1955–56* (Accra: Government Printer, 1958), p. 24; Ghana, *Survey of Cocoa Producing Families in Ashanti, 1956–57* (Accra: Government Printer, 1960), pp. 16–17; Bjorn Beckman, "The Distribution of Cocoa Income, 1961–65" (Department of Economics, University of Ghana, 1970); Bequele, "Stagnation and Inequality in Ghana," p. 226.

14. World Bank, *Accelerated Development in Sub-Saharan Africa*, pp. 12–13; USDA, *Food Problems and Prospects*, pp. 57–62; Sara Berry, "The Food Crisis and Agrarian Change in Africa," *African Studies Review* 27, no. 2 (June 1984): 67–70; Michael F. Lofchie and Stephen K. Commins, "Food Deficits and Agricultural Policies in Tropical Africa," *Journal of Modern African Studies* 20, no. 1 (March 1982): 13–18.

15. Ghana, *Economic Survey 1968* (Accra: Government Printer, 1969), p. 70. Regarding the 1968/69 sharp fall in cocoa production, "The sharp decline in production . . . was partly due to the adverse weather conditions which characterized the second half of 1968. The *excessively rainy weather* [my emphasis] made spraying difficult and affected adversely the flowering, pot setting and ripening. Harvesting was also delayed and incidence of black pod disease increased" (ibid., p. 68). Excessive rainfall also resulted in damage to the cocoa crop in 1979, increasing black pod disease, pod-rot, and black beans (Ghana, *Economic Survey 1977–1980* [Accra: Government Printer, 1981], p. 51).

16. "Ghana's Northern Food Crisis," *West Africa*, August 15, 1977, pp. 1661–1664; Andrew Shepherd, "Agrarian Change in Northern Ghana: Public Investment, Capitalist Farming and Famine," in Judith Heyer, Pepe Roberts, and Gavin Williams, eds., *Rural Development in Tropical Africa* (New York: St. Martin's Press, 1981), pp. 181–187.

17. On the impact of the 1983 drought on a previously prosperous village, see Merrick Posnansky, "Hardships of a Village," *West Africa*, October 29, 1984, pp. 2161–2163. Posnansky notes that most of West Africa has suffered an absolute reduction

in rainfall in the 1942–1983 period as compared with the 1922–1941 years: roughly 40 percent less in the Sahel, 20 percent less in the forest areas, 10 percent less in the village he studied. In the ten-year period 1973–1983, nine of the ten years had less than the mean rainfall for the forty-year period. In 1982–1983 the rainfall was 30 percent below the mean, with extremely low humidity (p. 2161). On the collapse of the transport system in 1982–1983, see "Ghana: Road Transport Crisis-1" and "Road Transport Crisis-2," *West Africa*, October 17, 1983, pp. 2404–2406; October 24, 1983, pp. 2447–2449.

18. World Bank, *Accelerated Development in Sub-Saharan Africa*, pp. 178–181.

19. William Steel, "Data on Labor Force Size, Growth, Composition and Underutilization by Sex, Firm Size, Sector, and Occupation: Ghana 1960–70," statistical tables prepared for the World Bank, unpublished, November 1978, Tables A4, A5.

20. See Cyril Daddieh, "The Political Economy of Food and Agriculture and Social Change in Nzimaland, Southwestern Ghana," (Ph.D. diss., Dalhousie University, 1983). Daddieh uses as his primary example the impact of the widespread planting of oil palm farms in the Nzima area and the removal of land from food farming.

21. See Polly Hill, *The Migrant Cocoa-Farmers of Southern Ghana* (Cambridge: Cambridge University Press, 1963), pp. 182–185; R. Szereszewski, *Structural Change in the Economy of Ghana, 1891–1911* (London: Weidenfield and Nicolson, 1965), pp. 73–77.

22. See Jon Kraus, "The Political Economy of Agrarian Regression in Ghana," Stephen Commins, Michael Lofchie, and Rhys Payne, eds., *Africa's Agrarian Crisis* (Boulder, Colo.: Lynne Rienner Publishers, 1986), pp. 114–115, for other evidence.

23. The most sophisticated neo-Marxist analysis is by Bjorn Beckman, "Ghana, 1951–78: The Agrarian Basis of the Post-Colonial State," in Heyer, Roberts, and Williams, *Rural Development in Tropical Africa*, pp. 143–165. He emphasizes the structural contradictions of a large state sector built on the finances of a weak export economy and, as related to food production, the state's attempt to bypass the peasantry.

24. The internal terms of trade of food farmers rose by 32 percent in real terms during 1960–1967 (Killick, *Development Economics*, p. 94). On internal terms of trade between cocoa and food farmers, 1962–1981, see Kraus, "The Political Economy of Agrarian Regression in Ghana," p. 125. On the rising prosperity of a food-farming village in the 1970s, see Merrick Posnansky, "How Ghana's Crisis Affects a Village," *West Africa*, December 1, 1980, pp. 2418–2420.

25. G. Helleiner, "The Question of Conditionality," in Carol Lancaster and John Williams, eds., *African Debt and Financing* (Washington, D.C.: Institute of International Economics, 1986), pp. 64–66; David Wheeler, "Sources of Stagnation in Sub-Saharan Africa," *World Development* 112, no. 1 (January 1984): 1–24.

26. Robert Bates, *Markets and States in Tropical Africa: The Political Basis of Agricultural Policies* (Berkeley and Los Angeles: University of California Press, 1981).

27. On perceptions of the political and bureaucratic elite, see Killick, *Development Economics*, pp. 33–50, 188–195; Ghana [really J. H. Mensah, Progress party finance minister], *One Year Development Plan* (Accra: Government Printers, 1970), pp. 50–65.

28. Inexplicably, the World Bank's famous *Accelerated Development in Sub-Saharan Africa* gives data on the (net barter) terms of trade for three years—1960, 1970, and 1979—and then calculates the average annual growth rate in the terms of trade as if the intervening years (when the terms of trade were much lower) did not exist.

29. World Bank, *World Development Report 1979* (New York: Oxford University Press, 1979), p. 140; World Bank, *World Development Report 1980* (New York: Oxford University Press, 1980), p. 124.

30. World Bank, *Accelerated Development in Sub-Saharan Africa*; USDA, *Food Problems and Prospects*; Carl Eicher and Doyle Baker, *Research on Agricultural Development in Sub-Saharan Africa* (East Lansing: Agricultural Economics, Michigan

State University, 1982), pp. 55–59; John C. de Wilde, "Case Studies: Kenya, Tanzania, and Ghana," in Robert Bates and Michael Lofchie, eds., *Agricultural Development in Africa* (New York: Praeger, 1980).

31. On the "parallel economy," see Ernesto May, *Exchange Controls and Parallel Market Economies in Sub-Saharan Africa: Focus on Ghana* (Washington, D.C.: World Bank, Staff Working Papers, No. 711, 1985), pp. 65–91; on the poorly conceived price controls, see Tony Killick, "Price Controls in Africa: The Ghanaian Experience," *Journal of Modern African Studies* 11, no. 3 (1973): 406–412; on aspects of the economic policy making, see Naomi Chazan, *An Anatomy of Ghanaian Politics* (Boulder, Colo.: Westview Press, 1983), pp. 162–179.

32. On authority structures and relationships under Acheampong's SMC, see Chazan, *An Anatomy of Ghanaian Politics*, pp. 95–108.

33. Note that in Table 5.2 the local food price index increased more than the general consumer price index (CPI) in fourteen of nineteen years between 1965 and 1983, in nine of the fourteen by a large percent. Kodwo Ewusi argues that 89 percent of the total 59 percent increase in the CPI during 1960–1969 was the result of local food price increases. See "The Rate of Inflation, Variation in Local Food Prices and the Effect of Transport Facilities on Local Food Prices in Ghana in the Sixties," in I. M. Ofori, ed., *Factors of Agricultural Growth in West Africa* (Legon, Ghana: Institute of Statistical, Social and Economic Research, 1973), p. 282.

34. Richard Jeffries, *Class, Power and Ideology in Ghana* (London: Cambridge University Press, 1978), pp. 38–57; Jon Kraus, "Political Economy of Industrial Relations in Ghana," in Ukandi G. Damachi, Hans Dieter Seibel, and Lester Trachtman, eds., *Industrial Relations in Africa* (London: Macmillan, 1979), pp. 113–131.

35. The Mine Workers' Union (MWU) strike of 1955/56 involved demands partly based on the increased cost of living and of food in the mining areas. Similar demands came from trade unions negotiating with the government for increased minimum wages in 1955. After the MWU strike started, a wage salary commission was appointed that awarded increases in 1956 and 1957. On MWU claims, see Gold Coast, *Report on the Gold Coast Mines Board of Inquiry*, 1956, pp. 44–47.

36. Gold Coast, *Report of the Commission of Enquiry into the Affairs of the Cocoa Purchasing Company* (1956); Bjorn Beckman, *Organizing the Farmers* (Uppsala: Scandinavian Institute of African Studies, 1976), pp. 59–70.

37. Killick, *Development Economics*, pp. 46, 185–186.

38. Ghana, *Economic Survey 1966*, pp. 52–53.

39. Killick, *Development Economics*, pp. 192–195; Marvin Miracle and Ann Seidman, *State Farms in Ghana*, Land Tenure Center No. 43, University of Wisconsin, 1968.

40. Bates, *Markets and States in Tropical Africa*, pp. 46–47.

41. Ghana, *Report of the Committee of Enquiry on the Local Purchasing of Cocoa* (Accra: Government Printer, 1967), pp. 14–21. Farmers catalogued their charges of "dishonesty, fraud, intimidation, victimisation, extortion, theft and outright roguery against many of the [UGFCC] officials," especially the local secretary-receivers (p. 14).

42. Ghana, *Parliamentary Debates* (Accra: Government Printer) vol. 30, cols. 15–42 (December 4, 1962), cols. 157–168 (December 13, 1962); vol. 34, cols. 256–294 (October 24, 1963), cols. 457–458 (October 30, 1963); vol. 38, cols. 503–505, 518–521 (January 29, 1965); vol. 39, cols. 207–234 (May 21, 1965); vol. 40, cols. 49–50 (August 26, 1965); vol. 43, cols. 165–169 (February 7, 1966). CPP officials sought to divert SFC produce to themselves. Citing this, the SFC director said "I know they are comrades, but a comrade cannot use 20 bags of rice in a week" (vol. 40, col. 108 [August 27, 1965]).

43. Ghana, *Report of the Commission of Enquiry into Trade Malpractices in Ghana* (Accra: Government Printer, 1966) [Abraham Commission], pp. 12–13. Cf. Rowena

Lawson, "The Distributive System in Ghana," *Journal of Development Studies* 3, no. 2 (January 1967): 202–203; Ernest Dumor, "Commodity Queens and Distributive Trade in Ghana," paper prepared for African Studies Association meeting, Los Angeles, 1978, pp. 11–12; Claire Robertson, *Sharing the Same Bowl* (Bloomington: Indiana University Press, 1984), confirms price agreements among market women in some commodities (pp. 92, 110, 114). None of these writers believe market women were responsible for a large proportion of food price increases.

44. Calculated from Ghana, *Economic Survey 1965* (Accra: Government Printer, 1966), p. 17, and Ghana, *Economic Survey 1969*, pp. 30, 114.

45. Kraus, "Political Economy of Agrarian Regression in Ghana," p. 121. Some of the budget decline, but not all, is explained by the closing of many state farms.

46. N. O. Addo, "Employment and Labour Supply on Ghana's Cocoa Farms in the Pre- and Post-Aliens Compliance Order Era," *Economic Bulletin of Ghana*, 2nd series, 2, no. 4 (1972): 33–50; J. Adomako-Sarfoh, "The Effects of the Expulsion of Migrant Workers on Ghana's Economy," in Samir Amin, ed., *Modern Migrations in Western Africa* (London: Oxford University Press), pp. 138–152.

47. Ghana, *Economic Survey 1969–71* (Accra: Government Printer, 1976), p. 68, suggests increases in many root crops in 1966–1969 (yams, cocoyams, cassava) and slight increases in grains except maize, which declined.

48. See Ghana, NLC, Finance Commissioner [J. H. Mensah], *Budget Statement for 1969–70* (Accra: Government Printer, July 15, 1969), pp. 7–8; J. H. Mensah, "The Wealth of the Nation," *Legon Observer* 6 (July 2, 1971), insert pp. i–x, in which he makes private accumulation a vital prerequisite for economic growth *and* social equity, in part a product of his experience with the perverse equity consequences of public spending under Nkrumah, which in many ways benefited the relatively well-to-do.

49. Ghana [J. H. Mensah], *One Year Development Plan, July 1970 to June 1971* (Accra: Government Printer, 1970), pp. 50–64; Ghana, J. H. Mensah, *Budget Statement for 1971–72* (Accra: Government Printer, July 27, 1971), pp. 10–14.

50. Ghana, Agricultural Development Bank (ADB), *Agricultural Credit Programs in Ghana* (1973), p. 45.

51. Mensah and some thirteen others, mostly educated Ghanaians, made minimum investments in Odumase Farms, Ltd., J. H. Mensah acquired a ¢7,000 loan from the ADB and had a district agricultural officer manage the farm—though the officer was supposed to be a full-time Ministry of Agriculture employee. The farm was illegal also in that as a minister Mensah was not supposed to be actively involved in a business. See Ghana, *Report of the Taylor Assets Committee*, vol. 2, part 1, pp. 234–238. Other PP leaders, such as G. D. Ampah, a lawyer and minister, were able to acquire large pieces of good agricultural land at almost no cost (¢1 per .4 hectares); Ampah acquired 40 hectares of sugar land near Asutsuare, as did another minister, Jatoe Kaleo, who acquired 30 hectares (ibid., vol. 1, part 2, pp. 44, 177). Prime Minister Busia had acquired three substantial farms before he came to office, but he also used state personnel to improve his farms (ibid., vol. 1, part 1, pp. 86–87). See also the activities of modern farmers in Jack Goody, "Rice Burning and the Green Revolution in Northern Ghana," *Journal of Development Studies* 16, no. 2 (1980): 136–155.

52. *Daily Graphic*, September 3, 1971, p. 11.

53. Jon Kraus, "The Political Economy of Industrial Relations in Ghana," pp. 140–141.

54. Ghana, "Statement by Ghana TUC . . . ," Annex 1 in *Report of the Committee on Review of Salaries and Pensions in the Public Services of Ghana* (Accra: Government Printer, 1969), p. 65.

55. Jon Kraus, "Strikes and Labour Power in Ghana," *Development and Change* 10, no. 2 (April 1979): 259–286.

56. Jon Kraus, "Strikes and Labour Power in a Post-Colonial African State: The Case of Ghana," paper presented to Seminar on Third World Strikes, The Hague, 1977, Tables, pp. 23A, 33A.

57. *Ghanaian Times.* May 17, 1971, p. 1, on suspension of 530 students from Ashanti secondary school for food protest.

58. *The Spokesman,* May 16, 1971, p. 1.

59. *Ghanaian Times,* April 1, 1971, p. 1.

60. *Ghanaian Times,* February 3, 1971, p. 1.

61. TUC, "Proposals Submitted by the Trade Union Congress (Ghana) to the Salary Review Commission" [Campbell Commission] (mimeo., n.d.), pp. 24–32.

62. Kraus, "Strikes and Labour Power in Ghana," pp. 276–282; Jeffries, *Class, Power and Ideology,* pp. 133–139.

63. Acheampong called it the National Redemption Council initially and altered the name to SMC in 1975, when junior officers were jettisoned for service heads as members.

64. Ghana, *Speeches and Interviews by I. K. Acheampong* (Accra: Government Printer, 1973), vol. 1, pp. 21–24 (February 5, 1972). The debt burden was onerous, but incompetent SMC management of debt talks prolonged difficulties. The consequences of Acheampong's decision was a cut-off of virtually all official British export credit guarantees during 1972–1978, which greatly compounded import difficulties.

65. Ibid., esp. pp. 20–34.

66. Data from Kraus, "The Political Economy of Agrarian Regression in Ghana," p. 121.

67. World Bank, *Ghana Agricultural Sector Review* (Washington, D.C.: World Bank, 1978), vol. 2, Annex 2, pp. 11–15.

68. Ghana, Ministry of Cocoa Affairs, "Ashanti Cocoa Project, Annual Report, 1976–77" (mimeo.).

69. *Ghana Agricultural Sector Review,* vol. 3, Annex 6, Appendix Table 6; Agricultural Development Bank, *Annual Report(s),* 1971–1978.

70. "Ghana's Northern Food Crisis"; Shepherd, "Agrarian Change in Northern Ghana."

71. Felix Nweke, "Direct Governmental Production in Agriculture in Ghana," *Food Policy* 3, no. 3 (1978): 205–207.

72. Ghana, *Parliamentary Debates,* vol. 2, col. 54 (December 5, 1979).

73. Goody, "Rice Burning and the Green Revolution in Northern Ghana"; Shepherd, "Agrarian Change in Northern Ghana."

74. World Bank, *Ghana Agricultural Sector Review,* vol. 2, Annex 5, pp. 14, 16.

75. Goody, "Rice Burning and the Green Revolution in Northern Ghana"; Shepherd, "Agrarian Change in Northern Ghana"; Daddieh, "The Political Economy of Food and Agriculture and Social Change in Nzimaland."

76. Mohammed Ibn Chambas, "The Politics of Agricultural and Rural Development in the Upper Region of Ghana" (Ph.D. diss., Cornell University, 1980), pp. 145–167.

77. Razal El-Alawa, "Ghana's Expanding Cotton Industry," *West Africa,* October 24, 1977, pp. 2155–2157. However, the Cotton Development Board's monopoly buying authority also gave its officials leverage for extorting gifts and food (see *West Africa,* March 8, 1976, p. 320).

78. Ghana, Agricultural Development Bank, *Annual Report(s),* 1971–1979.

79. See Posnansky, "How Ghana's Crisis Affects a Village"; V. Southworth, Wm. Jones, and S. Pearson, "Food Crop Marketing in Atebubu District, Ghana," *Food Research Institute Studies* 17, no. 2 (1979): 157–195, based on a 1976–1977 survey; Jette Bukh, *The Village Woman in Ghana* (Uppsala: Centre for Development Research, 1979).

80. See Kodwo Ewusi, *Planning for the Neglected Rural Poor in Ghana* (Legon, Ghana: Institute for Statistical, Social, and Economic Research, 1978), pp. 25, 36, 43, 46, 58, 64.

81. Ghana, *Report of the Ad Hoc Committee on Union Government* (Accra: Government Printer, 1977), Appendix A-C, pp. 135–145.

82. Jon Kraus, "The Crisis Continues," *Africa Report* 23, no. 4 (July-August 1978): 14–21; *West Africa*, May 23, 1977, p. 1011, and May 30, 1977, p. 1061.

83. *West Africa*, March 3, 1976, pp. 294–295, 319; April 12, 1976, p. 511. Essential commodities included sugar, milk, baby foods, dry-cell batteries, soaps, washing powder, toothpaste, and mackerel.

84. *West Africa*, May 16, 1977, p. 969.

85. J. R. Campbell, "The Politics of Food: Marketwomen and the Military in Ghana" (Paper presented at History Department seminar, August 1982, University of Dar es Salaam), covers the crisis in Koforidua.

86. *West Africa*, April 25, 1977, p. 833; May 30, 1977, p. 1061; July 4, 1977, p. 1385; August 8, 1977, p. 1648; June 27, 1977, p. 1310; TUC, Organization Department, H. T. Mbiah, "Report on the Distribution of Maize to Traditional Kenkey Producers" (typed, June 22, 1982), with extracts of annual reports on maize distribution.

87. *West Africa*, June 26, 1978, p. 1215.

88. *Daily Graphic* (Ghana), July 20, 1979, p. 12.

89. Naomi Chazan and Donald Rothchild, "Politics in a 'Non-Political' System: The March 30, 1978 Referendum in Ghana," *African Studies Review* 22, no. 1 (April 1979): 177–208.

90. *Daily Graphic*, July 20, 1979, p. 1; see Chazan, *An Anatomy of Ghanaian Politics*, pp. 279–284, on AFRC.

91. *Daily Graphic*, July 18, 1979, p. 3.

92. *Daily Graphic*, July 16, 1979, p. 7.

93. *Daily Graphic*, July 14, 1979, p. 1.

94. Claire Robertson, "The Death of Makola and Other Tragedies," *Canadian Journal of African Studies* 17, no. 3 (1983): 472–475, gives some estimates of which groups of marketwomen are relatively prosperous or poor, suggesting that the largest numbers, the petty traders without fixed stalls, make little money. She cites Ewusi's estimates that among self-employed persons the top 10 percent make 43 percent of the income, the bottom 10 percent only 1.8 percent, suggesting that most traders would fall in this category (but Ewusi's sample is self-employed income-tax payers). My own nonrandom inquiries among five sellers of bread or prepared foods in summer 1985, in the quarter around Danquah Circle in Accra, suggests, by a rough compilation, that these five sellers made 4–6 times the earnings of a minimum-wage earner, whose earnings then were roughly 50 percent of the salary of the highest civil servant grade.

95. Nii K. Bentsi-Enchill, "Destruction of Accra's Makola Market," *West Africa*, August 27, 1979, pp. 1539–1541, and "Losing Illusions at Makola Market," *West Africa*, September 3, 1979, pp. 1589–1592.

96. *West Africa*, September 8, 1980, pp. 1700–1701, noted by successor government; also, TUC, Mbiah, "Trade Union Congress Report on Maize Distribution," extract from *Annual Report, 1980* (Accra: TUC, 1980), reports that the FDC was unable to purchase enough maize in 1979–1980 because of farmer fears of soldiers, so less was available for distribution in 1980.

97. See Chazan, *An Anatomy of Ghanaian Politics*, pp. 284–301, on the 1979 election.

98. Jon Kraus, "The Political Economy of Conflict in Ghana," *Africa Report* 25, no. 2 (March-April 1980): 9–16; Chazan, *An Anatomy of Ghanaian Politics*, pp. 307–314.

99. See David Brown, "The Political Response to Immiseration: A Case Study of Rural Ghana," *Genève-Afrique* 18, no. 1 (1980): 61–63, on the "bingo mentality" in Ghanaian politics.

100. See K. Ata-Bedu, "Ghana's Prices Problem," *West Africa*, April 20, 1981, pp. 856–857, and "Sharing Ghana's Shortages," *West Africa*, April 13, 1981, p. 836; Ghana, *Economic Survey 1981* (Accra: Government Printer, 1983), pp. 257–260, on the distribution system.

101. See Ghana, *Economic Survey 1977–1980*, pp. 33–37; Ghana, *Economic Survey 1981*, pp. 17–26.

102. *West Africa*, March 9, 1981, pp. 521–522.

103. Ghana, *Economic Survey 1981*, p. 23.

104. *West Africa*, March 30, 1981, p. 684.

105. *Daily Graphic*, October 1, 1980, p. 1.

106. Ghana, *Economic Survey 1981*, p. 43.

107. Ibid., p. 44. The 130,000-metric-ton figure, a minimum, is calculated as the difference between cocoa purchased and cocoa exported.

108. On *kalabule*, see Ben Ephson, Jr., "Understanding *Kalabule*," *West Africa*, October 4, 1982, pp. 2571–2572, and "To Lomé and Back," *West Africa*, October 11, 1982, pp. 2626–2627; "Workers' Share of Production," *Legon Observer*, May 1982, p. 114.

109. *West Africa*, May 17, 1982, p. 1352 (on mental hospital conflict); May 10, 1982, p. 1288. Seized and imported goods piled up in GNTC warehouses with no arrangements for distribution; paychecks could not be processed because the acting managing director had no authority to do so; the WDC demanded a restructuring of the GNTC.

110. Radio Ghana, February 17, 1982.

111. *West Africa*, December 16, 1982, p. 2103.

112. Ibid., May 3, 1982, p. 1227; Deborah Pellow, "Kalabule Out, Warabeba In: Coping in Revolutionary Ghana" (Paper presented at the African Studies Association meeting, November 1982), pp. 10–11.

113. John Dadson, "Food and the Nation," *West Africa*, July 11, 1983, p. 1597.

114. *West Africa*, June 27, 1983, p. 1528.

115. Pro-PNDC views: "The Protests and the People," *West Africa*, May 16, 1983, pp. 1157–1158; "Roots of Student Protest," *West Africa*, June 6, 1983, pp. 1143–1145; also "The Uses of Student Protest," *West Africa*, July 18, 1983, p. 1654; *West Africa*, May 30, 1983, p. 1332.

116. "Road Transport Crisis," *West Africa*, October 17, 1983, p. 2405; October 17, 1983, pp. 2447–2449.

117. Ghana, *Summary of PNDC's Budget Statement and Economic Policy for 1983* (Accra: Government Printer, April 21, 1983), p. 22.

118. An FAO assessment indicated 35 percent, or 154,000 metric tons, of standing crops and stored cereal were destroyed (*West Africa*, March 3, 1986, p. 463); also *West Africa*, April 25, 1983, pp. 984–986.

119. Dadson, "Food and the Nation."

120. Posnansky, "Hardships of a Village," pp. 2163–2165.

121. *West Africa*, November 9, 1981, p. 2631; April 22, 1985, p. 797. The 1983/84 loans averaged ¢4,000, roughly $114 per farmer at 1984 exchange rates.

122. *African Research Bulletin/Economic* 24, no. 3 (April 30, 1987):8639–8640; *Primary Commodities: Market Developments and Outlook* (Washington, D.C.: IMF, 1987).

123. Elizabeth Ohene, "Words, Deeds, and Cocoa," *West Africa*, August 16, 1982, pp. 2103–2105; Rogers-Akpatah, "Chequing in the Cocoa," *West Africa*, March 7, 1983,

pp. 599–600; J. Osei-Kwame, "Banking on Farmers," *West Africa*, December 5, 1983, pp. 2811–2812. Two million cedis were lost through fraud during the two seasons, 1982–1983, less than previously (*West Africa*, June 11, 1984, p. 1245).

124. *West Africa*, January 26, 1987, p. 180.

125. TUC, "TUC Memo on the 1983 Budget" (typed), presented to PNDC.

126. Ben Ephson, "Margin for Maneuver," *West Africa*, May 12, 1986, p. 980. This data was from the Social Security and National Insurance Trust; the finance and bank sector paid the highest allowances and benefits.

127. TUC, "Press Statement by the TUC (Ghana) on the Recent Trade Increases of Some Commodities" (mimeo.).

128. TUC, "Resolution by the Executive Board on the Appraisal of the Economic Situation," October 25, 1984 (mimeo.).

129. The People's Stores were grass-roots cooperatives to which the state undertook to deliver directly certain food and essential commodities. Individuals subscribed small amounts for the capital to buy the commodities. Informants indicate that the supplies made available were very little. Three stores that I examined in Accra in the summer of 1985 were so small (4 meters by 8 meters) that they could not have accommodated many goods. By summer 1986 those in Accra were all closed; only a larger Tema People's Store ever made public its accounts. In 1987 several executives of the People's Stores organization were arrested for fraud.

130. TUC, "Position Paper of Executive Board of TUC on National Situation," February 18, 1985 (mimeo.), pp. 1–13.

131. See Nii K. Bentsi-Enchill, "Ghana: Masses or Asses?" *West Africa*, March 9, 1984, pp. 597–598, and "PNDC + PDCs + IMF = ?" *West Africa*, March 26, 1984, pp. 654–656; "'Hard and Painful Truth,'" *West Africa*, February 4, 1985, p. 201; Onyema Ugochukwu, "The Lost Revolution," *West Africa*, February 25, 1985, pp. 346–347; "Education: What Kind of Reform?" and B. Ephson and N. K. Bentsi-Enchill," *West Africa*, January 12, 1987, pp. 68–72; a radical defense of PNDC policy is R. A. Martins, "Ghana: Friends and Enemies," *West Africa*, May 7, 1984, pp. 974–976.

132. "'A Shameful Affair,'" *West Africa*, May 5, 1986, p. 920. On other detentions of trade unionists, "'Protect Our Rights,'" *West Africa*, October 27, 1986, pp. 254–255.

133. "Workers and the PNDC," *West Africa*, January 27, 1987, p. 152.

134. World Bank, *World Development Report 1984* (New York: Oxford University Press, 1984), p. 218.

·5·

Food and Agricultural Strategies and Popular Responses in Côte d'Ivoire

CYRIL KOFFIE DADDIEH

Ivorian agriculture is distinguished by its great diversification both at the level of export commodities—cocoa, coffee, oil palm, copra, rubber, bananas, pineapples, cotton—and of food crops—yam, plantain, cassava, rice, taro, etc. The country is not suffering from famine.

The future of Côte d'Ivoire hinges on agro-industry. It will require that our youth intensify their efforts in search of increases in productivity, processing and commercialization.

These excerpts from President Félix Houphouët-Boigny's silver jubilee independence anniversary message to his nation[1] represent the most current political thinking among Ivorian leaders about the state of their country's food and agricultural economy. The message also charts a course to an anticipated future of continued economic growth based chiefly on agroindustrial processing and external trade. However, the slightly veiled reference to famine is an indication that there is some skepticism about the country's record of food self-sufficiency.[2] But by responding to the critics, these remarks may well have placed Côte d'Ivoire squarely in the eye of the stormy academic as well as policy debate over the degree to which there is complementarity as opposed to a dialectic between commodity production either for export or for local agroindustry on the one hand and food production for domestic consumption on the other hand.[3]

Meanwhile, the president's remarks do serve as a useful point of departure for our analysis and understanding of the politics of food and agriculture in Côte d'Ivoire, partly because such ruling-class perceptions dictate national priorities, policies, and programs that, in turn, provide the socioeconomic and political parameters within which popular responses to national food and agricultural strategies are (re)formulated or simply stimulated. Second, in many ways the remarks reflect the government's renewed determination to press ahead with its brand of development that, in recent years, has consisted largely of increased intensification and diversification—a reinforcement of precisely those extroverted growth strategies that created the much-vaunted economic miracle of the first decade and a half of independence. Third, they are perhaps the most explicit reaffirmation yet at the highest political level of the need to relate industry even more closely than ever before to agriculture or to use agriculture as a basis for industrialization, not just in terms of providing the raw material inputs to industry but, more important, by providing the necessary capital to finance the industrialization drive. The government continues to search for a sustained role for the country's rural youth by exhorting them to take up agricultural production and thereby develop a stake in the existing social order.

Notwithstanding the optimistic tone of the remarks by the president and other leading government officials, several private and official reports reveal some rather disquieting trends involving agricultural personnel shortages, rising consumer prices, of which the food component is very high, depressed rural incomes, supply shortfalls, some as a result of deliberate neglect and even wanton destruction of some crops in protest over stagnant producer prices.[4] The degree to which such developments in the agricultural sector is viewed with official concern was reflected in part in the 1977 decision to regionalize the efforts of CIDT (Ivorian Textile Development Company), SATMACI (Technical Assistance Company for Agricultural Modernization in the Ivory Coast), and SODEPALM (State Company for Oil Palm Development in the Ivory Coast) in the savanna area of the north and in the center and forest zones of the south, respectively, and to extend the scope of their responsibilities to include the promotion of food crops in their areas of jurisdiction. As we shall see, these semiautonomous development companies have proved ill equipped to deal with their added responsibilities in the area of promotion of staple food production.

Partly as a result of their inability to stimulate the desired increases in food production, a new portfolio, Rural Development and Civil Defense, was created as part of the November 1983 cabinet reshuffle. The first minister of rural development, Vally Gilles Laubhouet, has been charged with trimming the country's imported food bill by encouraging Ivorian farmers to grow food as well as export cash crops. The association of rural development with civil defense was also an indication that the government had come to the realization that growth with equity and national security or domestic tranquility are ultimately inseparable.

Meanwhile, what we know about the current food situation in Côte d'Ivoire underscores the necessity, yet intractability, of striking a healthy balance between staple food production and supplies and export cash crops in the African context. I will therefore argue in this chapter that an enhanced understanding of the politics of food can only be achieved by relating the politics of cash-crop production to those of food and by extrapolating from that relationship the kinds of strategies or responses that are being pursued by various social groups either to take advantage of emerging opportunities or to limit the extent of any disadvantages to themselves. In other words, by following the history of the development of certain crops, I hope to be able to sketch the outlines of the agricultural strategy, its impact on rural economies, and some of the responses emanating from the perceived outcomes of the strategy. The central, related point of this chapter is that, as pricing is the critical policy instrument used by the government to stimulate the responsiveness of Ivorian farmers, the politics of pricing becomes equally critical to the understanding of popular responses to food in the country. The politics of pricing is here defined in its broadest and most meaningful sense to reflect not just the guaranteed prices paid for certain crops and not others—particularly food crops (except for the special case of rice, to which we will return later)—but also cash grants and subsidized inputs, as well as the effectiveness of the organizational infrastructure with which different crops are endowed—research, extension, market arrangements, etc. Finally, popular perceptions and responses are affected by the availability of alternative economic opportunities. With these introductory remarks in mind, I shall turn now to an examination of the Ivorian agricultural record.

· AGRICULTURAL PERFORMANCE ·

One of the outstanding features of the Ivorian political economy since independence is not just its continued heavy dependence on the production of export commodities—a continuation of its colonial inheritance—but that the country is apparently successful at such production.[5] This success is reflected in consistently high production figures for a variety of crops, most notably cocoa and coffee, the two leading export crops, but also oil palm, coconuts, rubber, cotton, pineapples, bananas, etc. The 1974 agricultural census revealed that 60.3 percent and 37 percent of the agricultural labor force were engaged in coffee and cocoa production, respectively. However, as Dian Boni points out, the distribution of the labor force between these two premier crops may be misleading as almost all of those who cultivate coffee also cultivate cocoa.[6] As Table 5.1 suggests, both the area planted to the two crops and their yields have risen dramatically since independence. At independence, the total area of harvested robusta coffee amounted to only 396,000 hectares, with a total production output of 185,500 metric tons and a yield of 468 kilograms per hectare. Coffee production has witnessed a greater degree of fluctuation, and yields have been consistently on the decline, as Table 5.1 demonstrates. Both production and yields had plummeted to 85,203 metric tons and 79 kilograms per hectare respectively during the 1983/84 agricultural campaign, according to the figures recently released by the Ministry of Agriculture.[7]

By contrast, the achievements in cocoa production have been quite dramatic, made all the more impressive by the fact that in 1908, the year the Gold Coast (Ghana) was exporting 20,000 metric tons of cocoa, the total Ivorian output was hardly 2,000 metric tons. Since independence, the area planted to cocoa has risen from 372,800 hectares to 1,163,000 hectares. Whereas total output stood at only 93,600 metric tons at independence in 1960, it had risen almost fivefold to 418,300 metric tons in 1980/81. During the 1983/84 campaign a total of 411,081,000 metric tons were harvested, with an average yield of 432 kilograms per hectare. Given this record, one has to concur with John C. de Wilde that even after conceding that possibly 30,000–40,000 metric tons of this total may have been smuggled from Ghana, the achievement is remarkable.[8]

The achievements in oil palm and coconut production are no less impressive. Both tree crops have long existed in natural stands in the country. A number of derivatives from the oil palm were used in a variety of local sociocultural and religious functions.[9] Two of these products—palm oil and palm kernels—also entered European-African exchange relations during the era of the so-called Legitimate Commerce following the abolition of the slave trade. The entry of palm products into European-African relations was at first facilitated by the discovery of palm oil as a substitute base raw material for the manufacture of soap and margarine.[10]

At the turn of the century, a serious effort was made by colonial interests to promote oil palm production and exports from Africa. Not unlike the beginnings of coffee and cocoa production in this colony, Europeans tried to monopolize the production of the commodity by establishing the first oil palm estates in 1912–1913. Exports grew from 6,000 metric tons of oil palm and kernels to a peak of 22,602 metric tons in 1925. Prices collapsed during the Depression of the 1930s and 1940s, seriously undermining exports from the country. Exports plummeted to a paltry 1,095 metric tons of kernels and not a single drop of oil in 1947. Even the opening of a processing factory at Acobo in 1950 did little to revive popular enthusiasm for the crop beyond ensuring local household or community needs. By 1959, Côte d'Ivoire was already a net importer of palm oil.[11]

Given the previous history of local production and the foreign-exchange flight that the imports represented, it is hardly surprising that soon after independence the Ivorian government elaborated (1961) and successfully executed (1963) an oil palm production promotion strategy called the Plan Palmier involving high-yielding varieties of oil palm. As Table 5.2 reveals, many of the gains were actually made within a very short period between 1967 and 1970. During that period, expenditure on oil palm accounted for 45 percent of all government investment in agriculture. Oil palm represented the single largest government investment in the 1960s. Between 1963 and 1973, about CFAF 35 billion were invested in the oil palm sector. (The unit of currency used in the Côte d'Ivoire is the West African franc. In 1968 $1 was equivalent to CFAF247; CFAF278 in 1971; CFAF230 in 1976; CFAF307 in 1982; and CFAF302 in 1987.)

It must be noted parenthetically that by African, or even Third World, standards of relative sectoral distribution of public expenditures, the share of government budgetary allocation going to oil palm was substantial, influenced, no doubt, by the potential for capital accumulation by the government and those external associates who were willing to make available the additional investment capital. And so, roughly a decade and a half after the Plan Palmier was launched, a total of fifteen integrated industrial oil palm complexes, each complete with its own plantation (nucleus estate); a factory to process the output of each estate complex and the supplementary output of outgrowers contracted to produce for the company; an administrative block; a *cité* for cadres, equipped with a center for social events; villages for mill and plantation workers; a few self-settling villages; along with such amenities as schools, health clinics, supermarkets, and places of worship had all been constructed. By 1978 these industrial complexes covered an area of 52,000 hectares, or some 57.9 percent of all oil palm plantations in the country. With the exception of Djibi, Frescoe, and Mopoyem, each of these integrated complexes exceeded 2,000 hectares. Ehania, the earliest and most important of these complexes, covers an uninterrupted area of 12,159 hectares. There are an additional 17,059 hectares belonging to various private capitalist individuals and associations, either European or Ivorian.

Similarly, although much less dramatically, coconut production has grown by leaps and bounds. As of September 30, 1984, a total of 29,532 hectares had been planted to coconut, of which 27,625 hectares were already producing fruits. Of that figure, the industrial plantations belonging to the parastatal Palmindustrie (Palm Oil Industries), covered an area of 18,225 hectares, with outgrowers and the Ivorian branch of the French research institute, IRHO (Research Institute for Edible Oils), contributing 9,904 and 1.403 hectares, respectively. An additional 1,500 hectares had been planted by private capitalists and were characterized as semiindustrial, and a further 18,500 were owned by peasant producers who are not beneficiaries of extension and related services going to the sector.[12]

In contrast to cocoa and coffee, oil palm and coconut production is not, strictly speaking, a peasant affair. The government is much more heavily involved through the activities of the vast industrial complexes and the supervisory role of its semiautonomous development companies; there is also the involvement of capitalist and semicapitalist producers—absentee or weekend farmers for the most part. However, even here the role of peasant producers has been significant. In addition to the figures cited for coconut outgrowers, oil palm outgrowers have increased their numbers and the total area cultivated since the inception of the program. In the mid-1980s, some 8,582 outgrowers and their families, not to mention some 6,000 agricultural workers employed by them, cultivate 34,373 hectares, representing roughly 42.1 percent of the total oil palm plantations in Côte d'Ivoire. The total area planted to selected oil palm stands at 98,206 hectares, according to the figures released by the Ministry of Agriculture for 1984.[13] Table 5.1 provides additional evidence of some of these achievements.[14]

If we turn to the government's promotion of the hybrid allen cotton in the north of the country, a move designed to remedy the increasing gap in income-earning opportunities between the savanna north and the forested areas of the south, we encounter similar evidence of success, at least at the level of aggregate production and yields. Efforts to promote cotton cultivation were initiated in the late 1950s by the CFDT (French Company for Textile Fiber Development), which provided extension services, introduced higher-yielding varieties of cotton, as well as provided an assured market for the producers' output. In 1974, the CIDT, Ivorian parastatal, took over responsibility for the promotion, purchase, and ginning of cottonseed and the marketing of the fiber, with CFDT retaining a minority interest in the company and providing technical assistance. In 1977, CIDT's mandate was broadened to include all crops grown in the north, including rice.

The output of seed cotton has grown from only 5,570 metric tons in 1961 to 142,975 metric tons in 1979/80, 156,983 metric tons in 1982/83, and back to 142,347 metric tons in 1983/84. By 1983/84 there were 93,519 farmers growing cotton. Average yields improved quickly to a little over 1 metric ton per hectare (1,161 and 1,040 kilograms per hectare for 1979/80 and 1983/84, respectively) and the ginning output improved from 36 percent in 1961 to a little more than 40 percent in the 1970s, largely as the result of the adoption of better varieties and the use of chemical fertilizer. The value of the crop to farmers increased from CFAF176 million to 11,140 million.[15]

· SOURCES OF SUCCESS ·

Because this record of achievement is made possible by the production activities of thousands of Ivorian peasants and agricultural workers from elsewhere in the subregion, particularly Burkinabe and Malians, it is fair to assume that the popular response to the government's promotional strategies has been quite positive. But this assumption begs the question of why Ivorian peasants have responded positively to government initiatives, whereas elsewhere African peasants have resisted official efforts to extract more production out of them. It also obfuscates the very real, albeit largely passive, resistance that some Ivorian peasants have engaged in over the years since independence and which are reflected in some of the fluctuations in the yield and production data that are available.

Favorable Climate and Resource Endowments

Ivorian peasant enthusiasm for these promotional schemes has come from several sources, not least of which is the fact that the country is endowed with excellent soils and climatic conditions. With the exception of the Sudanian zone of the north, which has only one rainy season, the rest of the country enjoys two rainy seasons with generally ample rainfall to allow for the cultivation of a wide variety of crops: bananas, cocoa, coffee (robusta), coconuts, oil palm, rubber, pineapples, cassava, yams, and rice in the forest zone of the south; maize, yams, rice, sorghum, millet, cotton, and groundnuts in both the Sudanian zone of the north and the transitional savanna of the central part of the country.[16]

Flexible and Secure Land Tenure System

In addition to favorable climatic and soil conditions, until recently, because of low population density (for the most part less than forty inhabitants per square kilometer, according to the 1974 agricultural census), land had been generally available for anybody serious enough about wanting to engage in commodity production, particularly in the central-west and southwest. The relative abundance of land and the flexibility of the traditional land tenure system of the south combined to make it possible for "strangers" and autochthons alike to gain access to land for the cultivation of new crops and the expansion of old crops. As the commercialization of agriculture has been accompanied by land commercialization—a phenomenon that has been condoned by the government and lineage elders who control the allocation of communal lands in the forest zone—some stranger farmers have secured access to land through land purchases. The majority—for the most part Baoule—have, however, availed themselves of the opportunity of access provided by the traditional system of sharecropping known as *abunsa* (a third-share) and *abunu* (half-share). As for the foreign migrants (Bukinabe, Malians, and Guineans), many have relied on the hospitality or intercession of their former employers to gain access to land for cultivating export cash crops.[17]

Plentiful Cheap Foreign Labor

Evidence is beginning to accumulate that suggests that labor is, and perhaps always has been, a serious constraint on African agriculture. Stated differently, labor is not as plentiful a commodity for most household and village/community production units as is often supposed. But fortunately for Côte d'Ivoire, the historical underdevelopment of its francophone neighbors—Mali, Niger, and Burkina Faso—and their common membership in the West African Monetary Union (UMOA) and the use of a common currency have combined to attract a sustained flow of a large number of cheap unskilled migrants to work on peasant farms, industrial plantations, and in urban centers in the country. Membership of the franc zone has facilitated downward migration to Côte d'Ivoire in part because remittances of workers' wages could be effected with a minimum of encumbrance.

Some of these foreign migrants have transformed themselves into important commodity producers in their own right. However, the majority remain ordinary wage earners on peasant farms and industrial plantations. Thus, 80 percent of the 5,147 workers employed in the industrial sector of the oil palm industry in the mid-1980s consisted of Burkinabe. These data are confirmed by the results of a survey conducted between 1977 and 1979 in Moronou, the heart of the cocoa belt, by J. M. Gastellu. As may be seen in Table 5.3, 1,697 workers (or 80.8 percent) of a total of 2,100 agricultural workers were Burkinabe; 100 (or 4.8 percent) were Malians, and only 117 (or 5.6 percent) of the total were Ivorians. These foreign workers have facilitated the rapid growth of commodity production in the southeast, east, and, recently, the central part of the country.[18]

Until the 1980s, peasant producers could afford to hire migrant agricultural workers partly because the modalities of compensating them combined both precapitalist and capitalist elements/forms. Among the more interesting aspects of this combination is the diversity in modes of payment for the tasks workers perform. No formal minimum-wage legislation is adhered to, a situation that is generally considered to be advantageous to agricultural workers because nationally legislated minimum wages for the agricultural sector are notoriously low. Various combinations of this flexible system of compensation may be identified. In some cases, the informal contractual agreement calls for boarding and lodging. Or the worker might be lodged on the farm but not fed; workers are expected to produce their own subsistence right there on the farm. Some arrangements call for a monthly payment. In others, wage earners are paid annually, although the employer may be obligated to give them an advance on their wages periodically as circumstances warrant. In still others, particularly in the cocoa/coffee sector, the workers are partly compensated in the form of *abunsa* or *abunu* of the crop. Such flexibility has made it possible for peasant producers to hire the necessary labor for extensive production.

Effective Research, Extension, and Marketing Infrastructure

Much of this growth has been spurred by a strong program of research and development of new hybrid varieties initiated by the government in collaboration with French institutions, some of these initiatives dating back to the colonial period. Thus the IFCC-GERDAT (French Institute for Coffee and Cocoa) has been very instrumental in developing Amazonian hybrids capable of increased photosynthetic activity in response to increased fertilizer use. The cotton/textile, oil palm, and coconut industries have benefited immensely from the research activities of the IRCT (Research Institute for Cotton and Textiles), which later became the CFDT and the IRHO. The adaptive research of the various institutes has produced arabusta, a cross between robusta and arabica coffee (offering the high yield of robusta without sacrificing the high quality and flavor of arabica; allen cotton, in place of the more familiar mono cotton; and SODEPALM/Palmindustrie's dwarf varieties of oil palm and coconuts.

The research efforts of these institutes have been nicely complemented by the extension activities of SATMACI and CIDT in the south and north, respectively. These extension agencies ensure that the seeds delivered by the research stations are properly treated; that their cultivation complies with the prescribed production techniques and that the right amounts of fertilizer, insecticides, pesticides, etc., are applied. Officials of these specialized crop agencies exercise supervisory control and leverage over peasant producers. The latter have to comply with company production and delivery techniques and schedules in return for the inputs and subsidies administered by these agencies.

In the south, coffee and, particularly, cocoa continue to receive increased official attention. (Re)planting with new varieties is a major objective of the government's agricultural policy. Recent figures indicate that 19 percent of the Ivorian cocoa tree stock was twenty-five years old or older, and 27 percent was five years old or younger in 1974. It was anticipated that hybrids would represent 90 percent of all new plantings by 1984–1985. Average yields have also improved appreciably over the years and are much higher that those prevailing in Ghana, but they are still much lower that those of Brazil. There is obviously room for improvement.[19]

However, the high level of peasant participation already achieved has come about in part as a result of an elaborate marketing strategy that has proved effective in mobilizing the output of thousands of smallholder cocoa and coffee producers dispersed throughout the cocoa/coffee belt. Part of that success derives from the fact that, in contrast to the situation that has obtained in Ghana for a number of years, peasant producers in Côte d'Ivoire receive prompt payment for their products and have had access to a wide variety of consumer durables on which to spend whatever income they derive from their farming endeavors. In accordance with the marketing strategy, the government itself does not participate directly in the purchasing of the cocoa/coffee crops. Rather, the collection, transport, storage, treatment, and shipping of Ivorian smallholder output is left to private initiative. Through the CSSPPA (Agricultural Products Stabilization Fund, or the Caisse, as it is usually known), the government limits its role to the fixing of the producer price before each buying campaign and licensing the buyers, who must buy all the produce in their designated zone of operation and keep a record of their activities in the zone if they hope to participate in the following year's campaign. These private buying agents are able to penetrate the countryside in the south and buy up the output of the entire season in part because of an extensive and well-developed network of motorways and feeder roads throughout the forest zone, a situation that contrasts sharply with the poverty of transport infrastructure in the north.

However, although marketing has remained reasonably competitive and efficient, the complicated system of licensing has contributed to the concentration of marketing activities in the hands of foreign firms and has undermined indigenous capital formation. The Lebanese dominate the buying and transport of cocoa and coffee in the countryside, and the French firms control international marketing and shipping. Meanwhile, the system allows the Caisse to keep a watchful eye on, literally, each available bean, all the way from the direct producers to the principal importing nations (where the Caisse has established offices of its own).[20]

Subsidies and Cash Grants

Furthermore, since the early 1960s the government has paid cash bonuses as inducement for farmers to cultivate new areas with selected high-yielding varieties of such crops as cocoa, coffee, cotton, oil palm, etc., and to adopt innovative production techniques involving the use of fertilizer, insecticides, herbicides, and tree spacing and pruning. The government has supplied a number of these inputs at subsidized prices. As Robert Hecht has noted, these cash bonuses have tided over some peasants financially during those critical first years before their farms could produce an income and have enabled others to purchase much-needed wage labor. It has been estimated that 10,450 hectares were planted in the Divo area alone under the bonus scheme during 1972–1980, representing 15 percent of the total cocoa farms.[21]

There are indications that the lion's share of the subsidies have gone to the sugar, cotton, and rice industries. Together, these three crops accounted for 93 percent of all government subsidies to agriculture. As the cotton and sugar schemes are located in the north, these transfers may be taken to reflect the government's desire to make good on an earlier promise that the savanna will catch up with the forest: hence, to achieve not only balanced economic growth but also to bring about a better redistribution of income.

It would be erroneous to think that the Ivorian government has granted these subsidies and bonuses out of official generosity. Such tactics have been indispensable to the continued expansion of commodity production. Under prevailing producer prices, peasants could not have afforded these new varieties and inputs at market prices. And if the new varieties are clearly more productive in response to the application of fertilizer and other inputs, they also require more labor time. Meanwhile, labor has become as costly as it is in short supply because of competition from industrial plantations and Abidjan, where the opportunities for migrants to earn a higher income are greater. Moreover, aging producer families no longer enjoy the luxury of assistance from sons who are either away at school or have migrated to Abidjan in search of what they anticipate to be a better life than agricultural work.[22] Further, some of the new crops (for example oil palm) and production techniques call for cessation of intercropping. This prohibition puts an additional economic burden on peasant producers who must turn to the market to procure some of their basic staples.

These factors explain why these bonuses, grants, and subsidies are indispensable if expansion in the area under cultivation is to be achieved, but also why the government has engaged in attracting migrants as cheaply as possible.

Sociocultural Effects

These tactics have certainly made a few large producers very affluent. And that affluence has created what I have characterized as sociocultural effects. Although the benefits of the economic miracle for most Ivorian peasants remains open to serious debate,[23] the existence of the few local producers who have become immensely economically powerful and even politically successful has acted as a strong incentive for others to continue to produce for the market. The affluence of this small planter bourgeoisie has demonstrated that there is money to be made from producing cocoa/coffee, oil palm, and other cash crops. Thus, although few peasant producers would ever become members of the class of large producers often referred to as the planter bourgeoisie, many are willing to participate in the process in the hopes of improving their economic situation and perhaps even becoming rich and powerful some day. Meanwhile, the ability of these peasant producers to hire labor has thus far given them a sense of *embourgeoisement* that not only sustains their involvement in commodity production but, by implication, militates against any serious effort to oppose governmental decisions/policies toward the agricultural sector. When we asked a group of fifty oil palm outgrowers whether they had considered forming an outgrowers' association to look after their interests, all but one said no; upon reflection, they did not think it would do them any good.[24]

Role of Government and External Associates

Earlier, we had noted that the role of the government is vital to understanding the propensity of Ivorian peasants to engage in export commodity production on such a large scale. Some of the previous discussion makes it clear that in general the government's role has been promotive rather than dysfunctional. First, the government's attitude toward the land has ensured security of tenure for migrant, or stranger, farmers. Since independence, government officials at the local level and village elders who mediate land disputes have taken as their cardinal operating principle the axiom that land belongs to whoever brings it into productive use. This dispensation has permitted migrants from other parts of the country and from neighboring countries to secure access to land in the forest zone.

Operating under the same principle and making convenient use of the precedent set by the colonial administration, which sought with some difficulty to seize control of the land, the PDCI (Democratic Party of the Ivory Coast) government moved quickly after independence to expropriate large tracts of land once communally owned. This move has enabled the government to establish the crop development agencies with their industrial plantation for oil palm, coconut, rubber, cotton, sugar, etc., without, in contrast to the situation in Ghana, having to confront the thorny issue of land compensation.[25]

Meanwhile, the Franco-Ivorian protocol of 1961 reinforced the existing propensity to pursue export-led development strategies by maintaining the preferential tariffs that already existed for coffee and cocoa and extending them to other exports—such as bananas, pineapples, and wood—from the newly independent country. It was also agreed to subsidize prices for coffee and bananas entering the French market. It has been estimated that the price support for Ivorian coffee and bananas was of the order of CFAF4.9 billion.[26]

Further, the willingness of the French government (through the CCCE [Central Fund for Economic Cooperation] and FAC [French Aid and Cooperation Fund]) and international capital to enter into partnership with the Ivorian government by providing generous funding for the various crop-promotion programs has been crucial to the success of the agricultural strategy. To take the example of the oil palm industry, by 1969 international capital had provided 68 percent of the capital required to launch the program, with the European Development Fund and the World Bank each contributing 31 percent and 20 percent, respectively. Total Ivorian official investment at the time was CFAF10,319 million, or 32 percent of total investment. The government has recently completed negotiations with international financiers for capital to enable Palmindustrie to initiate a major program of replanting between now and 1990 involving some 42,574 hectares and the development of a further 20,628 hectares of new oil palm plantations, a total of 64,702 hectares of new and replanted plantations. According to *Afrique Financement Agriculture*, the total cost of the program is estimated at $184.9 million, or CFAF70 billion. Palmindustrie (read: the government) will assume $78.7 million of the cost of financing the program; the Fund for Extension and Renewal (FER) will provide an additional $10.6 million; the smallholders and middle peasants will contribute $28.8 million, and the EEC, the Commonwealth Development Corporation (CDC), and the World Bank will each contribute $13.4 million. An additional $26.6 million will be shared equally between the European Development Fund (EDF) and the European Investment Bank (EIB).[27]

It is not surprising that the Ivorian political leadership, and especially President Houphouët, has been rather effusive in its praise of French development assistance since independence. In return, the Ivorian government has been rather supportive of French military and diplomatic engagements on the continent: a convergence of economic and foreign-policy interests.[28] It has been suggested that this preferential trade regime and the granting of these subsidies—a partial return of some of the surpluses the French had extracted from the Ivorian producers—were too enticing to turn down and that the arrangement conditioned the Ivorian government's export orientation.[29]

Popular Responses

Understanding the government's agricultural strategy and, in particular, its pricing policies is central to an understanding of popular responses. We have already seen how the government tries to mediate the apparent contradiction between the quest for increased peasant production and the extraction of surplus from the peasantry: by investing in research and development of high-yielding crops; by providing grants and subsidies and effective extension advice; and by making it possible for peasants to gain access to a cheap source of labor by tolerating the presence of foreign migrant workers even in periods of economic downturn.[30] These policies are but one side of the politics of pricing. The other side, to which we now turn, relates to producer price and income potentials and how these affect popular responses.

Although the combination of subsidies, bonuses, cash grants, technical advice and other nonprice incentives, and the guaranteed producer price for the major cash crops has been generally conducive to increased commodity production on the part of the Ivorian peasantry, an examination of different producer prices and production levels reveals fluctuations in popular responses to the politics of agriculture. These various responses include popular, perhaps even enthusiastic, support for government initiatives; shifts in favor of some commodities to the detriment of others; multiple cultivation of different crops in order to maximize income potentials or to hedge against potential losses from crop and/or price stagnation; diversion of crops to parallel markets; abandonment of farms; and rural outmigration.

Coffee had been the premier export crop from Côte d'Ivoire—in terms of area harvested, exportable output and yields—until roughly the end of the first decade of independence. As is revealed by the data in Table 5.1, however, it continued to hold its own until it was finally eclipsed in value by cocoa in 1977/78. This demonstrable shift in favor of cocoa production transpired as a result of official price discrimination against coffee. John C. de Wilde has determined that the average producer price for coffee in the four-year period 1977–1980 was 4.2 percent below that of 1970–1973, whereas the average cocoa producer price was 17.1 percent higher than in the earlier period. As the data in Table 5.4 indicate, in 1975 and 1976 cocoa producer prices were raised for the first time above those of coffee, and beginning in 1977 identical prices were fixed for cocoa and coffee despite the fact that coffee requires more labor time and hence costs more to produce. As De Wilde correctly stresses, the price and yield differential between coffee and cocoa means that the gross income per hectare of cocoa has substantially exceeded that of coffee since 1973. The income potential, coupled with the fact that the government provided additional assistance to producers by not only subsidizing their inputs and interest rate on planting credit but, beginning in 1974, actually giving a cash bonus of CFAF60,000 per hectare to those undertaking to plant cocoa in accordance with new standards, clearly encouraged the growth in cocoa production.[31]

And yet, as the production data indicate, though there may have been shifts away from coffee, the crop has not been completely abandoned. In fact, 59,089 hectares of selected coffee were apparently planted under the auspices of SATMACI between 1970/71 and 1978/9. The generous terms under which such (re)plantings took place played a role in maintaining a respectable level of production. Peasant familiarity with the crop and previous history of good income may have prevented its total demise. In any event, rather than put all their eggs in one basket, most peasant producers simply cultivated a few hectares of cocoa, coffee, and oil palm and some amount of staples primarily for domestic consumption.

The growth of oil palm and coconut (in the south) and cotton (in the north) is similarly revealing. The government had attracted peasant producers to these industries through offers of subsidies, credit facilities, and extension advice. In the case of oil palm, a continuous rather than seasonal crop, peasant producers had been lured by the additional prospect of a more regular (monthly) income, a more attractive proposition than the uncertainty of the annual income offered by cocoa and coffee. In other words, most producers clearly saw themselves as engaged in multiple dependencies.

However, the price paid to outgrowers for palm fruit was not only kept low, but it stagnated for nine years at CFAF4 per kilogram; it was raised to CFAF8 in 1974 and to CFAF10 in 1976 and has remained there since. "Deflated by the very substantial increase in consumer prices, the producer price of palm fruit in 1981 was only half that in 1974. . . . Similarly, the price paid for coconuts [CFAF7 per nut] has remained unchanged since 1974 despite an increase of 156 percent in the consumer price index."[32] The upshot of such deteriorating terms of trade was a crisis in the industry in the mid-1970s brought on partly by peasant resistance. This took several forms: Ivorian peasants neglected their trees when they reached a height that increased harvesting costs; they also diverted produce illegally (under the terms of their contracts) to the more remunerative open market, where prices were roughly three times those offered by the government. It has been speculated that such sales outside official channels might have been higher but for the fact that the new SODEPALM varieties are less suited to home cooking because they do not have the familiar taste of the traditional variety. The neglect and even abandonment of farms that have plagued the industry had resulted in further reductions in output and a concomitant serious underutilization of factory capacity (45 percent).[33]

As for cotton, its growth has been interrupted twice. In 1970, cotton production dropped precipitously in an apparent response to the producer price freeze at the CFAF33.5 level and the progressive rise in consumer prices. In the absence of viable alternatives and in view of the provision of government subsidies for fertilizer, pesticides, land clearing, etc. (until January of 1978 and free provision of such inputs thereafter), the industry still curried favor with most producers. However, in 1974 and 1975, the expansion was again halted temporarily by the government's decision to increase the producer price of paddy from CFAF28 to CFAF65 per kilogram (no less than 132 percent), a move designed to lessen the country's dependence on rice imports.[34]

The data (see Table 5.5) indicate that peasant response to the increase in producer price for paddy was apparently so strong that the increased output stretched SODERIZ (State Company for Rice Development) milling and storage facilities to the breaking point. There is reason to believe that the increased supplies came at the expense of cotton cultivation. Paddy deliveries to SODERIZ mills jumped from only 15,000 metric tons in 1972 (before the price hike) to 115,000 metric tons in 1975. However, the full benefits of the government's price increase could not be realized by the producers partly because SODERIZ did not have the necessary financial resources to buy all the paddy offered; it relied instead on wholesalers, who paid no more than half of the minimum "guaranteed" price.[35] It has even been estimated that as a result of these difficulties, less than a quarter of the rice produced actually ever reaches SODERIZ mills or the Abidjan market.[36]

Meanwhile, the coupling of the increase in the producer price for paddy in 1974 with an increase in the consumer price for milled rice pushed rice prices beyond the budgetary means of many consumers. In response, they simply reduced their consumption of rice. The reduction in consumption, the increase in domestic output following the producer price hike, and already available stock of imported rice resulted in a temporary reduction of rice imports to their lowest levels in many years. The political costs, primarily in terms of urban agitation and the very real possibility of a decrease in the flow of immigrants to the country as a result of the high cost of living, compelled the government to reduce the consumer price from its 1974 high of CFAF125 per kilogram to CFAF100 in 1976. The new price level contributed to a recovery of rice consumption. This renewed consumption and the decline in deliveries to SODERIZ mills, partly because the company lacked the financial wherewithal to buy paddy and partly because producer gains had been eroded by inflation, led to a new round of rice imports (see Table 5.5).

The difficulties of the industry continued even after the government initiated a number of institutional changes in 1977 in an effort to arrest the situation. SODERIZ was abolished and CIDT, SATMACI, and SODEPALM were given responsibility for promoting paddy production in their respective areas of operation. OCPA (Commercial Office for Agricultural Products), which took over responsibility for the buying of domestic paddy, fared no better than its predecessor, SODERIZ. In 1980/81 OCPA's production of milled rice had fallen to a mere 35,000 metric tons and imports had risen to 320,800 metric tons in 1984 at a cost of CFAF34,238 million. If wheat flour (205,496 metric tons valued at CFAF14,883 million) and maize (3,542 metric tons at a cost of CFAF345 million) are added, the total volume of cereal imports had reached 529,955 metric tons at a value of CFAF49,484 million.[37]

The financial burdens imposed on the government by the subsidies to OCPA and the continuing need for rice imports led to another round of reductions in the farmgate and mill buying price of domestic paddy from CFAF65 and CFAF75 to CFAF50 and CFAF60, respectively. Wholesale and retail prices were also raised. However, as de Wilde suggests, the new buying prices were below what farmers could obtain in the uncontrolled rural markets, and they responded by curtailing paddy deliveries to OCPA. In January 1982, the government decided to raise the farmgate price of paddy by 20 percent to CFAF60 per kilogram in the hope of at least partially restoring the farmers' incentive to deliver their paddy to OCPA.[38]

Meanwhile, the government's guaranteed pricing policies, including the provision of subsidies, cash bonuses, and grants, as well as the ease of marketing these cash crops, have conditioned Ivorian peasants popularly to associate cash crops with monetary gains and to treat domestic staples as subsistence crops. Affou Yaapi and Ori Boizo represent this outcome thus:

export crops = monetary income + foreign exchange (for the government)
food crops = consumption

They argue persuasively that, psychologically, those who are engaged in the cultivation of such export crops as cocoa and coffee enjoy, and are accorded, pride of place in their communities. Those who devote the same amount of land to the cultivation of, for example, maize or cassava are considered second-class farmers. They note that the equation is reflected in the kinds of ideological opposites that both official and popular discourse takes when it juxtaposes field and plantation, cultivator and planter, hence food and commercial crops.[39]

The practical outcome of such an association is that much of the best arable land is taken up by commercial crops, with only marginal lands left for food crop production. The pressure of cash for both the government and the peasant producer has fixed the parameters of policy and response and has put tremendous pressure on the available land. It is not surprising that individuals and corporatist groups are seeking access to or protection of land rights through litigation.[40] As land hunger increases, the fallow periods grow progressively shorter, seriously affecting yields, particularly of food crops, unless the use of chemical fertilizers can be increased. This devaluation of food crops has become such that only women devote much time and effort to their production. Plots are spread out, and this extensive mode of production has greatly increased the distance between villages and farms. The difficulty of daily return trips to the farms has led to the peculiarly Ivorian phenomenon of camping on farms. This course of action is not easily open to women because of their numerous other obligations. Their limited output is, therefore, intended primarily for auto-consumption. Perhaps as much as 90 percent of the food produced is consumed by the original producers. What is sold on the market is what the producer cannot consume or wishes to sell in order to be able to purchase a few essentials that she cannot produce herself: cloth, utensils, salt, dried fish, kerosene, soap, etc.[41] Meanwhile, between 1965 and 1975 subsistence production decreased from 45 percent to 32 percent of the overall output in the forest zone and from 64 percent to 46 percent in the savanna. Hence, the subordination of the food sector to the financial imperatives of the Ivorian government and of male planters and the marginalization of women go hand in hand.[42]

· CONCLUSIONS ·

Given the situation I have described, Côte d'Ivoire is fortunate not to have experienced a more serious food deficit. There is of course no guarantee of continued future success. In fact the combination of aging farms and producers, an urban growth rate of 8.5 percent per annum during the decade from 1973, a slowdown in the flow of cheap migrant labor, and recent difficulties in commodity markets provides cause for concern about the ability of the country to meet its food needs either through domestic production or through food imports unless government policy shifts dramatically in favor of the food crop producer. The same creativity that has marked the government's policy with respect to the politics of pricing and marketing structures needs to be summoned in the interest of food producers, the majority of whom are women.

TABLE 5.1 Development of Area, Yield, Output, and Prices of Principal Cash Crops
(area in thousands of hectares, production in thousands of metric tons, yield in kilograms per hectare)

| | Cocoa | | | | | | | Robusta Coffee | | | | | | |
| | Prices | | Total planted area | New area planted to hybrid cocoa[a] | Harvested area | Production | Yield | Prices | | Total planted area | New village plantings to selected coffee | Harvested area | Production | Yield |
Year	Producer	Export						Producer	Export					
1960/61	89/74	–	372.8	–	261.2	93.6	358	90	–	–	–	396	185.5	468
1961/62	64	121.0	388.0	–	267.7	81.0	303	75	–	–	–	460	97.1	211
1962/63	64	114.0	401.1	–	277.2	103.0	372	75	–	–	–	516	194.6	377
1963/64	70	126.0	416.8	–	291.8	98.2	377	80/90	174.0	–	–	560	260.7	466
1964/65	70	112.0	434.3	–	307.8	147.5	479	90	141.1	–	–	587	202.1	344
1965/66	55	80.0	452.8	–	327.3	113.3	346	75	164.0	–	–	615	272.6	443
1966/67	70	125.0	472.9	–	342.8	149.7	437	90	171.5	–	–	632	130.8	206
1967/68	70	160.0	493.7	–	358.0	146.6	410	90	166.0	–	–	649	287.8	443
1968/69	70	201.5	516.8	–	371.1	144.5	389	90	162.8	736	–	665	210.1	316
1969/70	80	226.8	539.2	–	386.8	180.7	467	95	208.8	868	–	652	279.6	429
1970/71	85	177.0	562.3	2.514	404.3	179.2	443	105	230.2	887	0.841	674	239.7	356
1971/72	85	140.2	586.3	6.817	422.8	225.8	534	105	220.4	910	2.133	695	268.8	387
1972/73	85	175.2	611.0	8.071	440.5	185.4	421	105	222.5	955	6.768	741	301.8	407
1973/74	110	303.6	898.5	11.312	497.0	208.5	420	120	275.6	1,060	6.231	847	195.9	231
1974/75	175	370.2	815.0	16.126	471.0	241.5	512	150	266.3	1,176	7.361	863	270.4	313
1975/76	175	362.7	840.0	19.491	498.0	231.1	464	150	416.8	1,214	8.373	901	308.1	342
1976/77	180	543.4	863.0	20.930	526.0	232.3	442	180	1,012.5	1,254	8.903	921	291.3	316
1977/78	250	780.0	896.5	21.777[b]	557.0	303.6	569	250	763.1	1,292	9.001	951	195.6	206
1978/79	250	724.0	946.5	–	586.0	318.4	543	250	679.5	1,362	9.478[c]	1,010	277.0	274
1979/80	300	591.0	1,076.0	–	610.0	379.4	622	300	660.0	1,174	–	1,046	248.7	238
1980/81	300	433.0	1,163.0	–	721.0	418.3	579	300	524.0	–	–	–	366.8	–
1981/82	300	–	–	–	456.7	–	–	300	–	–	–	–	241.8	–

Year	Oil palm				Coconuts		Copra production	Rubber production	Export banana production	Pineapple production			Seed cotton			Unit export price of lint
	Producer price of fruit[d]	New village plantings	Production of selected oil palms	Export price of palm oil	Plantation nut production					Fresh for export	For canning	Producer price[e]	Area	Production	Yield	
					Industrial	Village										
1960/61	—	—[f]	—	—	—	—	2.4	0.1	98.0	11.8	2.1	—	—	5.57	—	—
1961/62	—	—[f]	—	—	—	—	2.3	0.2	131.3	14.4	2.3	33.5	—	8.24	—	—
1962/63	—	—[f]	—	—	—	—	2.9	0.6	139.4	21.1	2.9	33.5	—	12.06	—	—
1963/64	—	—[f]	—	—	—	—	3.1	2.0	126.0	31.0	4.2	33.5	—	8.97	—	—
1964/65	4	—[f]	—	—	—	—	3.5	3.6	138.3	33.5	4.6	33.5	—	10.43	—	—
1965/66	4	—[f]	71.7	—	—	—	4.4	5.0	154.5	48.0	6.8	33.5	11.7	13.82	—	—
1966/67	4	—[f]	71.7	—	—	—	5.6	5.9	165.4	67.7	10.0	33.5	23.8	25.04	—	—
1967/68	4	—[f]	72.2	—	—	—	7.5	6.9	174.6	69.7	13.7	33.5	39.0	35.28	—	—
1968/69	4	—[f]	115.5	—	—	—	8.0	8.7	172.2	70.4	12.6	33.5	48.1	44.24	—	—
1969/70	4	17,670	223.2	—	—	—	10.3	11.0	178.9	86.6	16.5	35.0	33.3	34.32	—	—
1970/71	4	1,986	281.3	—	—	—	11.0	13.7	188.4	109.0	22.1	40.0	35.9	31.32	—	167
1971/72	4	2,271	435.9	—	—	—	11.5	14.5	212.3	155.8	39.4	40.0	51.4	49.53	944	178
1972/73	4	2,372	440.4	—	—	—	12.5	15.2	177.2	146.9	45.0	40.0	56.4	53.80	935	196
1973/74	8	2,350	670.9	—	—	—	13.5	16.5	207.8	157.0	63.1	45.0	58.2	59.46	1,005	327
1974/75	8	1,250	712.0	—	10,062	—	15.9	16.5	192.3	140.5	69.2	70.0	58.8	60.94	1,020	299
1975/76	10	3,957	718.8	—	19,801	952	16.9	16.9	147.2	172.3	65.2	70.0	65.5	66.04	994	293
1976/77	10	2,997	605.5	94.0	33,507	3,883	17.7	17.7	163.7	148.7	70.0	70.0	64.8	76.41	1,164	342
1977/78	10	3,948	676.0	127.0	41,556	6,535	19.2	19.3	196.8	181.9	102.8	80.0	87.5	102.93	1,176	316
1978/79	10	—	597.6	135.5	70,757	11,440	20.1	20.1	168.6	162.8	98.3	80.0	107.3	114.89	1,071	330
1979/80	10	—[g]	879.7[h]	139.5	101,400	15,100	30.0	21.8	162.7	—	92.0	80.0	123.0	143.00	1,160	376
1980/81	10	—	755.0	129.4	—	—	—	—	—	—	—	80.0	126.3	136.60	1,081	466
1981/82	15	—	—	—	—	—	—	—	—	—	—	80.0	—	135.37	—	—

aProbably unreliable.

bAt the end of 1978, the total new plantings were 107,128 hectares.

cAt the end of 1979, the total new plantings were 59,089 hectares.

dGuaranteed to smallholders who sell their fruit to large producers/processors.

eFirst quality.

fTotal new plantings in calendar years 1962–1970.

gOut of a total area of 100,350 planted to selected oil palm by 1980, smallholders accounted for 37,900 hectares, of which 31,860 hectares were harvested.

hOut of a total of 214,500 metric tons were from smallholder village plantings.

Source: John C. deWilde, Agriculture, Marketing, and Pricing in Sub-Saharan Africa (Los Angeles: African Studies Center and African Studies Association, 1984), pp. 94–95. Reprinted with permission.

TABLE 5.2 Evolution of the Size of Industrial Oil Palm Plantations (hectares)

Plantations	1963	1964–1965	1966–1967	1968–1973	1974–1978	Total
Eloka	824	1,857				2,681
Anguededou		908	1,927			2,835
Toumanguié	454	1,740	826	261		3,281
Ehania			2,127	8,283	1,749	12,159
Tiegba Irobo		816	1,334	–		2,150
Tamabo			1,142	1,105		2,247
Boubo			1,953	2,420		4,373
Yocoboué			1,406			1,406
Bolo			703	2,839		3,542
Soubré			718	3,914		4,632
Dabou	1,794	721	799	158		3,472
Fresco				75		75
Djibi				400		400
Iboke-Dewake					6,300	6,300
Okrouyo					2,452	2,452
Total	3,072	6,042	12,935	19,455	10,501	52,005

Source: SODEPALM-Palmindustrie, quoted in Dian Boni, *L'Économie de plantation en Côte d'Ivoire forestière* (Abidjan: Les Nouvelles Éditions Africaines, 1985), p. 185.

TABLE 5.3 Identity of Agricultural Workers in Moronou

Ethnic group		Permanent Number	Permanent Percent	Temporary Number	Temporary Percent	Total Workers Number	Total Workers Percent
Mossi		550	69.7	1,002	76.4		
Lobi	Burkina Faso	64	8.1			1,697	80.8
Zerma				81	6.2		
Malinké	Mali	20	2.5	59	4.5	100	4.8
Samogo				21	1.6		
Baoulé	Côte d'Ivoire	28	3.6	44	3.4	117	5.6
Agni		25	3.2	20	1.5		
Others		102	12.9	50	3.8	152	7.2
No response				34	2.6	34	1.6
Total		789	100.0	1,311	100.0	2,100	100.0

Source: J.-M. Gastellu, "Disparition de la main-d'oeuvre?" *Cahiers du CIRES*, no. 23 (1979), pp. 17–46.

TABLE 5.4 Comparative Yields, Prices and Gross Income for Coffee and Cocoa

Year	Yield[a]		Producer price (CFAF/kg) (in real terms)[b]		Producer price as percent of export price		Producer gross income (CFAF/ha in real terms)[c]	
	Coffee	Cocoa	Coffee	Cocoa	Coffee	Cocoa	Coffee	Cocoa
1961	468	358	90.0	81.5	n.a.	n.a.	42,120	29,177
1962	211	303	76.2	65.0	n.a.	52.9	16,078	17,695
1966	443	346	70.2	51.5	45.1	68.7	31,099	17,819
1970	429	467	72.8	61.3	45.5	35.2	31,231	28,259
1971	356	443	81.1	65.7	45.6	48.0	28,872	29,105
1972	387	534	80.7	65.4	47.6	60.6	31,231	34,924
1973	407	421	73.0	59.9	47.2	48.5	29,833	24,881
1974	231	420	70.9	65.6	43.5	36.2	16,378	27,552
1975	313	512	80.0	92.9	56.3	41.9	25,040	47,565
1976	342	464	70.9	82.5	36.0	48.2	24,248	38,280
1977	316	446	66.6	66.6	17.8	33.1	21,048	29,457
1978	206	569	82.1	82.1	32.7	32.1	16,913	46,715
1979	274	543	70.6	70.6	36.8	39.5	19,344	38,336
1980	238	622	75.3	75.3	45.5	50.8	17,921	46,837
1981	–	579	69.2	69.2	57.2	69.3	–	40,067

[a]Yields expressed in kg per hectare.
[b]Current producer price deflated by the consumer price index for African families in Abidjan (1961=100).
[c]Yields in kilograms multiplied by real producer price per kilogram.

Source: John C. de Wilde, *Agriculture, Marketing, and Pricing in Sub-Saharan Africa* (Los Angeles: African Studies Center and African Studies Association, 1984), p. 97. Reprinted with permission.

TABLE 5.5 Rice Production, Prices, and Imports

Year	Paddy Produce price (CFAF/kg) A	B	Domestic production Area (thousand ha)	Paddy (thousand metric tons)	Milled rice equivalent (thousand metric tons)	Rice imports (thousand metric tons)	Total supply milled rice (thousand metric tons)	Domestic rice prices (CFAF/kg) WP	RP	Approx. import price (CFAF/kg)
1961				156				49	54	32
1962				229				46	51	32
1963				219				49	54	31
1964				248				41	46	33
1965	18		261	250	157.5	58.8	216.3	46	51	30
1966	18			275				50	56	38
1967	20	19		340				55	61	36
1968	20			365				52	58	41
1969	22			303				55	61	33
1970	22		289	316	199.1	78.8	277.9	67	74	26
1971	22		282	385	242.6	97.3	339.9	45	50	22
1972	28		282	320	201.6	77.1	278.7	45	50	28
1973	65	75	290	335	211.1	147.9	359.0	57	63	59
1974	65	75	317	406	255.8	73.0	328.8	107	116	113
1975	65	75	390	460	289.8	1.6	291.4	97	108	
1976	65	75	398	426	268.4	2.3	270.7	87	100	
1977	65	75	409	440	277.2	147.5	424.7	87	100	
1978	65	75	428	520	327.6	141.7	469.3	87	100	
1979	65	75	448	534	336.4	217.8	554.2	87	100	71
1980	50	60	461	511	321.9	242.4	564.3	87	100	74
1981	60	70		546				100	100	69
1982					344.0	360.0	704.0	110	130	88

aFirst quality: A = farm-gate; B = mill
bAt Abidjan: WP = wholesale price; RP = retail price

Source: John C. de Wilde, Agriculture, Marketing, and Pricing in Sub-Saharan Africa (Los Angeles: African Studies Center and African Studies Association, 1984), p. 101. Reprinted with permission.

· NOTES ·

1. President Houphouët-Boigny, "Message à la nation," Special issue of *Fraternité-Matin*, 7 December 1985.

2. One such persistent skeptic is Laurent Gbagbo. See "Ivory Coast: Houphouët's Critic," *West Africa*, May 16, 1983, pp. 1164–1165.

3. This debate has ideological overtones as well as practical policy implications. The case for complementarity is set out in the Berg Report: World Bank, *Accelerated Development in Sub-Saharan African: An Agenda for Action* (Washington; D.C.: IBRD, 1981). For an initial exposition of the dialectical nature of the relationship between the two sectors, see Cyril D. Daddieh, "Recovering Africa's Self-Sufficiency in Food and Agriculture," in Adebayo Adedeji and Timothy M. Shaw, eds., *Economic Crisis in Africa: African Perspectives on Development Problems and Potentials* (Boulder, Colo.: Lynne Rienner Publishers, 1985), pp. 187–200; and Cyril K. Daddieh, "Contradictions in the Political Economy of Sub-Saharan African Agriculture" (forthcoming monograph).

4. The proceedings of a May 1982 conference organized by the *Centre Ivoirien de Recherche Économique et Sociale* in Abidjan, at which a number of these findings were exposed, are produced in two impressive volumes entitled *Les cultures vivrières: Elément stratégique du développement agricole Ivoirien* (Abidjan: Université d'Abidjan, 1983).

5. The virtues of success were first extolled by the World Bank in *Ivory Coast: The Challenge of Success* (Baltimore: Johns Hopkins University Press, 1978). For some comparative findings, see J. Hinderink and J. J. Sterkenburg, "Agricultural Policy and Production in Africa: The Aims, the Methods, and the Means," *Journal of Modern African Studies* 21, no. 1 (March 1983): 1–23, and John C. de Wilde, *Agriculture, Marketing, and Pricing in Sub-Saharan Africa* (Los Angeles: African Studies Center and African Studies Association, 1984).

6. See Dian Boni, *L'Économie de plantation en Côte d'Ivoire forestière* (Abidjan: Les Nouvelles Éditions Africaines, 1985).

7. See de Wilde, *Agriculture, Marketing, and Pricing*. The data have been updated using the recent release from the Ministry of Agriculture, *Annuaire des statistiques agricoles et forestières 1984* (Abidjan: République de Côte d'Ivoire, n.d.), p. 124.

8. De Wilde, *Agriculture, Marketing, and Pricing*, p. 96.

9. See Boni, *L'Économie de plantation*, esp. pp. 187–190; and Cyril K. Daddieh, *Contract Farming and Outgrower Schemes: Case Study of Ghana and Côte d'Ivoire* (Binghamton, N.Y.: Institute of Development Anthropology, December 1986).

10. See A. G. Hopkins, *An Economic History of West Africa* (London: Longman, 1973), esp. ch. 4, "The Economic Basis of Imperialism."

11. Boni, *L'Économie de plantation*. See also Eric R. Hermann, *Analysis of Selected Agricultural Parastatals in the Ivory Coast* (Study prepared for USAID under Contract REDSO/WA 79-177, June 1981), p. 170.

12. Boni, *L'Économie de plantation*; Hermann, *Analysis of Selected Agricultural Parastatals*.

13. The figures produced in the tables are sometimes at variance with those reported in the *Annuaire des statistiques agricoles et forestières 1984*. However, as the differences are not so great as to affect the conclusions, they have been left unaltered.

14. De Wilde, *Agriculture, Marketing, and Pricing*, p. 95.

15. Ibid., p. 98.

16. See Affou Yapi and Ori Boizo, "L'Organisation de l'agriculture et son impact sur la production vivrière," in vol. 1 of *Les cultures vivrières*, pp. 289–311.

17. Boni, *L'Économie de plantation*, esp. pp. 375–393.

18. Ibid., and J-M. Gastellu, "Disparition de la main-d'oeuvre?" *Cahiers du CIRES*, no. 23 (1979): 17–46. For some theoretical as well as sociopolitical implications of such widespread use of hired labor by Ivorian peasants, see J-M. Gastellu and Affou Yapi, "Un Mythe à décomposer: La 'Bourgeoisie de planteurs,'" in Y-A. Faure and J-F. Medard, eds., *Etat et bourgeoisie en Côte d'Ivoire* (Paris: Editions Karthala, 1982), pp. 149–179.

19. See Mathurin Gbetibouo and Christopher L. Delgado, "Lessons and Constraints of Export Crop-Led Growth: Cocoa in Ivory Coast," in I. William Zartman and Christopher Delgado, eds., *The Political Economy of Ivory Coast* (New York: Praeger, 1984), p. 125.

20. For more on this marketing arrangement, see, among others, the highly suggestive study by Robert M. Hecht, "The Ivory Coast Economic 'Miracle': What Benefits for Peasant Farmers?" *Journal of Modern African Studies* 21, no. 1 (1983): 25–53.

21. Ibid., p. 32.

22. See Boni, *L'Économie de plantation*, pp. 375–401.

23. For a sample of this debate, see (in addition to the work of Hecht, Gbetibouo, and Delgado, Hinderink and Sterkenburg, already cited) Eddy Lee, "Export-Led Rural Development: The Ivory Coast," *Development and Change* 11, no. 4 (October 1980): 607–642; Alex Rondos, "The Price of Development," *Africa Report* 24, no. 2 (March-April 1979): 4–9; Jon Woronoff, "The Value of Development," *Africa Report* 24, no. 4 (July-August 1979): 13–19; and Bonnie Campbell, "Inside the Miracle: Cotton in the Ivory Coast," in Jonathan Barker, ed., *The Politics of Agriculture in Tropical Africa* (Beverly Hills: Sage Publications, 1984), pp. 143–171.

24. The government understands the salutary ideological implications of this phenomenon of peasant producers hiring other peasants as wage earners and has participated actively in facilitating the inflow as well as recruiting of migrant workers.

25. See Boni, *L'Économie de plantation*, pp. 92–95. For a comparison with Ghana, see Daddieh, *Contract Farming and Outgrower Schemes*.

26. See Lynn K. Mytelka, "Foreign Business and Economic Development," in Zartman and Delgado, eds, *The Political Economy of Ivory Coast*, p. 152. It was suggested that the actual subsidy may have been much higher, as the 1960/61 subsidy was 65 percent higher than prevailing world prices.

27. See *Afrique financement agriculture*, no. 16 (May 1986): 272; also from interview with resident representative of the World Bank, Abidjan, July 1986.

28. For more on this subject, see Félix Houphouët-Boigny, "Black Africa and the French Union," *Foreign Affairs* 35, no. 4 (July 1957): 593–599. The political economy of foreign policy in Côte d'Ivoire is explored in Cyril K. Daddieh, "Ivory Coast," in Timothy M. Shaw and Olajide Aluko, eds., *The Political Economy of African Foreign Policy: Comparative Analysis* (New York: St. Martin's Press, 1984), pp. 122–144.

29. See P. Anyang Nyongo, "Liberal Models of Capitalist Development in Africa: Ivory Coast," *African Development* 3, no. 3 (1978): 5–20; Bonnie Campbell, "The Fiscal Crisis of the State: The Case of the Ivory Coast," in Henry Bernstein and Bonnie Campbell, eds., *Contradictions of Accumulation in Africa* (Beverly Hills: Sage Publications, 1985), pp. 267–310.

30. Incidentally, substantial subsidies and tax exemptions have also been extended to bananas, pineapples, and soybeans and have benefited not peasant producers but an elite group of bureaucrat/politician, or weekend, farmers. Most prominent among the producers of fresh and tinned pineapples are the president himself, Philip Yace, and Mathieu Ekra, all stalwarts of the party and government.

31. De Wilde, *Agriculture, Marketing, and Pricing*, p. 96.

32. Ibid., p. 98.

33. See Henrik S. Marcussen, "The Ivory Coast Facing the Economic Crisis," in Jerker Carlsson, ed., *Recession in Africa* (Uppsala: Scandinavian Institute of African Studies, 1983), pp. 1–27. An earlier version appeared in Henrik S. Marcussen and Jens Erik Torp, *Internationalization of Capital: Prospects for the Third World. A Re-examination of Dependency Theory* (London: Zed Press, 1982).

34. De Wilde, *Agriculture, Marketing, and Pricing*, p. 99. See also Campbell's "Inside the Miracle," pp. 151–152, in which she argues that peasant producers withdrew from cotton cultivation and devoted more time to rice or food production because the returns to cotton were neither immediate nor very secure.

35. De Wilde, *Agriculture, Marketing, and Pricing*, p. 100.

36. See Cheryl Christensen et al., *Food Problems and Prospects in Sub-Saharan Africa: The Decade of the 1980s* (Washington, D.C.: Foreign Agricultural Research Report no. 166).

37. See Ministry of Agriculture, *Annuaire des statistiques agricoles*, p. 181.

38. De Wilde, *Agriculture, Marketing, and Pricing*, pp. 101–102.

39. Yapi and Boizo, "L'Organisation de l'agriculture," p. 299.

40. Hecht, "The Ivory Coast Economic 'Miracle'," p. 33. For a suggestive study of the pressure of cash on the evolution of land commercialization and social conflict in neighboring Ghana, see Kwame Arhin, "The Pressure of Cash and Its Political Consequences in Asante in the Colonial Period," *Journal of African Studies* 3, no. 4 (Winter 1976/77): 253–468.

41. Yapi and Boizo, "L'Organisation de l'agriculture," p. 301. See also Abdoulaye Sawadogo, *L'Agriculture en Côte d'Ivoire* (Vendôme, France: Presse Universitaire de France, 1977).

42. For more on women's role in agricultural development in Africa, see Cyril K. Daddieh, "Production and Reproduction: Women's Contributions to Agricultural Resurgence in Africa," in Jane Parpart, ed., *Women and Development in Africa* (Washington, D.C.: University Press of America, 1988). On the contributions of women in Côte d'Ivoire, see François Kouakou N'Guessan, "Les Cultures vivrières et la division sociale du travail," pp. 151–168, and François Ruf, "La Contribution des femmes à la production alimentaire," pp. 105–126, both in vol. 1 of *Les cultures vivrières*.

·6·

Tanzania's Agricultural Decline

MICHAEL F. LOFCHIE

Tanzania is almost bankrupt.

Africa Confidential, July 16, 1980

Tanzania is today in the middle of a debilitating economic crisis, one which threatens the living standards and the basic needs fulfillment of much of the Tanzanian nation.

International Labour Office, 1982

In 1982-83, Tanzania faced its most disastrous year economically since independence in 1964.

Africa Contemporary Record, 1982–1983

Tanzania is now suffering its worst economic crisis since independence.

Uma Lele, 1984

The so-called Tanzanian "experiment" is now commonly seen as a complete and dismal failure.

John Shao, 1985

Tanzania had the highest rate of increase in domestic food production for the entire African continent during the decade of the 1960s. According to United Nations figures, Tanzanian food production increased by more than 70 percent, or about 7 percent per year, between 1961 and 1970.[1] During this period, Tanzania was regularly able to export grain to such nearby countries as Malawi, Zaire, and Zambia. Since the mid-1970s, Tanzania has become a consistent food importer to meet a persistent food gap. Though the level of food imports has fluctuated considerably from one year to the next, it had grown to about 200,000 metric tons of grain per year by the late 1970s and throughout the first half of the 1980s, averaging more than 300,000 metric tons per year.[2] Food imports in the mid-1980s account for about 20 percent of all imports by value and are necessary to meet a "structural" food gap that has little to do with climate or the quality of the country's natural endowment. Indeed, there is a virtually unanimous consensus among the country's close observers that the decline of its food-producing sector is but one symptom of an overall pattern of severe economic deterioration.

The widespread attention directed toward Tanzania's economic plight reflects the country's long-standing role as the embodiment of the deepest hopes and aspirations of the international Africanist community. It is also occasioned by Tanzania's current status as the epitome of independent Africa's worst economic performance. Even the country's more ardent sympathizers acknowledge an economic deterioration of such calamitous proportions that meaningful recovery may be all but out of reach. Critics of the country's experiment in socialist development forecast an even bleaker future.[3] They anticipate continuing economic decline characterized by worsening balance-of-payments difficulties and a worsening shortage of foreign exchange that will further strangle Tanzania's already crippled industrial sector; further declines in marketed agricultural production caused by a variety of factors including the disintegration of the country's physical infrastructure; continued expansion of the informal economy that evades taxation, thereby lowering government revenues and causing major cutbacks in social services, once Tanzania's principal source of national self-esteem; and, a growing atmosphere of cynicism and corruption on the part of the country's political leadership.

Observers at all points on this spectrum concur that Tanzania today is at a crossroads. The presidential succession of October 1985 set the stage for a renewed dialogue with international donors such as the IMF and for a more public internal debate about the causes and remedies for the country's economic collapse.[4] In August of 1986, Tanzania and the IMF signed an agreement for a standby loan of approximately $80 million, thereby signaling the imminence of economic reforms that seem likely to end the country's long-standing commitment to a socialist approach to economic development. But Tanzania's future economic course is still by no means certain. For the final years of the Nyerere regime were marked by an increasingly visible political cleavage between segments of Tanzanian leadership committed to a continuation of socialist development strategies and political institutions and those favoring more market-based approaches. And the outcome of the power struggle between Tanzania's "reds" and "experts" cannot, as of 1987, be foreseen.

Even if the reformist faction prevails, there is not overwhelming evidence that policy reform alone can stimulate economic recovery in an economy as badly undermined as Tanzania's. Tanzania will, at the very least, require substantial infusions of capital to restore its industrial base and agricultural infrastructure. The Tanzanian government will also need to restore the confidence of entrepreneurial classes that have been badly demoralized by years of economic limbo.

In the early years of its independence, Tanzania became a test case for those who believed that socialism could provide a basis for humane and egalitarian economic development. In the early years of its second presidency, Tanzania may become a test case of a different sort: whether policy adaptations can help initiate a process of economic growth.

· THE SYNDROME OF ECONOMIC DECLINE ·

A major part of the problem lies in the fact that once an economy has declined, its malaise becomes enormously complex and multifaceted. The symptoms of economic decline form an interlocking syndrome in which the various component factors reinforce one another as cause and effect. It is this quality of interrelatedness that makes the search for solutions so difficult. For it means that economic reforms must simultaneously address many different sectors of the economy. Because Tanzania's economic decline is so advanced, it provides an especially dramatic illustration of this problem.

In addition to chronic food deficits, the principal features of its present economic crisis are as follows.

Declining Export Volumes

Agriculture is the epicenter of Tanzania's economic system. It provides for most of the country's employment, about 80 percent, at least two-thirds of foreign-exchange earnings, and the largest single portion of GDP, about 47 percent.[5] Other sectors of the Tanzanian economy, such as industry and transportation, depend almost entirely on the foreign-exchange earnings generated by agricultural exports. For all these reasons, the major symptom of Tanzania's economic decline has been a sharp drop in export volumes and, as a consequence, in the country's foreign-exchange earnings from agriculture. Tanzania's export volumes have declined steadily since the end of the 1960s, and by 1980 the value of its agricultural exports was only about 40 percent of that in 1970.[6]

For certain of the country's major exports, the fall was precipitous. Between 1964 and 1980, for example, Tanzania's sisal exports, for many years the country's major source of foreign exchange, dropped from more than 230,000 metric tons to less than 20,000 metric tons, by more than 90 percent. Between the mid-1970s and mid-1980s, cashew nut exports, which had briefly emerged as the major source of foreign exchange, fell from more than 140,000 metric tons per year to less than 25,000 metric tons per year. Other crops dropped less precipitously but with no less grave consequences for the country's export earnings. Cotton exports, for example, fell from about 75,000 metric tons per year in the early 1970s to less than 50,000 metric tons annually in the early 1980s, a drop of more than 33 percent.[7]

Coffee and tea exports remained remarkably stable throughout the 1970s and seemed to some degree to be immune to the general trend toward falling export volumes. But their apparent resilience was principally the result of heavy capital and project assistance by several of Tanzania's donor countries rather than domestic factors. And in both cases, the quality of Tanzania's exports dropped markedly so that there was a downward trend in export earnings because of price discounting.[8] By the mid-1980s, both these commodities began to show signs of falling volumes, with tea exports falling to about 90 percent and coffee exports to about 75 percent of their all-time highs. If Tanzania had been able to maintain the export levels it attained in the late 1960s or early 1970s, the current economic situation would be far less bleak; and if Tanzania had only been able to achieve production increases comparable to those of many African states, it might have been averted altogether.

Balance-of-Payments Difficulties

As a direct outgrowth of falling export volumes and the price penalties that result from lowered quality levels, Tanzania has been experiencing severe balance-of-payments deficits since the late 1970s. Despite strenuous attempts to reduce imports, the country's balance-of-payments deficits on international trade have been enormous. In 1980, for example, Tanzania's trade deficit was more than $700 million, and since that time its trade deficits have varied between about $450 million and $650 million annually. One consequence of these deficits is that Tanzania's level of foreign debt has skyrocketed. At the end of 1984, Tanzania's foreign debt was about $3.3 billion and the country's debt-service ratio (annual debt burden as a percentage of export earnings) had risen calamitously to almost 70 percent. Tanzania has been able to service only a fraction of its foreign debt and as a result is accumulating an increasing arrears in its external financial obligations.

Balance-of-payments deficits have been the principal source of a foreign-exchange crisis of unprecedented severity, and the extreme scarcity of hard currency has, in turn, had an adverse impact on virtually every aspect of the country's economic life. To deal with foreign-exchange shortages, Tanzanian authorities have imposed sharp limitations on imports, and these have led to serious scarcities of a wide variety of goods, including petroleum products, consumer items, and inputs vital to the agricultural, industrial, and transportation sectors. The foreign-exchange shortage offers the best possible illustration of the self-reinforcing quality of Tanzania's economic predicament. For just as the foreign-exchange scarcity critically reduces the country's capacity to process and transport its exports, lowered exports in turn produce even deeper shortages of foreign exchange.

Low Industrial Capacity Utilization

Extreme scarcities of foreign exchange have had a profound effect in lowering Tanzania's rate of industrial capacity utilization. For much of the country's industrial sector was developed on the principle of import substitution. As industries that are designed to produce consumer goods for domestic consumption do not generate their own foreign-exchange reserves, they are dependent upon the hard-currency earnings of other sectors, principally agriculture. As the value of Tanzania's agricultural exports has declined, so has its capacity to import the raw materials, spare parts, replacement equipment, and energy necessary to sustain its consumer goods industries. The International Labour Office (ILO) estimated that, by the early 1980s, Tanzania's industries were operating at a rate of only about 20–30 percent of installed capacity.[9] As economic conditions have continued to deteriorate, that figure may now be substantially lower. Because of input shortages, a number of industrial plants have been shut down altogether, thereby adding the problem of growing urban unemployment to the country's other economic difficulties. And because of the scarcity of consumer goods, especially in the rural areas, it has become increasingly difficult to induce market-responsive behavior on the part of the country's smallholder agricultural producers, who find little value in the acquisition of cash income.

High Rate of Inflation

Another symptom of Tanzania's economic malaise is the country's high inflation rate.[10] According to official estimates, Tanzania's urban cost of living increased more than 400 percent, or about 65 percent per year, during the six-year period from 1978 to 1984.[11] But even this extraordinary figure probably underestimates the true rate of inflation by a considerable amount. For the Tanzanian government's consumer price index (CPI) is constructed partially on the basis of food prices as set by official marketing agencies.[12] Because most Tanzanians must now acquire their food in informal markets where price levels are much higher, the effective rate of inflation is substantially greater than that acknowledged in government figures. If the cost of illegally imported consumer goods, such as automobile parts, were included in Tanzania's CPI, the effective rate of inflation would be astronomic. It now seems indisputable that Tanzanians have had to cope with a high rate of inflation by accepting a steady lowering of their material standard of living.

Deterioration of Physical Infrastructure

One of the most visible symptoms of Tanzania's economic plight is the problem of infrastructural decay. The deterioration of the country's road and railroad systems is now so severe that transportation problems alone constitute a serious constraint on the prospect of economic recovery. The road from Arusha/Moshi to Dar es Salaam, for example, is vitally necessary for its role as the transportation route for both coffee exports and food supplies to the nation's capital city. Once well surfaced and easily traversable, stretches of this road have sometimes become so badly potholed as to be virtually impassable. Similar deterioration has prevented the shipment of foodstuffs from the country's other major grain-producing area, the southwestern highlands, to Dar es Salaam or to food-deficit regions such as Shinyanga.

Rise of the Informal Economy

The emergence of a sizeable informal economy[13] in Tanzania has been so well established that several government agencies have conducted price studies in the parallel sector to determine the differentials between official and free market prices. The informal economy has flourished as a result of the chronic inability of the country's official marketing agencies to provide adequate supplies of vital consumer necessities. The extent of the informal marketplace cannot be precisely determined, as the transactions that occur there are by definition covert. But Tanzanian officials readily acknowledge that for such key items as food staples, this market provides a larger percentage of the country's needs than does the official marketing system.

Tanzania now has two food supply systems. The largest is the informal market. Composed of small-scale private traders who procure their food supplies from local producers, the informal market delivers grains and other staples to the country's entire population outside Dar es Salaam. The second is the country's official grain-marketing mechanism. Based on the National Milling Corporation (NMC), the country's official grain procurement and distribution parastatal, the official food supply system is heavily dependent upon imported grains, including large volumes of food aid, to provide food for the capital city. Some observers offer an even more circumscribed description of the role of the official marketing system, suggesting that it does not even provide for the entire population of Dar es Salaam but, rather, only for the country's major institutional consumers, such as the army, police, schools, and hospitals. Whichever of these descriptions is correct, it seems clear that the informal market provides for the food needs of approximately 90 percent of the population.

For the entire range of consumer durables, such as bicycles, sewing machines, refrigerators, and automobile parts, which are no longer legally imported except in very small volumes, the role of the informal market may be even greater, providing nearly 100 percent of the country's total supply. As informal trade is outside the official jurisdiction of the Tanzanian state it is carried on tax-free. This may help account for Tanzania's declining tax revenues.[14] Despite rigorous efforts to reduce expenditures and increase taxes, Tanzania's budget deficits in the mid-1980s amounted to more than 25 percent of total expenditures, thus contributing additionally to the problem of inflation. The growth of the informal market also casts doubt on Tanzania's claim to have achieved a high degree of social equality, as this market has begun to sustain a growing and highly prosperous class of private traders whose incomes are not subject to the regulatory and distributive mechanisms of the Tanzanian state. And because the informal market depends upon the active collaboration of government officials at all levels, it has also begun to fuel the pervasive atmosphere of corruption that now infuses the Tanzanian public sector.[15]

· THE CAUSES OF ECONOMIC DECLINE ·

Tanzania's worsening economic malaise has evoked a voluminous outpouring of journalistic, academic, and official commentary. Its current economic plight is commonly referred to as a "crisis," but that term is inappropriate to the extent that it conveys the impression of a sudden, short-term situation from which a dramatic recovery is either likely or possible. Tanzania's economic predicament is not only the culmination of nearly two decades of steadily worsening economic performance but the product of a set of factors that includes some long-term casualties. Broadly speaking, three strands of causality may be usefully identified: (1) external factors, including the severe economic "shocks" to which Tanzania has been subjected in the last dozen years; (2) the country's policy of socialist development and the consequent tendency to constrain productive economic activity by private entrepreneurs; and (3) economic policies that have generated extreme disincentives for agricultural production. The intellectual debate among the proponents of these factors has generated an enormous literature on Tanzanian development.[16] Although the predominant weight of evidence suggests that internal economic policies are primarily responsible for Tanzania's current state, each of these three schools of thought helps shed some light on the process of economic decline.

External Factors

Tanzania has much in common with innumerable other countries that depend upon the export of primary agricultural commodities. These countries have been severely buffeted by international economic factors since the early 1970s. Among the factors most commonly cited by those who stress external considerations are the oil price increases of 1973 and 1979, generally depressed international price levels for agricultural products, and, especially in recent years, sharp declines in the terms of trade. During this period, Tanzania has also suffered at least two episodes of severe drought, first in 1973–1974 and the disastrous East African drought of 1984. Some observers also count Tanzania's costly war against Uganda in the fall of 1979 as an external factor, as it was largely necessitated by Uganda's persistent military intrusions into the West Lake Region. That war not only exerted a burdensome financial toll, most frequently estimated at about $500 million, but caused severe disruptions in the country's transportation system.

Inasmuch as Tanzania is heavily dependent upon oil—some 90 percent of its energy needs are met by petroleum derivatives—oil price increases have been especially harmful. By the mid-1980s, petroleum imports accounted for approximately 25 percent of all imports by value, and this had profoundly negative implications for the performance of other sectors. Petroleum imports, like food imports, compete directly with other categories of imported goods. The high cost of petroleum meant that there was less money available to acquire other necessities such as industrial machinery or agricultural inputs. By diminishing the available supply of consumer goods, increased petroleum costs have also reduced the incentives for Tanzanian farmers to produce marketable surpluses of both food and export crops.

Adverse shifts in the international terms of trade have also been held accountable for Tanzania's poor economic performance. Although this factor has been cited more frequently than almost any other in discussions of external impacts upon Tanzania, its precise effects are almost impossible to calculate. For there is almost no consensus on how to construct a terms-of-trade equation that will accurately reflect the country's actual economic experience since 1970. Economists disagree fundamentally over such basic issues as what time period to select, which commodity prices should be included, especially in the marketbasket of imports, and how to figure in changing export volumes.[17]

The reasons for these disagreements are often political. Observers sympathetic to Tanzania's socialist strategy of development generally seek to maximize the economic effects of external considerations in order to exonerate avowedly socialist policies of primary responsibility for economic failure. Those more critical of Tanzanian socialism are more apt to show that changes in the terms of trade, although important, are not so great over long periods of time as to constitute the primary reason for Tanzania's economic collapse. ILO has provided dramatic evidence of how widely terms-of-trade surveys can vary depending upon the base period chosen. "The results of this exercise [terms of trade analysis] would look different if different base years had been chosen: from a 1975 base year, the 1980 terms of trade would still represent an improvement. In the previous chapter we emphasized the swift deterioration of the terms of trade with 1977, the all-time high, as the base point."[18] By beginning its principal survey during a year in which commodities' prices boomed (1977) and extending the duration of its analysis through the collapse of these prices and the oil price increase of 1979, the ILO was able to spotlight the suddenness with which international economic trends shifted against Tanzania in the late 1970s and early 1980s. During this brief period, the prices of Tanzania's major imports increased by nearly 50 percent, while the price index of its exports remained basically stable.[19]

Some expert observers doubt altogether that declining terms of trade have had an effect on Tanzania's economic performance. Uma Lele, for example, argues that the country's economic decline is not "in any significant measure a result of the declining prices of Tanzanian exports in relation to imports," and her figures show that Tanzania's terms of trade actually improved slightly between 1973 and 1981.[20] Viewing the same period, Jennifer Sharpley also argues that changes in the international terms of trade, although negative, were not so great as to have had an appreciable effect on Tanzania's overall economic performance. "Whilst not an improvement, the adverse movement in the international terms of trade was not very large. Between 1973 and 1980, the net barter terms of trade averaged 99% of the 1973 base year, and even excluding 1977, when world coffee and tea prices reached an all-time peak, the index averaged 95% of the base year."[21] Lele and Sharpley both believe that the major source of Tanzania's acute balance-of-payments difficulties was not falling prices for its key agricultural exports but, rather, the country's tendency to show steep declines in its export volumes.

The available data on Tanzania's terms of trade may be roughly summarized as follows. Between 1973 and 1980, Tanzania's terms of trade declined gradually. The fall was about 11 percent, or approximately 1.7 percent per year.[22] Though this change was probably not great enough to have had a major effect on the country's economy, it did mean that export earnings would have had to grow appreciably simply to maintain the country's international purchasing power. Between 1977 and 1987, however, the decline in Tanzania's terms of trade has been more precipitous. Economists in Tanzania's donor organizations now calculate that changing price ratios between exports and imports have lowered Tanzania's international purchasing power by about half (at constant export volumes) during that decade. This drop has had a direct bearing on the country's ability to maintain export volumes. It has become more difficult to acquire the agricultural inputs necessary to maintain a stable level of exports.

In the final analysis, however, external factors do not provide a comprehensive or fully persuasive explanation of Tanzania's economic decline. In some respects, Tanzania's external environment has been highly favorable. During the beverage boom of 1976 to 1978, for example, Tanzania enjoyed a positive shift in the terms of trade, and this pattern may have been repeated briefly in 1984 and 1986 with soaring prices for tea and coffee. In addition, Tanzania has also had a great deal of assistance from the international donor community and has consistently enjoyed one of Africa's highest levels of per capita foreign assistance. The most important consideration, however, is that other countries with similar resource endowments and nearly identical export palettes have been able to achieve positive rates of economic growth during this period. Indeed, as most low-income, oil-importing countries have performed appreciably better than Tanzania throughout the 1970s and 1980s, it is impossible to avoid the conclusion that Tanzania's economic travails were primarily the outcome of internal factors, most notably persistent mismanagement of the productive sectors of the economic system, including agriculture.

Socialism and Agricultural Decline

Tanzania's attempt to implement a nationwide system of collectivized agriculture has been extensively documented and does not, therefore, call for detailed description.[23] Between 1969 and 1975, the Tanzanian government devoted prodigious energy and resources to a program intended to transform the socioeconomic basis of its entire rural economy. Its purpose was to replace existing patterns of largely individualized household production with a network of village communities in which land would be collectively held and production collectively organized. During this brief period of time, more than 5,000 new villages were created or existing villages designated as "socialist," and intensive efforts were undertaken to lay the basis for collective agricultural practices. Before the collectivization program began, less than 5 percent of Tanzania's rural population lived in villages. By the end of 1975, more than 60 percent of the rural population lived in settled village communities that had, to varying degrees, embarked upon the implementation of collective farming.

The attempt to introduce rural socialism contributed in a variety of ways to Tanzania's economic decline and was abandoned in 1975. Although efforts to promote villagization continued, the notion that this should be accompanied by collective production was replaced by more traditional patterns of production by individual households. The causes and developmental implications of the failure of rural socialism have been vigorously debated, but its impact in lowering the country's agricultural productivity is universally acknowledged.[24] There is little doubt, for example, that the socialist village program contributed directly to Tanzania's agricultural crisis of 1974–1975. The process of implementation sometimes interfered directly with agricultural production, as in cases where peasants were forcibly moved between planting and harvesting seasons or during one or the other of these periods of peak labor needs. There were also cases of peasants being moved to districts that were so environmentally different from their traditional areas of residence as to be unsuitable for crops they were accustomed to growing.

The major effect of socialist villagization, however, was on peasant morale. Against the background of Tanzania's long-standing traditions of individualized residence and production, state-induced collectivization promoted an atmosphere of confusion and uncertainty throughout the countryside. Apprehension about the program was so widespread that peasant resistance began to emerge even in regions of the country where the government was not attempting to bring about collective patterns of land use. By the early 1970s, peasant opposition to the collective village program was so strong that, in several regions of the country, the government began to use coercive means to implement it, a policy that only further heightened an already pervasive atmosphere of political and economic discontent.[25]

The socialist strategy of development also lowered Tanzania's ability to maintain food production. As one of the key purposes of collectivization was to promote social equality, it was sometimes accompanied by the outright confiscation of the farmlands of the country's larger-scale farmers. Inasmuch as this social stratum had accounted for a very large proportion of the country's marketed agricultural surplus, the land seizures caused a severe reduction in the available food supply. Larger farmers who were somehow able to retain their lands were treated with political disparagement, publicly reviled as "kulaks" or exploiters, and openly intimidated from engaging in market-oriented production, thereby further reducing the food reserve.

Socialism was also accompanied by implacable governmental opposition to any substantial admixture of capitalist practices in the nation's development and, therefore, precluded the use of open market incentives as a means of improving agricultural production or facilitating the growth of the mercantile sector. The tendency to treat capitalism as an imperialist practice adverse to the best interests of the Tanzanian people not only prevented the government from harnessing the considerable entrepreneurial talents inherent in its population, but led to a major flight of capital from the country during the late 1960s and early 1970s. It also discouraged major business corporations from making large investments in the country and thus eliminated foreign capital inflows as a stimulus of economic growth.

As articulated and implemented by the country's political leaders, the Tanzanian version of socialist development was an unbridled program of state regulation and control. As such, it is vulnerable to the charge that it was partly responsible for the uncritical expansion of state bureaucracy and for the rapid enlargement of public services, both of which grew out of all proportion to the country's financial or economic capacity. The commitment to socialism may also have contributed to the willingness of Tanzanian leaders to tolerate a high degree of inefficiency and corruption throughout the state bureaucracy and parastatal organizations. There was a profound conviction that state-administered development, however, inefficient, would produce more equitable results than if private traders and entrepreneurs were allowed to operate. Tanzanian socialism was based on the explicit premise that socialism, with all its ills, was greatly preferable to the alternative. As a result, the efforts at policy reform that did occur consisted largely of attempts to improve the operation of socialist institutions rather than to introduce corrective, market-oriented practices.

Socialism alone, however, does not provide an adequate explanation of Tanzania's economic decline any more than does the impact of external factors. Many of the economic policies pursued by the Tanzanian government since independence have been commonly adopted in a large number of African nations that have little or no identification with the idea of socialist development. Indeed, a large number of the social and political objectives that motivate public policy in Tanzania are virtually universal throughout Africa, and for this reason it would be inaccurate to view Tanzania as a unique case. Tanzanian political leaders, like others throughout the African continent, have felt impelled to implement the vision of a better society that was articulated during the nationalist period. That vision included a commitment to make public services, especially in the fields of education and health, more universally available. It also included the belief that development in the full sense of the term meant diversified economic growth and that it must therefore encompass the industrial as well as agricultural sphere. And, like virtually every other postcolonial society in Africa, Tanzania has been compelled to frame economic policies that would provide political stability by accommodating the demands and economic interests of potentially volatile urban constituencies.

The Policy Roots of Economic Decline

To achieve these objectives, the government of Tanzania has implemented a set of economic policies designed to extract economic resources from the countryside for the purpose of enlarging the country's public services and expanding its industrial base. Four policies merit special attention because of their ruinous impact on the country's once-thriving agricultural system. These are: (1) overvaluation of the currency exchange rate; (2) suppression of agricultural producer prices; (3) maladministration of the country's parastatal corporations; and (4) the pursuit of an industrial strategy based on the principle of import substitution. Although Tanzania shares these policies with numerous other African countries, it can be said to have pursued them with particular zeal. Tanzania therefore represents one of Africa's clearest and most dramatic examples of the degree to which inappropriate public policies can undermine agricultural performance and, thereby, engender structural food deficits.

Currency Overvaluation

The effects of currency overvaluation on the agricultural sector can be devastating. An artificially high exchange rate is, in effect, a hidden form of taxation on the agricultural producer.[26] Currency overvaluation has been a significant factor in reducing the real producer prices received by Tanzania's farmers. It directly affects the producers of export crops because the farmgate price levels for these commodities are, to a large extent, a function of the ratio at which the international price is converted into units of local currency. Tanzania's export farmers, like others throughout Africa, are paid for their crops in their national currency, and the prices they receive are calculated on the basis of the official exchange rate between the Tanzanian shilling and the U.S. dollar. The fewer the number of shillings per dollar (overvaluation), the lower the level of reimbursement to the farmer.

Overvaluation has equivalent but indirect effects on the producers of domestically consumed food staples and is, therefore, partially accountable for the country's structural food deficits. The relationship between the price levels of food crops and that for exportable crops is not allowed to vary randomly. In order to prevent farmers from substituting between these categories of crops, the producer price levels of noncash crops are generally set in a specific ratio to those for exportable commodities. As a result, overvaluation lowers the producer price levels of food staples by approximately the same amount that it lowers those for export crops.

It is difficult to measure the extent of overvaluation in Tanzania because there is no legal free market in its currency, and figures for unofficial conversions are, therefore, wholly unsystematic. Some indication may be derived from the fact that during the fifteen-year period from 1969 to 1984, while Tanzania's CPI indicated an average annual inflation rate of about 60 percent or more, the Tanzanian shilling was devalued only about 8 percent per year. By mid-1985, the shilling was probably overvalued by about 1,000 percent. Whereas the official rate of exchange was approximately TSh16 per $1, informal street traders were offering between TSh175 and 200. The Tanzanian government began to take steps to correct this situation in early 1986, in anticipation of an agreement with the IMF, but as of late summer 1986, when the IMF standby agreement was signed, the exchange rate had been devalued to only TSh42 per $1. As the informal exchange rate remained at TSh160 per $1, the overvaluation rate was still nearly 400 percent.

It would be a gross oversimplification to suggest that devaluation alone would stimulate a recovery in Tanzania's agricultural productivity.[27] The price levels received by Tanzanian farmers are affected by a variety of factors including direct governmental controls, the level of taxation, the operating margins of the country's agricultural parastatals, and the amount of subsidy provided for agricultural inputs. Exchange-rate policy is thus only one of a number of policies that determine whether or not there is sufficient incentive for farmers to produce a marketable agricultural surplus. But when overvaluation consistently exceeds 500 percent, its disincentive effects on producer prices are necessarily considerable.

Overvaluation has suppressed domestic food production in Tanzania in at least two additional ways. It has encouraged the importation of foods from overseas, thereby making it possible for foreign agricultural commodities, including grains, to be sold cheaply on the local market. And it has contributed to the relatively high cost of agricultural services.[28] Overvaluation has meant that Tanzania's food-producing farmers have faced an utterly dismal situation: low prices for the commodities they produce, high costs for the transportation and storage services necessary to market these goods, and difficult competition with artificially cheapened grain imports.

By discouraging exports and encouraging imports, overvaluation has also contributed to Tanzania's scarcity of foreign exchange and thus to the necessity for a system of foreign-exchange rationing. In Tanzania, as in so many other countries in independent Africa today, the process of foreign-exchange allocation is heavily influenced by political factors. Because farmers have been politically weak in comparison to urban pressure groups, their needs have not generally received the highest priority. The result has been a chronic shortage of agricultural inputs that has its origins not only in the country's overall shortage of hard currency, but in the fact that the rural sector has had great difficulty in asserting its claim to those foreign-exchange reserves that are available. Contrary to the claims of those who believe that overvaluation helps farmers by lowering the cost of imported agricultural inputs, it has had exactly the opposite effect. It ensures that imported inputs are almost always in short supply and thus results in the fact that they are generally obtainable only at inflated black market prices.

Regulation of Producer Prices

The government of Tanzania regulates the producer prices of all the country's major crops, both for export and for domestic consumption. Its tendency in both cases has been to set prices at far lower levels than might have prevailed under free market conditions.[29] The suppression of export-crop prices has been particularly marked and largely accounts for the drop in export volumes of key commodities. Between 1969/70 and 1980/81, the real producer price of cashew nuts, for example, fell by 27 percent, and even this represented a substantial recovery from the period 1976 to 1978, during which time the producer price of this commodity in real terms was only about one-half that in the earlier period. Similarly, in 1980/81, the real producer price of coffee was less than half its level in 1971/72; the real producer price of cotton, about 30 percent lower than its 1971/72 level; and the real producer price of tea, less than half its level in 1969/70.[30]

The relationship between Tanzania's food-pricing policy and its perennial food deficits is less clear-cut. During the mid-1970s, the Tanzanian government declared a policy of food self-sufficiency and, to implement this policy, raised the nominal producer prices of the country's principal food grains by vast amounts. Between 1967 and 1980, the nominal price of maize increased by about 450 percent; the nominal price of rice, by about 700 percent; and the nominal price of wheat, by about 360 percent.[31] These increases were so great that despite the country's high rate of inflation, the real producer prices of these commodities also showed apparent increases during this period.[32] The policy of pricing for food self-sufficiency did lead to an increase in the marketed volume of each of these three food staples, with maize production temporarily reaching about twice its 1967 level in 1977 and 1978.[33]

The gains from self-sufficiency pricing were both limited and short-lived, however. Of the three food staples, only maize production returned to its former peak, and this recovery lasted for only two years. The gains in rice and wheat production were extremely weak; Rice production rebounded from about 15 percent of its 1971 peak to about 35 percent, and wheat increased from about 25 percent to slightly over 50 percent of its 1972 peak. By the early 1980s, the country's pricing policy for food staples was beginning to show the same tendency as that for exportable goods. In 1980/81, the real producer prices for all three of the country's major food staples—maize, rice, and wheat—dropped below those for 1973/74, and the production levels of these crops began to fall accordingly, plunging the country more deeply than before into food deficits.[34]

The fall in the producer prices for foodstuffs in the 1980s provides only the beginning of an explanation of the country's persistent food deficits during this period. Pricing policy alone cannot account for the weakness of the recovery in food production during the mid to late 1970s, when prices were high. The relationship between producer prices for food staples and the persistence of chronic food shortages in Tanzania is highly complicated and not susceptible of unilinear generalizations based on simple assumptions about producer-price responsiveness. At least three additional considerations must be taken into account.

The first is the size of the gap between nominal and real producer prices. Many observers have suggested that Tanzania's official CPI understates the true extent of inflation in the country. If this is so, calculations based on this index that showed rising real prices were probably incorrect. It is at least conceivable and, indeed, likely that the real producer prices for food staples were not increasing during the late 1970s, as analyses by de Wilde and George Kahama, T. L. Maliyamkono, and Stuart Wells suggest, but, rather, that these prices remained on a basically downward trajectory despite dramatic nominal increases. The actual performance of Tanzania's food-producing sector between 1975 and 1979 is more consistent with the notion of falling real prices.

The second critically important issue in connection with the relationship between producer prices and food deficits is the distinction between prices and incentives. Although agricultural economists often use indices of producer prices as if these were synonymous with incentives, this is not the case in a country whose entire economic system has deteriorated badly. If valued consumer goods or social services are not available, the relationship between prices and incentives may be negligible. John Shao suggests that Tanzania's food problems are not as traceable to its pricing policy as to its overall economic malaise, the inability of food producers to improve their living conditions in a context of general economic decline.[35] His analysis indicates that Tanzanian food producers were unwilling to produce for cash returns because there was so little on which additional cash income could be spent.

The third and most important consideration is the relationship between official producer prices and those available on the informal market. Practically no systematic studies have been done of pricing patterns in Tanzania's parallel markets, but spot samples by researchers in donor organizations suggest that these have tended to be consistently higher than official prices, even during periods when official prices were increasing rapidly. If so, this suggests that a major factor underlying Tanzania's persistent food deficits is the tendency of the country's food producers to avoid the official marketplace in order to gain the higher returns available in informal markets. It may be extremely significant that Tanzania's two major maize-producing regions, Arusha/Moshi in the north and Sumbawanga/Rukwa in the southwest, are very near its borders with neighboring countries. There are persistent reports that large volumes of Tanzanian maize are traded for consumer goods in Kenya, Zambia, Zaire, and Malawi. Tanzania may well produce sufficient food for national consumption but still depend upon food imports because it is unable to capture this production within its domestic marketing system.

Parastatal Maladministration

Tanzania implements its price control system through a network of parastatal crop authorities. Typically these authorities are given a complete legal monopoly over the purchasing, storage, processing, and marketing, whether domestic or international, of a given crop. Agricultural parastatals are also frequently given sole jurisdiction over other critically important activities including crop research, fertilizer distribution, extension services, and the import and allocation of equipment and supplies, such as motor vehicles, tractors, and trucks. The parastatals' monopolistic status is entrenched by a complex set of laws and administrative regulations that forbid farmers from trading their crops on the private market or from obtaining agricultural services and inputs from any other source. The system of enforcement also prevents private traders from purchasing and marketing any crop that has been assigned to a parastatal authority. There are approximately one dozen major agricultural parastatals in Tanzania, including the National Milling Corporation, which has sole jurisdiction over the purchasing and marketing of all food grains.

Supporters of the parastatal system have defended these organizations as economically and socially functional. They argue that all countries use parastatals to provide economic services in sectors where competition between private-sector firms would be prohibitively expensive or where reliance upon the private sector might result in a failure to provide for the needs of poorer regions or social strata. They also contend that very few countries have been able to achieve a high level of agricultural development by relying upon the forces of the free market. Defenders of agricultural parastatals point out that governmental intervention in the pricing and marketing of primary commodities is commonplace in countries that wish to maintain a high level of exports and that certain vital economic functions, such as price stabilization, would never be provided for by the private companies, whose orientation is inevitably toward short-term profit maximization.

Tanzania's parastatal system is also the product of deep political conviction. One important driving force is a profound belief that if private traders were allowed to operate in the rural areas, they would engage in unbridled economic exploitation of helpless and vulnerable peasants. The intensity of this belief may be partly a result of racial feelings, as many government officials seem convinced that if private traders were allowed to operate, the majority would be of Asian descent. Tanzania's deep commitment to the parastatal system may also derive in part from the fact that key political leaders have tended until very recently to view governmental regulation of the agricultural sector in all-or-nothing terms. They believe that once private traders become established, the traders would gain such great political influence that it would be increasingly difficult to resist their political demands for a larger and larger economic role. As a result of this belief, there has been a reluctance to entertain proposals for mixed forms of economic management.

Despite these arguments, there seems to be little doubt that the operation of Tanzania's agricultural parastatals has been one of the major factors contributing to the country's economic crisis. These organizations have exhibited pervasive patterns of inefficiency, mismanagement, and corruption. Studies by the Tanzanian government show that the administrative and operating costs of the parastatal corporations have tended to absorb a higher and higher percentage of the corporations' sales revenues, and, as a result, parastatal overheads have contributed significantly to the downward pressure on producer prices.[36] Sometimes the parastatals' overhead costs have been so high that there has been no cash remainder for the farmers, and there are innumerable reports of producers' payments being delayed for months if not, in certain instances, for several years.

The final result of inefficient administration has been a vicious cycle of rising administrative costs, measured as a percentage of sales, and falling levels of marketed production because of lowered returns to the producers. This cycle is so well-established and so pervasive among Tanzanian parastatals that Frank Ellis has posited a law of rising parastatal marketing costs. He states this law in the following terms:

> [I]t is possible to discern the makings of a distinctive law of motion of the export crop parastatals of Tanzania. . . . The basic mechanism of the tendency rests on the impact on *unit* marketing costs of fluctuations in the volume of produce handled when the marketing system is characterized by fixed high overheads. The effect of a reduction in output is to increase the unit costs of marketing in approximate proportion to the share of overheads in total costs. These higher unit costs are then discounted from the export price . . . resulting in a lower producer price than would be warranted by the external market situation.[37]

There are reasons to doubt that rising unit costs are so inevitable as to constitute an economic law, as administrative reform is not theoretically impossible. But Ellis's conclusion does reflect the dismal economic performance of Tanzania's parastatal crop authorities and the disastrous impact this has had on the country's agricultural economy.

The Tanzanian government has publicly acknowledged the need to improve parastatal performance and has taken some steps toward this objective. In 1982, for example, the government published a lengthy statement on structural adjustment in which an entire section was devoted to specific proposals for improvements in the administration of the crop parastatals. This was followed in early 1983 by the appointment of a Presidential Commission on Cost Reduction in Nonfinancial Public Enterprises, which presented its recommendations to the government in early 1984. Many of these recommendations were incorporated in the 1984/85 budget address, in which the minister of finance committed the government to the eventual goal of transforming the parastatals into financially self-sufficient institutions. The principal concrete proposal was the restoration of the country's producer cooperatives, a step that, once fully implemented, may be expected to relieve the parastatals of significant portions of their crop-purchasing role. But in Tanzania there is a vast gulf between a policy proposal and its full implementation. Two years after the restoration of producer cooperatives had been announced, very little progress in this direction h ad actually occurred.

Industry and the Agricultural Sector

In the early 1960s, Tanzania, together with innumerable other newly independent African countries, adopted an industrial strategy based on the principle of import substitution. The basic idea was utterly compelling: to launch the growth of an industrial sector by beginning production of simple consumer goods that were being imported in large volumes. The advantages seemed overwhelming. Through simple import substitution, Tanzania could promote industrial employment in the cities, stimulate the growth of a managerial class, and begin to accumulate a background of industrial experience that might later be applied to larger-scale enterprises. Perhaps most important, import substitution could help conserve foreign-exchange reserves by reducing nonessential imports. Import substitution was widely acclaimed by leading development economists, and their enthusiasm helped reinforce the inclinations of national political leaders to move in this direction.

Throughout the 1960s, there seemed little reason to doubt the viability of this strategy. New industries devoted to the production of textiles, soft drinks, beer, concrete, household utensils, soap, shoes, cigarettes, and other consumer goods seemed to be thriving. Although the foreign-exchange needs of these industries was a matter of concern, owing to the need to import capital goods, raw materials, and spare parts, it seemed to be of manageable proportions. As claims on foreign-exchange receipts, which would later become enormous, including debt servicing and energy and food imports, were then relatively small, the productivity and earnings of the agricultural export sector seemed well up to the task. Moreover, there was considerable optimism in East Africa that the problems of creating a larger regional trading community would be overcome and that some of the new industries might well be able to earn foreign currency by developing export markets.

It is impossible to assign a precise date at which the import-substitution strategy began to appear doubtful. But by the end of the 1960s, it began to become clear that the capital and foreign-exchange needs of the industrial sector were having a negative effect on agricultural performance. Even before the agricultural crisis of 1974–1975, food imports had become a matter of serious concern, and the foreign-exchange requirements of the industrial sector seemed to conflict directly with the need to use hard currency to rebuild agricultural productivity. The early notion that some of the new industries could reduce their foreign-exchange costs by developing local resources also seemed a distant possibility, linked to the development of intermediate industries, rather than an imminent possibility. It had also become apparent that the East African Common Market, far from providing opportunities for consumer-goods exports, was subject to deepening political strains that would eventually break it apart altogether. And in any case, Tanzania had become a consumer-goods market for Kenyan industries to a far greater degree than it had been able to develop outside markets of its own.

The agricultural crisis of 1974–1975 exposed the inherent weaknesses in the program of industrialization by import substitution. This strategy had depended upon the premise that the agricultural sector, especially agricultural exports, would be able almost indefinitely to provide the financial wherewithal to capitalize emergent industries and to finance their continuing needs for spare parts, raw materials, and expatriate management. So long as agricultural exports were buoyant and so long as the country's terms of trade were relatively stable, it did not appear necessary to question this premise. But the agricultural crisis demonstrated the fundamental flaw in import substitution: Agricultural exports could not do everything. It was simply impossible for earnings from agriculture to finance the country's food needs, energy requirements, and provide hard currency for the industrial sector.

The operational success of import substitution depended upon a long-term transfer of capital from agriculture to industry. By the mid-1970s, this strategy was no longer feasible because it had taken too great a toll of the agricultural sector. Of the many causes of Tanzania's 1974–1975 agricultural crisis, one of the most important was sheer capital starvation in the agricultural areas.

Despite compelling evidence that import substitution was having adverse affects on agriculture, the country reaffirmed its commitment to this approach in 1975, introducing an enlarged program called the Basic Industry Strategy. The principal idea was to extend import substitution beyond the consumer-goods sector and to begin the production of more essential capital goods such as agricultural implements and construction materials. The underlying assumption was that Tanzania's foreign-exchange shortage had become so severe that it ruled out the continued importation of even these vital inputs. Tanzanian planners had come to believe that the very survival of such key sectors as agriculture, construction, and transportation depended upon the development of an internal capacity to provide internally for certain of their equipment needs.

In retrospect, the decision to expand upon import substitution is bewildering. The difficulty confronting the new basic industries was precisely the same as that confronting the earlier consumer-goods sector: The launching of new industries, however foreign-exchange-conserving their products might be in the long run, requires heavy inputs of foreign exchange and investment capital during an extended start-up period. As Tanzania had exhausted its foreign-exchange reserves to purchase nearly 600,000 metric tons of grain during 1974 and 1975, it was unclear where the financial resources for basic industries cold be obtained. To be successful, the Basic Industry Strategy would have had to be accompanied by an agricultural strategy that generated sufficient foreign-exchange earnings to provide for the capital requirements of the new industrial sector. And, indeed, the Basic Industry Strategy was given a temporary boost by the commodities boom (especially in beverages) of 1976/77.

The commodities boom was short-lived, however, and only concealed the fact that Tanzania's agricultural policy during this period was not designed to provide for increased export earnings. Rather, as its principal reaction to the country's food crisis of 1974–1975, the government had committed itself to the goal of food self-sufficiency, a policy that manifested itself in increased producer price levels for food staples relative to exportable agricultural commodities. The goal of this policy was to help conserve the country's foreign-exchange reserves by eliminating the heavy burden of large volumes of food imports from overseas. But, by raising the price for food crops out of proportion to those for export crops, the government of Tanzania was setting the stage for a sharp reduction in export earnings.

The basic industries approach continued the process of capital depletion from the agricultural sector. As late as 1975/76, agriculture, despite a decade of import substitution, still received approximately 35 percent of the country's capital resource allocations. In 1976/77 it was receiving less than half of that amount, and by 1981/82 the figure dropped to only about 11.5 percent.[38] Expressed in real terms, this meant that whereas capital allocations to all sectors including industry increased by about 33 percent during this six-year period, those to agriculture dropped by about 50 percent. Under these conditions, it is not surprising that Tanzania's agricultural economy has been so stagnant. Indeed, given the problem of capital starvation in addition to other adverse policies, the only surprise is that this sector performed as well as it did, a testimony perhaps to the willingness of smallholders to continue their efforts even under the most difficult conditions.

• CONCLUSION •

Tanzania since the end of the 1970s has given every indication of a nation pursuing utterly contradictory economic policies. On the one hand, it had committed itself to an industrial strategy that required a major enhancement of the country's foreign-exchange earning capacity by requiring the import of a large volume of capital goods. On the other hand, it had initiated an agricultural policy that diminished the economic incentives for export-crop production in order to achieve self-sufficiency in domestic food staples.

Even the country's food strategy seems, in retrospect, to have been poorly thought through. For, as Jennifer Sharpley points out, food self-sufficiency and foreign-exchange conservation are very different matters.

> The identification of food production with economic self-sufficiency was based on the false assumption that domestic food production requires relatively few imported inputs, saves on food imports, and benefits the balance of payments. On the contrary, food production in Tanzania remains heavily dependent on imported inputs and foreign exchange earnings and the supply of food is intimately linked with the performance of the agricultural export sector.[39]

Food production in Tanzania is nearly twice as import-intensive as is export-crop production; to be self-sufficient, therefore, Tanzania would have had to boost its hard-currency earnings considerably. Other than foreign public and/or private assistance, these hard-currency earnings could only have come from increased agricultural exports, a possibility that seemed wholly precluded by the country's adverse pricing policy for export crops.

Tanzania provides an almost textbook example of the adverse production effects of inappropriate agricultural policies. Indeed, its agricultural policies since the late 1960s seem to exemplify the policy mistakes outlined by Robert Bates in his now classic study, *Markets and States in Tropical Africa.*[40] For nearly twenty years, Tanzania has overvalued its exchange rate, suppressed real producer prices below shadow market levels, tolerated costly inefficiencies in its parastatal corporations, and engaged in an industrial strategy that depletes the agricultural sector of capital. Although Tanzania has been buffeted by a series of international economic shocks, the evidence suggests that these policies have been a far greater factor in accounting for the precipitous declines in agricultural production. Although it is uncertain whether Tanzania can reestablish a positive rate of growth without favorable improvements in the international economic system, it seems certain beyond any doubt that it will be unable to initiate a process of agricultural recovery without thoroughgoing reform of its policies toward the agricultural sector.

If Tanzanian agriculture is to recover, it is minimally necessary that this set of policies be corrected. The Tanzanian government has already accepted a substantial devaluation of its currency, but the continuing gap between official and unofficial exchange rates suggests that further steps in this direction are critically necessary. Increases in agricultural producer prices are also of critical importance. Tanzania has an immense capacity to increase its foreign-exchange earnings by increasing export volumes of coffee and tea. For this to occur, however, Tanzanian producers must be given sufficient price incentives not only to grow additional volumes of these commodities, but to market them through national marketing channels rather than through informal networks to border countries. This pertains directly to reform of the parastatal sector. Price increases alone are meaningless if the country's official marketing agencies continue to absorb an increasing percentage of the price to cover overhead costs. In practical terms, reform of the parastatal sector is a synonym for passing on the lion's share of the increased prices directly to the producer.

The most complex area of policy reform concerns the country's elaborate system of import-substitution industries. Although it is abundantly clear that these industries have contributed to agricultural decline by draining off much-needed capital, it seems premature to conclude, as one observer has, that many of the country's basic industries need to be closed down in order to assure a resurgence of capital flows to the agricultural sector.[41] It seems more realistic to suggest a review of import substitution on an industry-by-industry basis to determine whether certain of these industries might, in a more market-oriented policy environment, make a positive contribution to economic growth. If price increases are to represent real incentives for increased production, the official market will need to provide for an ample flow of both consumer goods and agricultural implements to the countryside. And import substitution, with all its faults, can help assure such a flow.

As innumerable observers have suggested, the most difficult issue concerning policy reform is political, not economic. However carefully implemented, policy reform appears to entail a period of severe austerity, whose burden falls most heavily on poorer urban classes. The Tanzanian government has traditionally been unwilling to accept this austerity, both because it seemed so inconsistent with its socialist commitment and, more pragmatically, because of the concomitant danger of volatile urban unrest. The present government of Tanzania gives every indication of having come to terms ideologically with the IMF formula. But, like virtually every other government in independent Africa, its capacity to sustain prolonged urban dissidence is unproven. The economic austerity that accompanies an IMF-sponsored program of policy reform could provide political fuel for the socialist wing of Tanzania's governing party.

· NOTES ·

1. UN, Economic Commission for Africa, *Survey of Economic Conditions in Africa, 1972* (United Nations, n.p., n.d.), p. 67.

2. John Shao, "Politics and the Food Production Crisis in Tanzania," *Issue* 14 (1985): Appendix I, 21. See also S. E. Migot-Adhola, "Rural Development Policy and Equality," in Joel D. Barkan, ed., *Politics and Public Policy in Kenya and Tanzania* (New York: Praeger, 1984), Table 8.6, p. 233.

3. For one such view, see Shao, "Politics and the Food Production Crisis."

4. For an extensive and extremely well informed account of Tanzania's past negotiations with the IMF and the economic arguments involved, see Reginald Herbold Green, "Political-Economic Adjustment and IMF Conditionality: Tanzania 1974–1981," in John Williamson, ed., *IMF Conditionality* (Washington, D.C.: Institute for International Economics, 1983), pp. 347–380.

5. Any statistical figures on Tanzania should be treated with utmost caution. For, as the International Labour Office (ILO) has pointed out in its report entitled *Basic Needs in Danger: A Basic Needs Oriented Development Strategy for Tanzania*, "All is not well with Tanzania's statistics." (Addis Ababa: International Labour Office, Jobs and Skills Program for Africa, 1982), p. 251. The best approach, therefore, is to treat the figures that follow as indicative of general trends rather than as exact approximations of Tanzania's economic performance.

6. Uma Lele, "Tanzania: Phoenix or Icarus?" in Arnold C. Harberger, ed. *World Economic Growth: Case Studies of Developed and Developing Nations* (San Francisco: Institute for Contemporary Studies, 1984), p. 166 and Table A-2, p. 193.

7. Additional figures on Tanzanian exports may be found in Shao, "Politics and the Food Production Crisis," Appendix II, p. 22, and in John C. de Wilde, *Agriculture, Marketing, and Pricing in Sub-Saharan Africa* (Los Angeles: African Studies Center and African Studies Association, 1984), Table 3.3, p. 36.

8. Lele, "Tanzania: Phoenix or Icarus?" p. 166, and de Wilde, *Agriculture, Marketing, and Pricing*, p. 35.

9. ILO, *Basic Needs in Danger*, p. 17. For detailed figures on an industry by industry basis for the period 1976 to 1980, see George Kahama, T. L. Maliyamkono, and Stuart Wells, *The Challenge for Tanzania's Economy* (Portsmouth, N.H.: Heinemann, 1986), Table 7.3, p. 347.

10. For an extensive discussion of this problem, see Kami S. P. Rwegasira and Louis A. Kanneworff, eds., *Inflation in Tanzania* (Dar es Salaam: Institute of Finance Management, 1980).

11. *Daily News* (Tanzania), June 20, 1985.

12. For a discussion of the various price and cost-of-living indices in Tanzania and the inflation rate these figures generate, see "Technical Paper 15: Price Indices in Tanzania," in ILO, *Basic Needs in Danger*, pp. 391–397.

13. The term "informal economy" is used here to describe an illegal trade in food staples and other consumer goods that, under Tanzania law, may only be purchased through official marketing agencies.

14. Lele, "Tanzania: Phoenix or Icarus?" p. 188.

15. See "Tanzania: End of the Dream," *Africa Confidential* 21, no. 15 (July 16, 1980): 2.

16. See, for example, Dean E. McHenry, Jr., *Ujamaa Villages in Tanzania: A Bibliography* (Uppsala: Scandinavian Institute of African Studies, 1981).

17. A terms-of-trade equation is normally constructed as the ratio of percentage changes in the prices of a marketbasket of exports over those in a marketbasket of imports.

18. ILO, *Basic Needs in Danger*, p. 44.

19. Ibid., p. 16.

20. Lele, "Tanzania: Phoenix or Icarus?" p. 165 and Table A-1, p. 192.

21. Jennifer Sharpley, "External Versus Internal Factors in Tanzania's Macro-Economic Crisis," (Unpublished ms., Institute of Development Studies, Sussex, 1984), p. 8.

22. See Kahama, Maliyamkono, and Wells, *The Challenge for Tanzania's Economy*, Table 9.1, p. 349.

23. For a thorough and excellent treatment of this program, see Dean E. McHenry, Jr., *Tanzania's Ujamaa Villages: The Implementation of a Rural Development Strategy* (Berkeley: Institute of International Studies, 1979).

24. The best discussion of the contending viewpoints about the failure of the ujamaa village program is Jonathan Barker, "The Debate on Rural Socialism in Tanzania," in Bismarck U. Mwansasu and Cranford Pratt, eds., *Towards Socialism in Tanzania* (Toronto and Buffalo: University of Toronto Press, 1979), pp. 95–124.

25. B. C. Nindi, "Agricultural Change in Tanzania: With Examples from Iringa Region," *Transafrican Journal of History* 14 (1985): 101–111.

26. The language is sometimes confusing. An overvalued exchange rate is one that involves too *few* units of local currency being traded for an external hard currency such as the U.S. dollar. The artificial cheapening of the foreign currency increases, or "heightens," the value of the local currency.

27. For an outstanding cautionary statement on the benefits of devaluation, see Delphin G. Rwegasira, "Exchange Rates and the External Sector," *Journal of Modern African Studies* 22, no. 3 (September 1984): 451–457.

28. Economists are generally agreed that overvaluation tends to lower the domestic prices of tradeable goods, both exports and imports, and to increase the costs of nontradeables, such as services.

29. The classic study of agricultural producer pricing in Tanzania is Frank Ellis, "Agricultural Price Policy in Tanzania," *World Development* 10, no. 4 (April 1982): 263–283. See also his article "Relative Agricultural Prices and the Urban Bias Model," *Journal of Development Studies* 20 (April 1984): 28–51, and de Wilde, *Agriculture, Marketing, and Pricing*, ch. 3.

30. These figures are taken from de Wilde, *Agriculture, Marketing, and Pricing*, Table 3.3, p. 36.

31. Kahama et al., p. 58.

32. De Wilde, *Agriculture, Marketing, and Pricing*, Table 3.3, p. 36.

33. Kahama et al., Table 6.2, p. 340.

34. De Wilde, *Agriculture, Marketing, and Pricing*, Table 3.3, p. 36. See also Kahama et al., Table 6.4, p. 342.

35. Shao, "Politics and the Food Production Crisis," p. 15.

36. United Republic of Tanzania, Ministry of Agriculture, *Crop Authorities: Financial Position and Financial Performance 1977 to 1981/82*, Part 1, *Summary and Conclusions* (Dar es Salaam: Project Preparation and Monitoring Bureau, 1983). See also, United Republic of Tanzania, *Analysis of Accounts of Parastatal Enterprises 1972–1980* (Dar es Salaam: Bureau of Statistics, 1983).

37. Ellis, "Agricultural Price Policy in Tanzania," p. 38.

38. Alberto Ruiz de Gamboa, "Resource Allocation and the Agricultural Sector" (unpublished ms., USAID, Dar es Salaam, n.d.), p. 9 and Table 1, p. 13.

39. Sharpley, "External Versus Internal Factors," pp. 16–17, and M.G.G. Schluter and M. A. Sackett, *Estimates of 1981/82 Import Requirements for the Production, Processing and Marketing of Major Crops in Mainland Tanzania* (Dar es Salaam: Marketing Development Bureau, Ministry of Agriculture, 1981).

40. Robert Bates, *Markets and States in Tropical Africa: The Political Basis of Agricultural Policies* (Berkeley and Los Angeles, University of California Press, 1981).

41. Lele. "Tanzania: Phoenix or Icarus?" p. 188.

·7·

Zaire

JANET MacGAFFEY

President Seko Mobutu advised his people to "Débrouillez-vous" (fend for yourselves) in order to cope with Zaire's recurrent crises, and the circumstances of life in Zaire make it possible for them to do so. Zairians find a variety of strategies for survival and are explicit about the ways they manipulate the system to their advantage. Using the preface "il faut se débrouiller"—one must manage for oneself—they describe how they survived when their families fled into the forest and lived there for months without any regular food supply during the rebellion of 1964–1965; how women and children in the cityof Kisangani made a living when they were left without a man to support them after this rebellion; how schoolteachers and university professors managed while they went unpaid for several consecutive months in 1980; or how storeowners coped with the difficulty of getting goods of any kind with which to make a living.

The stringent hardships undergone by the people of Zaire since independence vary in their nature and causes from one region of the country to another and over time. Zaire's abundant natural resources and agricultural potential make it one of Africa's richest countries; yet malnutrition is among the leading causes of death among children admitted to Kinshasa's hospitals, hunger in the cities is widespread, and localized famine conditions occur. Zaire's food crisis is not primarily the result of drought or other natural disaster or of war and the resulting displacement of the population. The reasons for it are primarily political. They have their roots in the colonial past and are determined by the country's place in the world economy and its internal social, cultural, and structural conditions since independence. All of these factors, as well as the responses to food shortages, are modified by particular local conditions within Zaire.

Rural-urban interdependence is a critical factor in the connection between politics and economics in the food crisis and in the popular responses to it. The social processes involved are obscured by a tendency to set up a rural-urban dichotomy or focus on either the struggle between peasants and capital or on the urban "informal sector." Such investigations falsify the interdependence of town and country. The problem is solved by the synthesis of rural and urban phenomena in an analysis of class relations.[1]

· ECOLOGICAL, HISTORICAL,
AND SOCIOECONOMIC CONSIDERATIONS ·

Zaire is potentially one of the richest countries of Africa. It has abundant natural resources in its minerals and fertile agricultural land, enormous hydroelectric potential, a vast network of navigable waterways connected to railways, and, in most areas, copious rainfall from the equatorial climate. Zaire ranks sixth in the world as a producer of copper, is the primary producer of cobalt, and is the source of 90 percent of the world's supply of industrial diamonds. Its other minerals include gold, tin, silver, manganese, iron, bauxite, and casseterite, and crude oil is exported from its offshore oilfield. Coffee has replaced palm oil as the major agricultural export; the country also exports tea, rubber, cotton, copal, and other crops; and it has huge, mostly undeveloped, timber reserves. Land is in general abundant, though pressure on it is increasing in some areas, for example arund Kinshasa, the capital city, and in the fertile areas of highland Kivu. The potential exists for abundant production of the staple food crops—manioc, beans, rice, and plantain bananas. Given the network of roads, railways, and river transport constructed by the Belgians, distribution should not be a problem either. The constraints on the plentiful production of food and its distribution and on the development of the export sector are thus sociopolitical rather than ecological. Their roots can be found in the nature of Zaire's colonial experience and the legacy that experience left after independence.

Belgian colonial administration was distinguished by the number of its administrators and the extent of its interference in peoples' lives. Crawford Young describes the "colonial trinity" of the church, the state, and the big companies, all of which organized the penetration of capitalism into African society.[2] This organization so effectively developed Zaire's resources that on the eve of independence in 1960 the Belgian Congo was the most industrialized country in Africa south of the Sahara, except for South Africa. Perhaps the most distinct difference between Belgian and other colonial systems was the establishment of an initial monopoly by the state over commercialization of the principal export products and an emphasis throughout the colonial period on the discouragement of indigenous trade, the marginalization of commercial capital, and the setting up of a privileged relationship for financial capital.[3]

The Belgians developed an economy oriented to the production of primary products, principally minerals, for export. The colonial state assisted in recruitment of labor for the mining companies and organized food production to feed their workers. It also granted huge land concessions to the big plantation companies.[4] Sufficiency of food in the colonial period was ensured by compulsory cultivation of food crops. From 1917 to 1957 the population was liable to sixty days of compulsory cultivation a year; until 1960, for forty-five days. The need for cash for taxes, fines, monetized bridewealth, and European goods imposed the use of money and drove people to wage labor and cash crops, but low minimum prices were never exceeded by monopoly buyers, and wage rates for long and arduous labor were very low.[5] These conditions have continued into the 1980s in low wages and high prices; they reduce incentives and lower production. The Belgian Congo survived and even prospered in the Depression and World War II by increasing agricultural exports through expansion of compulsory cultivation. But this enforced extension of the acreage under cultivation decreased fallow periods and, together with overpopulation in some areas, exhausted the soil.

These characteristics of the colonial economy had powerful long-term consequences. The emphasis was on development of mining rather than agriculture: Three-quarters of capital investment from 1920 to 1932 was for mining and its infrastructure.[6] The priveleged relationship between the state and the big companies constrained the development and nature of local initiatives; public resources were dependent on production of a few commodities; and the stultifying effect on the rural economy of the dependence of production on state control was manifested after independence when this control disintegrated and production dropped sharply.[7] The colonial legacy for the newly independent republic in 1960 was an export economy, subject to the price fluctuations of the global market for primary commodities, with a poorly developed food-producing sector.

Colonial policies also shaped the nature of the postindependence dominant class. This class was drawn from the African elite of the colonial bureaucracy, but most were grossly lacking in education and experience. The Belgians, unlike the British and French colonialists, had no policies to encourage an African elite capable of participating in administration and government. They did not permit Africans to rise above the level of clerk in the bureaucracy, excluded them from large-scale business and commerce by legal constraints and credit restrictions, and provided very little secondary or higher education until almost the end of the colonial period.[8] This lack of qualified and experienced personnel contributed to the weakening of the state after independence and to the resulting decline in administrative capability. In a continuation of colonial policy, government indifference to the agricultural sector was a significant factor in its decline after independence: By 1972, imports of food were equivalent to 45 percent of local production, in contrast to 1 percent in 1958;[9] between 1970 and 1978, agriculture received only 1–3 percent of current government expenditures, 2–3 percent of capital ones.[10]

The power of those in the new dominant class after independence was based on position in the state apparatus and alliance with the representatives of Western capitalism, who continued to control the economy. After Mobutu came to power in a coup in 1965, the centralization of political power was accompanied by concentration of economic revenues to benefit the small and privileged circle surrounding him. Like an absolutist monarch, Mobutu rules through this "political aristocracy," his chosen instruments, for whom personal loyalty to the president is the ultimate requirement for entry and continued membership. The new dominant class is not a bourgeoisie in the classical sense of the term, as it is not a productive class.[11] Its members have become rich, in some cases fabulously so, by siphoning off the state's revenues for their personal benefit. They also use this wealth to maintain the ties of patronage that support their political position. This new class used the state to move into the economy, especially in the takeover of part-ownership of large companies and the indigenization of foreign capital in the decrees of Zairianization and Radicalization in 1973–1975, which handed over foreign-owned enterprises primarily to the political aristocracy or those connected to them. The mismanagement of these concerns had disastrous effects on the economy, which were compounded by the world recession, the drop in copper prices, the tripling of world petroleum prices, and the Shaba wars of 1977 and 1978. In addition, the closing of the Benguela railroad since 1975, because of the Angolan civil war, interfered with copper production and export and decreased foreign-exchange earnings.

The often huge enterprises that the political aristocrcy have acquired are not managed in rational, capitalist fashion; profits are consumed in conspicuous consumption, invested in real estate, or stashed in foreign bank accounts rather than in expanding productive enterprise.[12] The arbitrary selection of those in authority and power and their general incompetence and corruption paralyze administration and render government ineffective.

· THE FOOD CRISIS: HIGH PRICES, SCARCITY, AND THE POLITICS OF DISTRIBUTION ·

By 1978, the economic crisis resulted in an output that was about 17 percent below the level of 1974; imports were 50 percent below; the manufacturing sector was operating at only 40 percent of capacity; inflation was almost 100 percent; and real wages and salaries were one-quarter of their 1970 level.[13] By the early 1980s, industry was working at only 20–30 percent of capacity. At the end of 1983 the foreign debt stood at about $4.2 billion. Prices spiraled higher and higher, wages and producer prices remained extremely low, and gross shortages of foodstuffs and imported commodities of all kinds became widespread.

The food crisis intensified from the mid-1970s on and is most acute in urban areas. It has primarily resulted from extremely high prices relative to very low wages and from scarcities, often locally acute, that are caused by inequitable distribution or induced by hoarding and speculation. Distribution problems have also aggravated localized famine conditions caused by occasional ecological disasters. In 1978 manioc disease resulted in a famine in Lower Zaire; the erosion and decline of soil fertility resulting from population pressure and discontinuance of colonial soil conservation measures in North

Kivu[14] was the indirect cause of severe malnutrition among children. In 1983, a drought in north and notheastern Zaire decreased palm oil production.

The severity of the food crisis is primarily attributable to problems of distribution rather than of production. The predatory and pillaging activities of the political aristocracy have resulted in shortage of foreign exchange, which has contributed in several specific ways to the food crisis. For one thing, Zaire needs to import increasing amounts of food for which it needs foreign exchange. Imports of wheat, wheat flour, and maize cost $51.4 million in 1984.[15]

Shortage of foreign exchange is also a major factor in the decline of the transportation system. Roads have deteriorated steadily since independence for lack of maintenance: Many rural areas have become completely inaccessible to vehicles, stretches of major roads are impassable for days after rain, bridges are out, ferries no longer function for lack of spare parts and fuel. Trucks, spares, and fuel are scarce and often only available at the high prices of the black market. Riverboat and airline services are erratic, infrequent, and subject to interminable delays and theft. Mail, telegraph, and telephone services are undependable. All these problems make food distribution very difficult. The government marketing boards barely function for lack of funds and vehicles, and farmers have great difficulty in marketing the crops they grow. Vegetables rot beside the roads in Kivu waiting to be picked up or are spoiled because a plane to Kinshasa is several days late; in one instance, thirty-six out of a truckload of fifty pigs died on the road from Kivu to Kisangani because of delays caused by bad roads. In 1983/84, production of palm oil and food crops by the Medail Company was restricted by lack of transportation; marketing of beef was held back by the poor state of the runway at Bunia Airport in Ituri and by the high freight rates and the appalling state of the Kisangani road.[16] Complaints appear in government reports blaming scarcity of food on the state of the roads, closing of ferries, and lack of fuel.

Urban food prices are impossibly high, given the completely inadequate wage rates at all levels of society. In 1982 a worker in Lubumbashi needed an average monthly salary of Z1,000 to buy basic necessities, but high administrators earned only Z832.12 and clerks earned only Z115.21.[17] In Kinshasa in 1983 a 40-kilogram sack of manioc flour cost Z900, of rice Z2,100, but the wage of the highest-paid domestic worker was only Z600 a month. (The unit of currency is the zaire, divided into 100 makuta. In 1982, $1 was equal to Z5.754; in September 1983, $1 equaled Z26.3; in February 1984, $1 equaled Z33.) In 1984, it took 80 days of work at the wages of an unskilled worker in Kinshasa to buy a 40-kilogram sack of manioc, the primary food staple; 2 days of work for 1 kilogram of rice; 3.3 days for 1 kilogram of sugar.[18] Not only is food extremely expensive, it is also often in short supply, and particular items are hard to find or unobtainable for varying periods of time. In rural areas producer prices are quite inadequate to allow farmers to pay for the commodities they need and do not themselves produce. In rural Kivu, for example, purchase of a length of cloth in 1983 required the sale of five times as much cassava as it did in 1979.[19]

One factor in the prohibitively high cost of food and its scarcity is the politics of distribution. Shortages of imported manufactured goods, foodstuffs, and fuel occur from lack of foreign exchange; they are compounded by middleman activity and speculation. Those who are in a position to control the allocation of scarce commodities enrich themselves and their clients. State officials use the power of their offices for access to resources; in allocating them, they maintain the relationships of patronage by which they sustain their class position. Large profits are made by middlemen. They obtain goods, including foods either imported or locally processed, by voucher at the official, controlled price; these vouchers are sold, often several times and each time for a higher price; by the time the goods are collected and sold to the consumer, they cost many times the official price. In Kinshasa in 1978/79, there was a 258 percent difference between the official prices of goods and their actual market prices.[20] Besides putting up prices, these wholesaler activities greatly increase the difficulty of supply for traders and storeowners who have to seek out illicit suppliers because they can obtain so little through legal channels at lower prices. Shortages also allow for large-scale profitmaking through speculation: Enormous price markups are imposed as goods are shipped from one part of the country to another where they are in short supply.

Attempts to stop these activities are doomed to failure because of the involvement in them of the very personnel charged with rooting them out. The various foreign experts and teams called in to head financial institutions and straighten out corrupt dealings or to staff customs posts and prevent rampant smuggling and fraudulent export have given up in despair. The religious missions are periodically charged with distributing essential food supplies imported through foreign-aid programs, to ensure equitable distribution and keep prices down, but it is impossible to prevent food being resold at higher prices after it is initially sold at low prices.

The government regularly imposes price controls on food and other essential commodities and attempts to increase supply by importing. Robert Bates points out that such policies are responses to pressure from urban consumers, whose disaffection the government fears, giving them more political clout than rural dwellers. Price controls, in fact, fail to stop price increases but offer many opportunities for corruption and result in redistribution of income from consumers to officials: It is all too easy to divert food from official marketing channels. Imports of food undercut local food prices because of the overvaluation of the currency.[21] Price controls also mean that farmers receive lower prices for their products, [22] whereas protective tariffs, tax incentives, and other protective measures for mostly foreign-owned domestic industry mean that farmers must pay more for consumer goods.

· POPULAR RESPONSES ·

Just as the food crisis itself is rooted in politics, so are the popular responses for dealing with it; they represent a challenge to the viability of the state. When people "manage for themselves," they go outside established, officially regulated institutions for solutions to their problems. One manifestation of this process has been a move into production by wage earners: Urban dwellers survive by growing their own food in gardens outside the town; rural workers abandon their poorly paid jobs to grow food, hunt, and fish for sale to obtain the cash to buy the foodstuffs and goods they cannot afford on their meager wages. A more specific challenge to the state is evident in "l'économie de débrouillardise"—the second, or parallel, economy—which has enormously expanded during Zaire's economic crisis, and which has its own system of production and distribution. Its activities are unmeasured and unrecorded; some of them are illegal, others not illegal in themselves but carried out in a manner that avoids taxation or in some way deprives the state of revenue. These are activities supposedly controlled by the state that either evade this control or involve illegal use of state position. They make this sector of the economy as much a political as an economic phenomenon,[23] a manifestation of class struggle as well as of coping strategies for economic exigency. Other responses to the food crisis in Zaire may be categorized as either complete withdrawal from any confrontation with the state into encapsulated enclaves or as abandonment of reliance on it through the use of self-help or ethnic ties to organize the production and distribution of food for the urban market.

The Return to the Countryside

It is obvious from the figures on wages and prices that urbanites must find some means of producing or acquiring food themselves in order to provide sufficient food for a family. There has been a move by both rich and poor, the powerful and the powerless, to acquire plots of land outside the city for growing food crops for subsistence and even for sale. Since land was nationalized in 1973, permission for the right to use land must be obtained from the government and a yearly tax paid according to the type of use. Concessions for 200 hectares must be obtained under signed contract to the regional government; for under 10 hectares, to the Land Title Office. In fact, in some areas, small plots can be obtained with a token payment to the local village headman. Otherwise, those whose villages of origin are in reach of the city can get access to land through kin ties, whereas those lacking such access may arrange for food to be sent to town by rural kin in exchange for commodities obtainable in the city but scarce in the villages, such as kerosene, salt, soap, and cloth. Some examples of this move into production follow:

- In Kinshasa, a former ministerial adviser now working for a foreign economic development agency has acquired a farm in the country to which he and his family repair on weekends to cultivate and oversee local workers growing food for the family's needs, to picnic, and to enjoy being out of the city.

- In Kisangani, a domestic worker, a member of a local ethnic group, is able to live on his low wage and send his children to primary and secondary school because he and his wife grow their staple food. Only one of his six children living at home has finished school, a son who works as a carpenter. This man took four months in between jobs to plant a lot of manioc. His wife goes back and forth from the city to harvest it. They basically live on the manioc tubers and greens, buying salt fish once in a while.

- A kisangani zone councillor, who is not local to the area, has a 150-hectare plantation 60 kilometers from the city. He has 50 hectares of food crops, chiefly manioc and maize, and 100 hectares of coffee and citrus fruit. He pays a small sum to the local chief for use of the land and tax and rent to the state, the real landowner. He hires the local Bakumu people as workers. This enterprise is primarily commercial but also supplies his family's food needs.

- A wealthy businesswoman in Kisangani has several hectares of cultivations about a forty-minute ride from town, in which manioc is interspersed with bananas and plantains. She also has avocado and papaya trees, grows spinach and tobacco (for her workers), and in 1979 was having more land cleared for rice and peanuts. In that year she employed twenty-three workers on this farm and was building a storage shed with a concrete floor. After her household's needs were filled, she sold manioc to the local textile factory for starch.

Nsaman O. Lutu quotes an urban councillor who was able to survive because of the fields he cultivated. "At the harvest I sell maize and sweet potatoes. With this money I pay for the clothes and school fees of my children. In addition, manioc and vegetables feed us and provide money for some expenses. The little money I get at the end of the month as salary allows me to buy maize flour.[24]

Rural wage earners are likewise moving into food production. Government reports from the early 1970s and after complain that plantation workers are deserting because they can make better money from selling food grown on their lineage land or by fishing and hunting game for sale than they can from wage labor. The zone councillor cited in the examples complained that his workers only showed up irregularly because they could make more than the Z2 a day he paid them by selling what they produced by fishing and cultivating their gardens. One plantation company stabilized its labor force by issuing daily payments of food if the worker had completed assigned tasks and giving out palm oil, salt, rice or manioc, canned fish, and pork twice a week. Palm oil production increased for the company from 4,397 metric tons in 1982 to 5,035 metric tons in 1983.[25]

The food produced in this way, however, tends to enter private channels of distribution and trade with the result that much more food is produced and distributed in Zaire than appears to be from the official figures.

The Expansion of the Second Economy

Production and distribution of food in the second economy make it very difficult to assess the exact dimensions of the food crisis. The drop in official figures on food production for Zaire[26] do not reflect reality: Much more food is produced than is officially recorded. Robert Bates gives sources for Tanzania that indicate that the cause of the decline in food purchased by the marketing agencies was not a decline in production but rather a flight from government-controlled marketing and a massive diversion into private channels of trade.[27] Bjorn Beckman writes that in Nigeria the official picture of stagnation and decline "conceals one of the major dynamic changes in the development of Nigerian capitalism: a dramatic increase in the commercialization of agriculture oriented toward the domestic food market and the consequent radical broadening of the rural market for manufactured goods."[28]

In Zaire, one response to the food crisis has certainly been increasing food production and distribution in the second economy. Fernand Bèzy, J.-P. Peemans, and J.-M. Wautelet consider that food production has increased in response to increasing demand from urban centers. They estimate that two-thirds of peasant production is noncommercialized and unregistered in statistics, so that total production is difficult to assess.[29] Such activities are outside the control of the state and are evidence of people's unwillingness to cooperate with it: Barter and unofficial channels of trade are not only unmeasured, they are also unlicensed and deprive the state of taxes.

Unrecorded production of palm oil by petty producers for direct sale to consumers, and thus unlicensed and untaxed, exists on a large scale. It seems likely that such production compensates sufficiently for the drop in official production to supply the internal market: Import of palm oil, foretold as necessary since 1974 to keep up the supply for domestic consumption, has never in fact occurred, despite the fact that palm oil is a necessary ingredient for staple dishes consumed regularly by the population.[30]

Furthermore, some of the food crops grown by petty producers are smuggled across the borders to neighboring countries where prices are higher.

One reason Kinshasa suffers food shortages is that foodstuffs produced along the Zaire River all the way to Upper Zaire are deflected from the Kinshasa market and fraudulently exported to Brazzaville, with the cooperation of the personnel of the parastatal shipping company ONATRA (National Transport Office for Zaire).[31] The activities of the second economy also provide various means to increase incomes that are otherwise inadequate to buy enough food to stay alive. I have described these in detail elsewhere[32] and so will give only a brief outline here.

The second economy's productive activity is mostly by small-scale farmers and workers. It consists of illegal production in clandestine gold or diamond mining; production for private distribution, or for smuggling, of food and export crops; ivory poaching and hunting rare game for valuable skins; and production in small-scale craft or manufacturing enterprises in urban or rural areas for nonlicensed trade. Distributive activities consist of smuggling and fraudulent export; theft; barter; speculation, hoarding, and wholesaler activity; usury; and bribery, corruption, and embezzlement. People solve transportation problems by organizing their own or participating in the arrangements of others. They pay a fee or offer some favor, rely on kin or ethnic ties to ride on company trucks, or in other ways participate in the organization set up by larger concerns, or they make "arrangements" with the personnel of official transport services for favored treatment.

The state is defrauded of huge amounts of revenue from its principal exports of copper, cobalt, and other minerals through embezzlement by government officials. It also suffers enormous losses from smuggling of export crops such as coffee and palm oil and of gold, ivory, and diamonds. The wealth generated by these activities enriches the powerful, but they cannot exert a monopoly; quite ordinary people can also smuggle coffee and diamonds and can dig for gold. Access to these activities, however, is highly uneven and intensely competitive; it does not result in a fair redistribution of resources. Opportunities to participate in the lucrative activities of this sector of the economy vary from one region of the country to another and depend on access to land and on its fertility, proximity to mineral and other natural resources, and location with regard to truck routes or frontiers.

A wide range of goods and services are also produced by small-scale craft and manufacturing enterprises and by the self-employed in the so-called informal sector of towns and cities; most of this activity is unrecorded and untaxed and thus part of the second economy. It constitutes a means of livelihood for the urban unemployed and also serves to supplement grossly inadequate wages.

The expansion of food production and distribution in the second economy is in response to demand. Although it cannot solve the food crisis, participation in it is one of the ways that individuals attempt to solve the problem of the scarcity of food and its prohibitive expense. Food shortages are still frequent, and anything other than a very minimal diet is unaffordable to the majority of people; malnutrition, hunger, and even starvation exist and become acute problems at particular times and in particular places or for individuals.

Withdrawal, Self-Help, and Ethnic Organization

Some groups have responded to the difficulties of life in Zaire by withdrawing to live autonomously from state and society deep in the forest, refusing to pay taxes or to carry out public works *(salongo)*. They subsist by growing their own food crops, hunting and fishing, and clothing themselves in animal skins. They run their own schools and dispensaries. They obtain some cash by selling ivory to poachers or by digging gold. Official reports by government administrators in Kisangani describe the existence in Upper Zaire of these enclaves for the religious sects of Kitawala, Monama, Lulwa, and Idome, living out of reach of the authorities deep in the bush. In Equateur, Kitawalists are estimated to number 15,000. A visitor to one of their camps estimated its population to be 800, with 165 huts, and described the people as very active in fishing and hunting.[33]

The state has conspicuously failed to maintain the necessary infrastructure to support development projects and the maintenance and expansion of food production. The result is that those organizations that can construct their own infrastructure are the ones that are functional in production and distribution. The missions, both Catholic and Protestant, run their own transportation services by air, road, and river and their own communication networks by radio telephone, importing the commodities necessary to keep them functioning. The big companies do the same. Bralima, one of Zaire's breweries, one example among many, runs its own river barge service to Kinshasa and has its own agricultural projects for which it supplies trucks, tractors, and tools. Two millionaire businessmen, one in Kivu in the east, another in Lower Zaire in the west, organize for themselves the services the state is incapable of providing. One, whose cattle ranches supply Kinshasa with meat, has an airstrip and a seven-passenger plane, a radio telephone communication network, has put Z 10,000 into the maintenance of public roads, and runs transportation for his agricultural laborers and ranch hands daily to and from the local town. The other, a ranch and plantation owner, has his own air freight and charter air service with four planes. A small airport has been constructed in Butembo, a predominantly Nande town in Kivu, financed entirely by local businessmen under the direction of the Nande Catholic bishop. Two small hydroelectric dams are also planned. The only electricity in the town is from private generators, and the central government has refused to allocate any funds, so this project will likewise be locally financed and organized. The construction is being organized by a committee of forty local businesspeople, headed by the bishop. This kind of withdrawal into self-sufficiency in necessary infrastructure differs from the near self-sufficiency and autonomy of organized enclaves.

The Nande furnish an example of the use of ethnic ties to expedite the commercialization of food and overcome distribution problems. They inhabit the productive agricultural zones of North Kivu. The fertile soils and temperate climate of the western mountains of the Rift Valley make this a prime area for the production of beans and other vegetables; it is also suitable for raising cattle to supply meat for the local market. The Nande have a near monopoly shipping vegetables by road from Kivu to Kisangani and thence downriver to Kinshasa. In 1979/80 North Kivu supplied 8,720 metric tons of beans, a food staple, to Kinshasa (66 percent of its total supply), 1,300–1,600 metric tons of potatoes, 105 metric tons of leeks, and 47 metric tons of onions, via Kisangani; Kisangani consumed 201 metric tons of leeks and 200 metric tons of onions from North Kivu.[34] This extensive trade in food is carried on by Nande living in Kisangani and Kinshasa and is organized through a network of kin and ethnic ties. In return they import commodities needed in Kivu, such as fuel, construction materials, beer from Kisangani's breweries, palm oil, and imported manufactured goods. Nande family members and friends cooperate in this trade: They organize the shipping and purchase of goods, transmit information and arrange the necessary credit. Control of all stages of the trade by one ethnic group helps to overcome the problems caused by the degeneration of the transport and communication system, the restricted access to capital, and the suspicion and mistrust that prevails between different peoples in Zaire.[35] Such trade is a prime example of an ethnic collectivity undergoing a process of politicization, through organization and the growth of consciousness, in the process of pursuing its interests. This use of ethnic ties has also overcome the marketing problems that contribute to the food crisis for at least one source of food supplies for two of Zaire's major cities.

· CLASS RELATIONS ·

Both the food crisis and the popular responses to it may be analyzed in terms of domestic class relations and class struggle within Zaire's particular historical, social, and economic context.

The historical context for Zaire's food crisis and the political situation that fosters it is the Belgian colonial legacy of an export economy dependent on the fluctuations of world market prices for primary commodities, a poorly developed food-producing sector, and a dominant class lacking qualified and experienced personnel. The decline in the administrative capacity of the state that followed independence and the indifference of the government to the agricultural sector, followed by the pillaging activities of Mobutu's political aristocracy, paralyzed and incapacitated the administrative apparatus and the government, brought about drastic deterioration of the economic infrastructure, and resulted in food scarcities and high prices.

Any political opposition to the regime and its policies and practices is brutally repressed. For all the decay of the administrative capacity of the state, the regime has been remarkably effective in stifling dissent and maintaining political control by means of a ruthlessly efficient secret police and network of informers, recourse to imprisonment and torture, and violent reaction to any signs of opposition. Several hundred people were killed when uprisings and dissent in Kwilu and Kasai in 1978 and 1979 were suppressed; student strikes and riots protesting against the regime, as well as against inadequate grants and food supplies, were violently put down by troops in 1979 and 1982; and criticism of conditions of life in Zaire by members of the legislative council have resulted in arrests and imprisonment.

Political repression and control is successful, but a critical element in class relations is the lack of control by Mobutu and his political aristocracy over economic processes. This is partly the result of the predatory nature of this class, its pillaging of the economy and the concomitant collapse of the administrative capacity of the state, and partly attributable to the incomplete penetration of capitalism in Zaire. Noncapitalist modes of production continue to exist in articulation with the capitalist ones in the Zairian economy, labor is not dispossessed from the means of production, and alternatives for subsistence exist besides wage labor. Such economies are widespread in Africa and contrast with the classical form of capitalist production in the industrializing sectors of the world economy, in which it is much more nearly the case that labor markets, in which labor power is sold as if it were a commodity, are the only means of subsistence and reproduction for the work force.

In Zaire, both petty producers and urban and rural wage earners can find alternatives to wage labor: They have access to land in noncapitalist modes of production through kin relations, and they can participate in the productive and distributive activities of the second economy. They thus earn money by petty commodity production. Some writers consider the price that these producers receive to be a concealed wage, so that they thus constitute a proletariat: From this viewpoint, they are in fact selling their labor power through the sale of products. Furthermore, the control of capital over the level of this price expresses its command of labor power. This form of capitalist production depends, then, "not on the constitution and automatic functioning of a labor-market, but on the coercive subjugation of the small commodity producer."[36] But an opposing point of view holds that "the process stops short of full proletarianization in that the separation of the producers and the means of production is not complete, and the individualized production of the household is not replaced by a socialized production process, 'set in motion' by capital."[37]

This latter view illuminates the popular responses to the food crisis in Zaire. Because of access to means of production and distribution outside the control of the dominant class, the subordinated classes have means to avoid the exploitation and oppression of this class. The low wages and high prices; the hoarding, speculation, and resulting scarcity of food; and the barriers to enterprise constituted by licensing, taxation, and the decay of the infrastructure represent mechanisms of this oppression. Resistance to, and evasion of, these mechanisms is a measure of the political aristocracy's inability to control labor processes and to extend capitalist relations of production. This situation provides opportunities for some individuals not only to subsist but to accumulate considerable wealth in noncapitalist modes of production and in the activities of the second economy.

In conclusion, town and country are integrated into one social system in the formation of the new postindependence class structure. Members of the political aristocracy oppress urban and rural wage earners and petty producers as they make use of position in the state to accumulate wealth and consolidate their class position. They exploit their privleged access to resources to engage in speculation, middleman activity, and smuggling. Their appropriation of public funds for private use and their mismanagement of the vast assets they have acquired have contributed to Zaire's economic crisis and to its severe food shortages.

Rural and urban workers struggle to survive on inadequate wages and to evade the depredations of the state by making use of kin and ethnic ties between town and country. They have moved into food production and engage in small-scale enterprise, smuggling, barter, private channels of trade, and middleman activity. Petty producers seek higher return for their labor in unofficial marketing channels for the crops they grow. Some people have withdrawn into self-sufficiency; some have found lucrative opportunities.

All this activity outside the control of the state has opened up society by providing a wider range of opportunities for social mobility. The state is no longer the primary means of class formation, and a small but significant indigenous capitalist class is beginning to emerge in at least some parts of the country.[38] The causes of the food crisis in Zaire and the popular responses to it are an integral part of an ongoing class struggle.

• NOTES •

1. J-L. Amselle and E. LeBris, "De la 'Petite production marchande' à léconomie mercantile," in P. Hugon and I. Deblé, eds., *Vivre et survivre dans les villes africaines* (Paris: Presses Universitaires de France, 1982), pp. 163–173.

2. Crawford Young, *Politics in the Congo* (Princeton, N.J.: Princeton University Press, 1965), p. 32.

3. Louis H. Gann and Peter Duignan, *The Rulers of Belgian Africa 1884–1914* (Princeton, N.J.: Princeton University Press, 1979), p. 125; J-P. Peemans, "Capital Accumulation in the Congo Under Colonialism: The Role of the State," in Peter Duignan and Louis H. Gann, eds., *Colonialism in Africa*, vol. 4 (Cambridge University Press, 1975), pp. 169–170.

4. See F. Bézy, J-P. Peemans, and J-M. Wautelet, *Accumulation et sous-développement au Zaire, 1960–1980* (Louvain-la-Nueve: Presse Universitaire de Louvain, 1981), pp. 13–16.

5. B. Jewsiewicki, "Rural Society and the Belgian Colonial Economy," in David Birmingham and Phyllis M. Martin, eds., *History of Central Africa*, vol. 2 (New York: Longman, 1983), pp. 112–115; Gann and Duignan, *The Rulers of Belgian Africa*, pp. 130, 204.

6. Bézy, Peemans, and Wautelet, *Accumulation et sous-développement*, p. 20.

7. Ibid, p. 35.

8. See V. Y. Mudimbe, "La Culture," in J. Vanderlinden, ed., *Du Congo au Zaire 1960–1980* (Brussels: CRISP, 1981), pp. 372–377. White settlers cultivated export crops while African farmers were forced into nonprofitable sectors. On the eve of independence in 1960, 95 percent of palm oil, 87 percent of coffee, 90 percent of rubber, 97 percent of tea, 35 percent of tobacco, and 99 percent of cocoa production was European-owned (T. Mukenge, *Businessmen of Zaire: Limited Possibilities for Capital Accumulation Under Dependence* [Ph.D. diss., McGill University, 1974], p. 137).

9. J-P. Peemans, "L'Etat fort et la croissance economique," *Revue nouvelle* (Brussels) (December), p. 525.

10. André Huybrechts and Daniel Van Der Steen, "L'Economie: Structures, évolution, perspectives," in Vanderlinden, *Du Congo au Zaire*, p. 277.

11. T. M. Callaghy, *The State-Society Struggle: Zaire in Comparative Perspective* (New York: Columbia University Press, 1984), pp. 184–185.

12. For details, see Crawford Young, "Zaire: the Politics of Penury," *School of Advanced International Studies Review* 3, no. 1 (1983); J-C. Willame, "Zaire: Système de survie et fiction d'état," *Canadian Journal of African Studies* 18, no. 1, (1984); J. Rymenam, "Classes sociales, pouvoir et économie au Zaire ou comment le sous-développement enrichit les gouvernements," *Genève-Afrique* 18 (1980): 41–54.

13. World Bank, *Zaire: Current Economic Situation and Constraints (Washington, D. C.: World Bank Country Studies 1980)*, p. iii.

14. Vwakyanakazi Mukohya, *African Traders in Butembo, Eastern Zaire (1960–1980)* (Ph.D. diss., University of Wisconsin, Madison, 1982), p. 329.

15. *Conjoncture économique* 23 (1984): 24.

16. Ibid., pp. 211, 266.

17. Nsaman O. Lutu, "Le Management face à la crise de l'administration publique zairoise," *Zaire Afrique* 175 (1983): 27.

18. Mubake Mumeme, "Crise, inflation et comportements individuels d'adaption au Zaire: Solution ou aggravation du problème?" *Zaire Afrique* 183 (1984): 269.

19. Catherine Newbury, "Ebutumwa Bw'Emiogo: The Tyranny of Cassava: A Women's Tax Revolt in Eastern Zaire," *Canadian Journal of African Studies* 18 (1984): 40.

20. Mubake, "Crise, inflation et comportements," pp. 266–267.

21. Robert Bates, *Markets and States in Tropical Africa* (Berkeley and Los Angeles: University of California Press, 1981), pp. 30–43.

22. In September 1983, a series of reforms backed by the IMF, were instituted to improve the economic situation. One of these reforms liberalized prices, including producer prices for agricultural commodities. Little data on the effect is as yet available, but a 1984 assessment indicated that production of food crops was still inadequate, although imports of maize had decreased (*Conjoncture économique* 23 (1984): 24).

23. This second economy should not be confused with the "informal sector," which generally refers to the small-scale enterprises of the urban poor.

24. Nsaman, "Le Management face à la crise," pp. 279–280 (my translation).

25. *Conjoncture économique* 23 (1984): 205.

26. World Bank, *Zaire*, p. 11; Bézy, Peemans, and Wautelet, *Accumulation et sous-développement*, p. 221.

27. Bates, *Markets and States in Tropical Africa*, p. 85.

28. Bjorn Beckman, "Imperialism and Cpaitalist Transformation," *Review of African Political Economy* 19 (1980): 88.

29. Bézy, Peemans, and Wautelet, *Accumulation et sous-développement*, p. 131.

30. M'Bela Bole Kolaka, "Crise de la production agricole au Zaire: Le Cas de l'huile de palme," *Zaire Afrique* 162 (1982): 77.

31. Mbumba Ngimbi, *Kinshasa 1881–1981* (Kinshasa: Editions Centre de Recherches Pédagogiques, 1982), p. 47. The same phenomenon is reported in Maniema and Kivu.

32. J. MacGaffey, "How to Survive and Get Rich Amidst Devastation: The Second Economy in Zaire," *African Affairs* 82 (1983): 351–366; "Fending for Yourself: The Organization of the Second Economy in Zaire," in Nzongola Ntalaja, ed., *The Crisis in Zaire: Myths and Realities* (Trenton, N. J.: Africa World Press, 1986); "Economic Disengagement and Class Formation in Zaire," in Naomi Chazan and Donald Rothchild, eds., *Balancing State and Society* (Boulder, Colo.: Westview Press, 1986).

33. *Rapport annuel affaires politiques, haut Zaire* 1973, 1976; *Rapport annuel, administration du territoire, haut Zaire* 1977; Michael Schatzberg, *Politics and State in Zaire: The Mechanics of Coercion in Lisala* (forthcoming).

34. Société de Développement International Desjardins, *Commercialisation des produits agricoles du nord-est du Zaire*, vol. 1 (Lévis, Quebec: SDID, 1981), pp. 67–80.

35. More details of this modern trading diaspora appear in Janet MacGaffey, *Entrepreneurs and Parasites: The Struggle for Indigenous Capitalism in Zaire* (Cambridge: Cambridge University Press, 1988), ch. 6.

36. J. Banaji, "Modes of Production in a Materialist Conception of History," *Capital and Class* 3 (1977): 34–36; see also C. Moser, "Informal Sector or Petty Commodity Production: Dualism or Dependence in Urban Development?" *World Development* 9/10 (1978).

37. Henry Bernstein, "Notes on Capital and Peasantry," *Review of African Political Economy* 10 (1977): 69. For a fuller discussion of this argument, see David Goodman and Michael Redclift, *From Peasant to Proletarian: Capitalist Development and Agrarian Transitions* (New York: St. Martin's Press, 1982), pp. 94–98.

38. See MacGaffey, *Entrepreneurs and Parasites*.

·8·

Weak State and Backward Agriculture in Zambia: A Case Study and Its Implications

KENNETH GOOD

After years of agricultural production that was significantly below domestic consumption needs for key commodities, Zambia in 1985 looked forward to a good harvest of maize, the nation's staple. The minister of cooperatives, Justin Mukando, in February anticipated more than 8 million bags of maize, and Prime Minister Kebby Musokotwane declared on May 13 that "about ten million bags" were expected.[1] In the Zambian system, purchasing, transportation, and storage of crops, like many other agricultural functions, were in the hands of the state. This was expressed not least through the involvement of political figures at the highest level and the continued reliance upon the established rural parastatal organizations, the National Agricultural Marketing Board (Namboard) and the provincial cooperative marketing unions.[2]

The harvest is, of course, a regular, annual exercise. Marketed maize production had been rather consistently low—in 1982, 5.7 million bags; 1983, 5.9 million bags; 1984, 6.3 million bags[3]—although around 1984 something like 9 million bags of maize (90 kilograms each) were required to feed the country's rapidly rising population. Zambia enjoyed notably good rains from the start of the rainy season in late 1984, and climatic factors clearly favored the 1985 harvest, which commenced around mid-June and was officially due for completion in mid-October. Nevertheless, the state's actual management of this vital, well-known, and limited-duration exercise was, if anything, worse than usual. The failures and inefficiencies that were displayed point again to serious structural weaknesses in the Zambian state and political economy.

· THE STATE'S MARKETING ARRANGEMENTS ·

An official report in March 1984 identified serious inadequacies in the organization of the national harvest. Between 560,000 and 770,000 bags of maize, about 5–10 percent of total marketable output, were lost each year in Zambia through poor marketing and storage arrangements. This represented almost a month's supply of food for the country.[4]

185

Losses to the national harvest as a result of the smuggling of produce into neighboring countries were also of serious proportions. This too was influenced by government policy, especially with regard to official producer prices. More than 400,000 bags of maize were believed to have been smuggled into Zaire from Mkushi District in Central Province in 1983. The official price for maize in Zambia in that year was K18.30 a bag, but a Zambian farmer could easily obtain at K35 by selling in Zaire.[5] (The Zambian unit of currency is the kwacha, divided into 100 ngwee. In 1980 $1 equaled K.8; K.9 in 1982; and K7.6 in 1987.) It was estimated that some 150,000 metric tons of maize, about 1.7 million bags, or almost three months' supply of food, was smuggled into Zaire from northern Zambia during 1983.[6]

Sources within the government pointed to important institutional deficiencies in the existing marketing arrangements toward the end of 1984. The minister of state for lands, Cosmas Masongo, said in late October that the existence of two official marketing organizations, Namboard and the provincial cooperatives, resulted in the duplication of functions and inefficiencies.[7] In parliament shortly afterwards, Michael Sata, member for Kabwata, declared that the functions of the two inefficient organizations overlapped and that one of them should be phased out or they should be merged.[8] The reality of the problems facing the state's marketing institutions was further reinforced in the same month when it was reported that the general manager of Namboard, George Chabwera, had been sent on indefinite leave, and the acting grains manager, Stephen Zimba, had been suspended indefinitely for incompetence.[9]

To improve the arrangements for the next harvest, the government eventually decided to increase the power and functions of Namboard. According to the minister of finance, Luke Mwananshiku, in his budget address in January 1985, "the Party and its Government have decided that in coming years, Namboard will be primarily responsible for the collection of maize and the distribution of fertilizers. Provincial cooperative unions will as in the past, act only as agents of Namboard where necessary."[10] This brief and somewhat ambiguous statement was enlarged upon in the following months,[11] when the finance minister told parliament that the government had decided to withdraw marketing functions from the cooperatives because of their prevalent weaknesses. Although Namboard had made mistakes, including cases of possible corruption, all was not well either, he said, in the provincial cooperatives. So those that were presently weak would be assisted by Namboard until they functioned properly: "In dealing with this [complex] matter . . . we must maintain a flexible posture." he also announced the formation of a new body, a so-called task force of five ministries, to work out plans to ensure the prompt collection and safe storage of crops in the forthcoming season.[12]

The precise nature of the new marketing arrangements between Namboard and the cooperatives remained, therefore, unclear, and one month after his first announcement, the finance minister stated that arrangements were still being worked out administratively.[13]

· THE WEAKNESSES OF THE COOPERATIVES AND OF NAMBOARD ·

Among all the uncertainties, however, the failures of the cooperative unions were a definite reality. These assumed a variety of forms, of which one of the most regular was the mismanagement of funds resulting in the nonpayment of farmers for the crops they delivered. Provincial cooperatives seldom made purchases from farmers with their own financial resources but, rather, used government grants or bank-guaranteed overdrafts or by a combination of both.[14] Mistakes and malpractices occurred easily. In December 1984 the Northern Cooperative Union owed farmers K3.5 million for produce purchased earlier that year, whereas checks issued by the Eastern Cooperative Union, valued at some K15 million and intended as late payments to farmers, were not honored by Barclays Bank.[15] This was when farmers all over Zambia were already heavily involved for a month or more in new plantings for 1985, for which they required seeds and fertilizers, which the majority of farmers—namely, the small peasants—could not hope to obtain without prior payment for their 1984 crops.

Mismanagement also resulted in some cooperatives experiencing large losses, notably the accumulated total of K8.5 million by the Northern cooperative at the end of 1982.[16] Inefficiencies could easily act as a cloak for embezzlement of public funds. Thefts were experienced by all nine of the country's provincial cooperatives, and between 1980 and 1984 they amounted to K1.4 million. Most cases did not involve mere petty pilfering. Southern provincial cooperative, for example, lost some K240,000 in thirty reported thefts; Central lost about K125,000 in nineteen thefts; Lusaka lost K121,000 through thirty-nine reported thefts; Eastern lost K29,000 in six thefts; and Northern experienced a loss of K504,000 in twenty-six reported thefts that resulted in only three convictions in the courts. The results of audits then current in both the Northern and North-Western cooperatives were not included in these figures.[17]

After revelations that about K1 million was missing from the Northern cooperative, the general manager was dismissed and the board of directors was dissolved.[18] Large-scale embezzlement was also discovered in the North-Western cooperative. The auditor-general reported that he had found a highly organized racket in which some K270,000 had vanished and that government loans between 1981 and 1983, totaling K450,000, had been diverted to an unprescribed purpose and not repaid.[19] It was most unlikely that embezzlement existed only in the Northern and North-Western cooperatives. The Registrar of Cooperatives stated in May 1985 that financial indiscipline was now "rampant" in the country's cooperative unions.[20]

The government was obviously right in recognizing, belatedly, the weaknesses of the cooperatives. According to the chairman of the rural development subcommittee of UNIP's (United National Independence Party) central committee, Reuben Kamanga, in February 1985, the cooperatives failed to pay farmers on time, made late collections of produce, and caused delays in the distribution of inputs.[21] In the same month, cooperatives minister Justin Mukando castigated the general managers of cooperatives: "You have allowed yourselves and your officers to borrow heavily from unions even when you know that this is against regulations. What is more, you are not paying back your debts. This has led to disasters."[22]

The case against the cooperatives as effective marketing agencies was clear, though there were some in government who appeared to dissent from the weight of critical evidence. President Kenneth Kaunda, at the beginning of February 1985, unconvincingly described cooperative societies as effective tools in removing the seeds of exploitation and as essential in the creation of wealth and employment for members.[23]

The criticism of the cooperatives was, however, only part of the equation, and it remained another matter to support Namboard as the undefined but supposedly primary state marketing organization. Referring to cases in the 1970s and in 1981, when Namboard had been responsible for the destruction of fertilizer costing tens of thousands of kwacha in foreign exchange, and to what were called many similar examples, the *Times of Zambia* declared that Namboard was an organization of "proven inefficiency," with "a notorious reputation of doing most of its work the wrong way round."[24] In the debate following the 1985 budget speech, members of parliament strongly attacked the decision to augment Namboard's powers. The member for Chikankata, Lazarous Cheelo, called the government's action an "unmistakable sign of confusion."[25]

The Zambia Cooperative Federation, of course, added its voice to this criticism. At a press conference in Lusaka in February 1985, the federation's chairman declared that Zambians knew of Namboard's problems and failures, and many were therefore asking why the government had suddenly acquired confidence in the organization. "If Namboard is deemed to be so efficient by the government," he went on, "why does it need the unions to act as its agents?" The federation, he noted, had not been consulted by the government before the recent decision.[26]

The government had implicitly rejected the suggestions that wastage in the harvest partly resulted from inefficiencies and duplication of functions in and between the two state marketing agencies. It had ignored the proposal that they should either be merged or one should be abolished. The state had instead chosen to retain both of these ineffective bodies, while also proposing to increase by some imprecise extent the powers of Namboard relative to the cooperatives. The outcome, as the rainy season drew to a satisfactory end, seemed to be one of more confusion than previously. The chairman of the

Truckers Association of Zambia, whose members were directly responsible for the haulage of crops, declared in early March 1985 that there appeared to be "too much talk and less action" on preparations for the harvest.[27]

Inactivity and confusion continued well into April. For example, by April 28—some three months after the announcement of the changes—in Southern Province, an area of comparatively advanced agricultural production, the government had not provided the provincial permanent secretary with any guidelines for how Namboard and the cooperatives would operate together.[28] President Kaunda, however, at the end of the month, reiterated what he termed his strong faith in cooperatives and said that he would soon announce changes to make Namboard more effective, as this had to be the main center in marketing arrangements: "There must be somebody we can blame when things do not work out."[29]

• THE PROGRESS OF THE HARVEST •

The appointment of the new prime minister, Kebby Musokotwane, on April 24, was followed by a flurry of statements apparently aimed at clarifying the functions of Namboard and the cooperatives.[30] On May 13 Musokotwane firmly declared that the government "will not tolerate professional rivalry from either Namboard or the unions. We expect the two organizations to work together. . . ."[31] Six days later he stated that all buying and transportation of maize and fertilizers would be done by Namboard, but only as a temporary measure. His clarification of Namboard's capacities was qualified further in the area of transportation and storage. Cooperatives should acquire trucks, said the premier at this late stage of the season, which would then be hired by Namboard for the carriage of produce. Where Namboard had insufficient storage facilities, it should use those of the provincial cooperative on payment of a fee. He concluded by giving cooperatives two weeks in which to hand over marketing functions to Namboard.[32]

The state implicitly intended that Namboard should have sole responsibility for the purchase, haulage, and storage of crops in 1985 but recognized that Namboard was in fact unable to fulfill its "sole" responsibility alone. It could play its role only with the assistance of the cooperatives. But as the time for the start of the harvest rapidly approached, it was clear that the cooperatives remained reluctant to accept the new arrangements. Although the finance minister had spoken in February of the state's "flexible posture," Musokotwane now expressed a stern rigidity: Namboard and the Zambia Cooperative Federation were now ordered to sign a haulage and marketing contract within a week. They should themselves solve the problems that obviously still existed within and between the two agencies, and the prime minister warned their representatives: "You will have to work day and night to solve [the] problems."[33] Both organizations were known for their inefficiency, but they were now required to work together closely, even though officials of some cooperatives were openly hostile to Namboard.[34]

Namboard, however, obtained a new general manager on May 20—Major General Charles Nyirenda, formerly head of TAZARA, the trouble-plagued Tanzania-Zambia Railway Authority. The minister of agriculture, General Kingsley Chinkuli, accurately said that Namboard required "not only an ordinary man but a crusader." The removal of the chairman of the board of directors was also announced.[35] Nyirenda, shortly after, assured farmers in Mkushi that his organization would this year pay them on the spot upon delivery of their produce.[36] The agency committed itself even further when, on June 3, it pledged to haul all maize to safe storage before the onset of rains.[37]

The government's preparations at the infrastructural level of the harvest—the state of the roads, the availability of spare parts, fuel, and grain bags—gave little encouragement. The minister of works, Haswell Mwale, admitted in early April that the condition of roads in Zambia was "very bad," and his permanent secretary added that most roads were in a "deplorable" state.[38] Those in Southern Province were described, later in the month, as in "a bad shape," and the grading of feeder roads would not be done before the haulage began because all fifty-four graders in the province had broken down.[39] President Kaunda correctly referred to feeder roads as the key to the success of the peasant farmer, but he complacently observed that "it was rather too late" to start work on repairing them, and, in any case, there was nothing the government could do, as it had no money.[40]

Preparations were inadequate with regard to other key transportation items. Tires, tubes, and spare parts were known to be in short supply throughout the country by early 1985, and at the beginning of March the chairman of the Truckers Association appealed to the ministerial task force, said to have been formed a month earlier, to ensure that these essential supplies were quickly made available to transporters. Without urgent action, the association chairman said, crops would be left to rot, especially in outlying rural areas.[41] In July, the Commercial Farmers Bureau reported that farmers too were gravely handicapped by the dearth of tires and tubes for pickups, lorries, and tractors.[42]

Mistakes in the management of the country's fuel supplies soon reached crisis proportions, for the availability of diesel fuel and gasoline was one of the most basic requirements of the harvest. Signs of a diesel shortage appeared near the end of May, with the Mpongwe Development Company, in Ndola Rural District, saying that it had fuel to last only ten days more. The shortage of diesel had already affected the transportation of more than 2,000 metric tons of soya beans and threatened the abandonment of the company's wheat project, in which K400,000 had been invested during 1984/85.[43]

In June, the operations of all major transport companies in the country were reported to be grinding to a gradual halt. The minister of power, Fitzpatrick Chuula, claimed that "the market [for diesel] would be flooded in a week."[44] Fuel was, however, available only on a sporadic and limited basis in July.[45] The acting minister of power, Haswell Mwale, simply denied reports that the shortage was affecting the maize haulage.[46] But later that month the situation was manifestly more serious. Chuula now said, on July 25, that the collection of maize from rural depots "hangs in the balance because of the shortage of diesel."[47] The problem worsened further, and at the end of the month the minister seemed unable or unwilling to indicate when fuel supplies would improve.[48] Desperate measures seemed called for, and in August the Truckers Association attempted to bring into the country 160,000 liters of diesel from Zimbabwe—the balance from supplies that had been purchased when the association had been importing Zimbabwean maize at the beginning of May.[49]

Only in mid-August, however, were fuel supplies ensured for the latter stages of the harvest, through the medium of financial aid from the United States. The U.S. ambassador to Zambia, Paul Hare, announced a grant of $3 million (K24 million), half of which would go toward the immediate importation of diesel and half for the importation of agricultural machinery and spare parts. Soon after, Chuula stated that Zambia was negotiating for the purchase of diesel from South Africa, using the U.S. grant.[50] When President Kaunda swore in former prime minister Nalumino Mundia as ambassador to the United States in late September, he bid farewell to him with the words: "Remember our bilateral relations with the U.S. are warm. They assist us in various fields. You are going to thank them and ask for more assistance. . . . Our problems are beyond our control."[51]

Later, at the end of October, President Kaunda offered an explanatory statement on the fuel crisis that the country had experienced over most of the harvest period. Two months earlier, he said, Zambia had been "on the verge of total collapse . . . within a matter of some ten days or so our total oil stocks would have been exhausted without any prospects of further supplies." Zambia had failed to meet its debt repayments to the foreign banks that normally financed the country's oil imports. The banks had declared, he said, that enough was enough and that unless they were paid all outstanding debts, they would not oblige. To meet these foreign debts, said Kaunda, the Bank of Zambia had to divert resources from some of the highest priorities. Fuel supplies resumed, he noted, "before the country ran completely dry."[52]

Although the president did not touch upon the interesting question of how he and his government had chosen the priorities from which they diverted finances, it would seem that one area that may have been adversely affected was Namboard's organization of the harvest. The importation of new grain bags and their distribution to farmers was a prime and well-established responsibility of Namboard. On April 9 a board spokesman announced that K8.6 million in foreign exchange had been secured from the Bank of Zambia to import 10 million jute bags from Bangladesh. This was already late in the season, and the official estimate of the total number of bags that would be required for all crops was 13 million. The spokesman and, shortly afterwards, Reuben Kamanga of the rural development committee were firm that Namboard had actually received the necessary foreign exchange and placed the order for the needed 10 million bags.[53]

Expectations of adequate supplies were short-lived.[54] Cooperatives in three of the most agriculturally advanced provinces—Central, Southern, and Eastern—had not received any bags from Namboard by early June.[55] Only near the end of the month did a shipment of 3 million bags arrive in the country, and Namboard began distributing them.[56] Even then, Eastern provincial cooperative received only 500,000 bags of the 3 million that it required, whereas the Southern and Central provincial cooperatives had been given no bags before the beginning of the harvest.[57]

According to the Commercial Farmers Bureau, there were virtually no new grain bags in the country by early July and only a small stock of used ones of doubtful quality.[58] Namboard's failure to supply Zambia's farmers with a vital requirement meant that a dismal prospect confronted many of them. As the Southern provincial political secretary, Wachuku Mwelwa, informed the regional party conference in September 1985, "Only about a million empty grain bags have been made available to farmers in the province. More than half the produce—especially from peasant farmers—will [possibly] be soaked by rains. . . ."[59]

Only in mid-August did it become known that the country's critical shortage of grain bags had been caused by mismanagement at the highest levels of Namboard and by the inadequate priorities actually accorded to Namboard's operations by the government. The minister of agriculture, General Chinkuli, then told parliament that Namboard had, in fact, not been allocated the necessary foreign exchange to import 10 million jute bags from Bangladesh. Instead, Namboard had been obliged to divert some foreign exchange that it had been allocated for the purchase of fertilizers, and which was sufficient to secure only 3 million bags, after the haulage was well under way. In the face of "mounting difficulties," Namboard had obtained a consignment of 3.5 million bags, from what he referred to as "another country," with financial assistance from the United States and West Germany. The first shipment had arrived in Zambia only three days earlier, and Namboard now expected to obtain "a total of nine million empty grain bags including the two million which would be recycled and these should be enough for packing of the estimated crop." But the minister added that 50,000 metric tons of maize had been ordered from Zimbabwe and another 40,000 metric tons from Malawi, in case of another shortfall in domestic marketed production.[60]

If problems with the importation of grain bags were the ultimate responsibility of the top levels of the state wherein foreign-exchange allocations were determined, Namboard itself introduced new problems into the distribution of those bags that became available. At the beginning of July, and without any apparent warning, Namboard put up the price of new grain bags from K1.20 to K4 and of used bags from 80 ngwee to K3, thereby increasing costs to farmers by more than 300 percent. The parastatal further aggravated the bad situation by terminating existing arrangements whereby farmers purchased bags on credit, the cost being subsequently deducted from what they received for their produce: Now farmers were suddenly required to pay in cash for bags purchased from Namboard or the cooperatives. An immediate consequence was that even available grain bags remained unsold to farmers. The district governor at Mkushi, Willard Ntalasha, reported over the weekend of July 6–7 that only about half of a recent consignment of grain bags had been sold after the price was increased.[61]

There were soon strong protests against these new constraints. The member of parliament for Mazabuka in Southern Province, Patterson Haamane, said on July 10 that the selling of bags for cash had caught farmers unaware. It would cause heavy waste in the existing crop, because farmers just did not have the money to pay cash. But it also represented great discouragement to farmers' future plans and efforts: "Even small-scale farmers have this year produced around 2,000 bags [of maize] each, but they do not have the K8,000 such production requires for the purchase of empty grain bags. We are defeating the purpose of going back to the land."[62] Five days later in Choma—like Mazabuka, an area of long-established commercial agricultural production—about 200 angry farmers reportedly stormed the offices of both Namboard and the Southern provincial cooperative. They accused the agencies of failing to tell the truth on the availability of bags and declared that they had lost patience with both of them.[63]

Not until July 17, however, did Namboard rescind its decision and again allow farmers to obtain bags on credit.[64] The Commercial Farmers Bureau welcomed this move but noted that the price of bags remained high. Kamanga admitted that this was true[65] but claimed that the government was working out new arrangements, thereby prompting a critical editorial comment in the *Daily Mail* that Namboard's decision both to increase prices heavily and to demand cash from farmers was "a clear case of lack of foresight.... Surely they should have seen that such a move was counter-productive...."[66]

Namboard's mismanagement was far from over. Under the new haulage arrangements that had belatedly been worked out with the provincial cooperatives, the cooperatives supposedly bought produce and paid farmers in Namboard's name, while Namboard supposedly released funds to the cooperatives to enable them to meet these payments and as commission to the unions. This was, under the circumstances, an uncertain and precarious setup from the outset, and toward the end of July it was reported that Namboard was failing to meet payments, contrary to the firm promise given by Nyirenda three months previously that farmers would be "paid on the spot." Central provincial cooperative already owed farmers thousands of kwacha for maize delivered to its depots,[67] and the Zambia Cooperative Federation alleged that Namboard was out to discredit the cooperative movement.

Kamanga stated on July 26 that "instructions have already been given to Namboard and to marketing unions to pay farmers without delay."[68] But many, if not most, farmers continued to be unpaid by the state agencies. The Eastern provincial cooperative stopped making payments to farmers toward late August,[69] at which time the Lusaka provincial cooperative owed farmers in its area more than K1.4 million.[70]

The reason for Namboard's failure to pay farmers was similar to, but much greater than, its failure to import grain bags from Bangladesh when they were required. Nyirenda announced in Lusaka on September 5 that the government had not provided Namboard with the money—which he said was K141 million—to pay farmers and complete the haulage of crops. "Because we have failed to get the money from the government which is supposed to fund us," he said, "we have resorted to asking for loans from banks which I am sure doubt our ability to pay them back." The setback with the grain bags was a separate problem, "aside [from] the K141 million needed to pay farmers, truckers and some cooperative unions." Nyirenda also admitted that Namboard was operating "in a haphazard manner," and right from the beginning there had been no proper planning of the haulage exercise. Namboard's acute problems, with the harvest due to end next month, "definitely require[d] immediate government action," he said.[71] Some three days later, Kamanga purportedly assured the nation that a committee under the chairmanship of the prime minister was looking into ways of raising funds for Namboard.[72]

In mid-September, with the end of the haulage season only one month away, unexpected rains in the Kalomo area of Southern Province were reported to have soaked more than 100,000 bags of maize awaiting transportation to storage.[73] By early October, more than 1.6 million bags of maize had been bought from farmers in Southern Province, but most had still not been moved to safety.[74] A few days later, Kamanga announced that more than 5 million bags of maize had been purchased nationally, of which only half had reached safe storage depots.[75] On October 11, General Chinkuli criticized "the panicky manner" in which grain bags had been recently distributed, as a result of which some areas received more than they needed and others less. He said that the 1985 marketing season had been "beset with problems from the very start" and then announced that instead of the season closing on October 15, as expected, it was extended to October 30.[76]

When the extended marketing season finished nationally at the end of October—though it was still further extended indefinitely in Northern Province—a quantity of maize remained threatened by rain. According to the then latest official figures, 5 million bags had been hauled to safety, and about 2.5 million bags had not reached storage.[77] A few days earlier, over 900 farmers near Choma had threatened to demonstrate against Namboard and the Southern cooperative because they had not been paid for produce delivered in July and August.[78] Much worse off was Northern Province, however, where thousands of bags of maize and rice were uncollected and unpaid for. At a provincial council meeting, at the end of October, several district governors were said to have spoken strongly against "the shame" of the government's urging the people to grow more food but failing to collect what they have grown.[79] A rather similar conclusion had earlier been reached by B. K. Susa of Mkushi in a letter to the *Daily Mail*, in which he referred to "the worst crop marketing season [Zambia] has ever witnessed" and concluded: "On the whole, this young nation seems not to possess the interests of [poor] peasant farmers at heart. . . . It is a mockery of the agrarian revolution our leaders preach about."[80]

· SYSTEMIC AGRICULTURAL MISMANAGEMENT ·

In expectation of a bumper harvest in 1985, the Zambian government had altered the existing functions of the two marketing agencies, established a ministerial task force, and appointed a new administrator for Namboard. Prime Minister Musokotwane was closely involved in the early stages of the harvest, and other ministers and party chiefs intervened frequently. The mismanagement that resulted had serious consequences for the whole country. Non-self-sufficiency in the staple represented a basic national weakness for Zambia, in sharp contrast to the situation in its smaller neighbor, Malawi. Both Malawi and Zimbabwe were surplus-producing countries from which Zambia imported maize at a cost to its foreign exchange. During the 1984–1985 season, 20,000 metric tons were imported from Malawi at a cost of K7.8 million in foreign currency, and 50,000 metric tons from Zimbabwe at a cost of K19.8 million.[81]

Nyirenda had announced in August 1985 that Namboard had ordered 40,000 metric tons of maize from Malawi and 50,000 metric tons from Zimbabwe in expectation of shortfalls in the current harvest. Even at the previous season's prices—which were likely to be exceeded—these planned imports would represent a sum above K30 million in foreign exchange. Moreover, every bag of maize imported from neighboring countries was estimated, in August 1985, to cost Zambia K48 in foreign currency, whereas the domestic price was only K28.32 a bag,[82] a differential of some 70 percent. The importation of maize was therefore a costly response to the problem of inadequate domestic production.

The state's manifest marketing inefficiencies have had many negative consequences for national food production: for example, the costly smuggling of commodities out of the country and the widespread practice of "retained production," through which farmers effectively boycott state marketing agencies and divert their produce elsewhere.[83] Some farmers with the capacity to choose have moved out of maize production in recent years and into more profitable alternatives such as wheat, soya beans, and cotton. With cotton, some have been spurred on by the fact that the responsible agency, the Lint Company of Zambia (LINTCO), has the unusual reputation of paying farmers on time. National marketed cotton output more than trebled during 1982–1984, when maize production was little more than static.[84]

In the case of wheat, the state raised the official producer price and introduced the floor-price system, which was particularly attractive to large-scale farmers with an organization like the Commercial Farmers Bureau to represent their interests.[85] Wheat production offered incentives to individual commercial farmers but was in a parlous condition nationally. The government's National Milling Company paid farmers K85 for a 90-kilogram bag of wheat in September 1985, whereas private millers were paying K120 a bag. Retained wheat production in 1984 was some 70 percent of Zambia's total output.[86] The country's domestic wheat production and marketing was totally inadequate, and compensatory imports by the state were comparably costly. The national output of wheat in 1985 was only about 12,500 metric tons, whereas domestic consumption stood at 150,000 metric tons. The National Milling Company announced in April that it required at least K4 million in foreign exchange monthly between then and September if it was to import 33,000 metric tons of wheat from South Africa.[87] Expensive imported wheat and critical shortages of flour and bread in the country were the results of inadequate domestic production.

The burden of the state's mismanagement of agriculture did not fall evenly on the whole country but fell most heavily of all on the small peasantry. Almost 90 percent of all rural households, small peasant farms were usually scattered in remote areas, over often impassable roads, and it was their maize that was most in danger of being uncollected by the agencies. As the farmers who were least likely to obtain any external financial, advisory, or other assistance, they were the ones most dependent on receiving early payment for their produce if they were to be able to replant the next season; for example, in 1980 about 80 percent of all rural households lacked sufficient income to meet even their minimum private consumption needs.[88] The spectacle of their crops being uncollected, marooned, and ultimately drenched with rain through Namboard's mismanagement was a strong disincentive to their efforts to try to maintain or increase production. Individually they were, of course, only small producers—of maize, groundnuts, beans, sorghum, etc.—but collectively they made a powerful contribution to national maize production.[89] Larger-scale farmers were most able to move out of maize when market prices suggested they should.[90] Sometimes large-scale farmers also retained the maize they produced, not for human consumption, but simply as feed for their cattle.[91] The state's neglect of the small peasantry had considerable significance for domestic marketed food production.

The range and kind of mistakes that occurred in 1985 inevitably brought greatest difficulties to peasants with small and middle-sized holdings. The better-placed areas suffered along with the others. Mkushi District is comparatively well served by road and railway, and the Central provincial cooperative usually handled a lot of produce from farmers there. But the district also experienced that year, according to the National Assembly's Committee on Agriculture, Lands, and Cooperatives, "serious problems" in securing inputs, and "a lot of produce" was left uncollected and consequently destroyed by rains. Farmers were paid late for their produce—despite Nyirenda's personal assurance to them to the contrary—and they were, near the end of the year, "demoralized." The committee pointed out that such problems were, however, "universal" to cooperatives in the country.[92] In mid-November 1985, farmers in Zambia were still owed K13.8 million by the agencies. Credit, thus particularly vital to the smaller peasant, was given too late and was also insufficient. The chairman of the Committee on Agriculture, Lazarous Cheelo, informed parliament in December, "Loans to farmers are not only inadequate but are in most cases given late. The interest rates are so high that farmers are now scared to obtain loans."[94] The haulage exercise was actually still continuing, with no end in sight, during the first weeks of the new year in Northern Province, with possible consequent disruption to many activities in the new farming season.[95] Despite such an extended harvest period, only about 7.2 million bags of maize had been collected by the end of January,[96] well below both the confident predictions and the national requirements that stood then at around 10 million bags.

The mismanagement of the 1985 harvest was worsened by the government's accumulated foreign indebtedness. But this accumulation of indebtedness occurred, not so much from a fall in Zambia's copper revenues, but from underlying structural weaknesses in the domestic economy brought about by the state's failure to invest in agriculture over very long periods. For example, during the five years of the Second National Development Plan, 1972–1976, the entire capital budget for the rural sector was only K152.5 million, which represented a mere 7.3 percent of total investment; it has been estimated that investment in agriculture was below 5.5 percent annually over the period.[97]

The very low priority accorded to agriculture by the state is shown in the heavy underutilization of the country's rural resources. Labor power was drained from the countryside as villagers were forced to seek a better chance of survival in the towns. Abundant land resources were left untapped. It has been estimated that some 42 million hectares of good land are available for agriculture in the country, of which only about 15 percent is presently cultivated.[98] The decline in copper revenues seriously affected Zambia, because the state had for too long invested far too heavily in this wasting, inherently doubtful asset. Extraneous climatic factors strongly favored the 1985 harvest, but climatic conditions were in any case only one factor influencing the outcome.[99]

Mismanagement of the 1985 harvest was little different from the state's mismanagement in agriculture generally. Consider, for example, the so-called Rural Reconstruction Programme, launched in 1975, supposedly to be completed in eight years at an estimated cost of K17.5 million a year. Five Rural Reconstruction Centres, the program's major units, were to be established by the government in each of Zambia's fifty districts. But, as the ILO carefully pointed out, the establishment of a total of 250 centers would involve, according to the government's plan, some 216,000 new farmers and between 1 million and 1.3 million ancillary personnel, which was equivalent to one-third of Zambia's total rural population in 1974.[100] Such an enormous concentration of personnel and other scarce resources would involve the severe dislocation of the whole agricultural economy, suggesting that the program was misplanned from the start. It was reported in 1985 that in fact only 55 centers—now called Rural Reconstruction Cooperatives—had been established after 1975, of which just 11 were said to have proved viable.[101] But even this assessment may have been optimistic, for General Chinkuli described the centers/cooperatives in July 1984 as a "terrible loss" and an "economic burden."[102]

Nitrogen Chemicals of Zambia (NCZ) is said to be the state's biggest single venture, after the establishment of Zambia Consolidated Copper Mines, since independence. When President Kaunda commissioned NCZ's plant at Kafue in September 1983, the company had received state investment totaling K350 million.[103] Its contribution to agriculture was expected to be important, because the country's fertilizer consumption had risen by some 58 percent from 1975 to 1982—without any comparable rise in production. In 1982 Zambia was importing around 212,000 metric tons of fertilizer, at a cost in foreign exchange of K74 million. The marketing and distribution of these imports, chiefly under the aegis of Namboard and the provincial cooperatives, resulted in a 30 percent annual loss of fertilizer in 1982, through wastage, theft, destruction, and smuggling.[104]

NCZ has, however, fallen far below its potential. It was experiencing serious financial problems as early as July 1985 and was failing to make payments to its suppliers. After less than two years of operations the company's Kafue plant was said to be in need of rehabilitation and restructuring. Reconstruction would cost more than K145 million, would involve further foreign borrowing, and 450 workers were to be declared redundant. The extent of the required reconstruction was indicative of NCZ's failures. New equipment, spare parts, and management contracts were necessary, and an Italian company would step in to operate the fertilizer plant for four years. According to NCZ's managing director, Ronald Fogg, all these costs were necessary if the company was to be saved from collapse: "The plant produces at only 25 percent of its capacity, but this is expected to rise to 85 percent after rehabilitation."[105] Improvements will not be completed until 1990.

Zambia has often been without sufficient agricultural machinery, and it is acutely so today. In 1982 the Ministry of Agriculture received 109 tractors and the same number of plows and planters, with appropriate spare parts, valued in total at K1.5 million, as a grant from Japan. The ministry did not, however, put this equipment directly to work, but instead transferred it to a Lusaka car dealer for sale on commission to the public, from which the ministry received K1.3 million. The auditor-general was unable to establish why this valuable equipment was not utilized by the government in its supposed food-production drives.[106] Near the end of 1985, following the state-engineered devaluation of the kwacha by more than 100 percent, tractors and other imported farm machinery were expected to rise enormously in price, making their future importation and sale prohibitive.[107]

The state's historic neglect and mismanagement of agriculture is hardly to be seriously gainsaid.[108] The country's copper-dominated and import-oriented economy, maintained by the independent government, has now accumulated heavy foreign indebtedness, which weakens the institutions of the state and limits or preempts resources essential to the management of agriculture.

• THE INCREASING RELIANCE ON LARGE-SCALE FARMING •

The sharp contrast between rhetoric and reality in the government's approach to agriculture, and the lack of any coherent program, does not disguise the underlying trends within Zambian agriculture. On the one hand, many failures and inefficiencies in agriculture, not least the 1985 harvest, bear most heavily on the small peasantry, the great bulk of the rural population. On the other hand, government actions, purposeful and even less purposeful,[109] seem directed toward the strengthening of the large-scale farming sector. Various pronouncements and decisions are explicable in terms of a growing commitment of the state to capitalized farmers and a concomitant abandonment of the rural poor.

Official producer prices have been increased more extensively in the mid-1980s and have been announced as important incentives to all farmers. But such changes by themselves chiefly represent higher potential incomes for large-scale farmers, for without extensive improvements in the whole marketing system—far-better roads, good credit facilities, available inputs, efficient marketing agencies, etc.—poor and middle-income peasants cannot begin to take advantage of higher producer prices.[110] The floor prices, introduced by the government for all crops except maize in May 1985, were, as already suggested, clearly most advantageous to organized commercial farmers. The state's fertilizer subsidy is similar in its effects. Despite stiff reductions in state subsidies, especially to consumers, in the mid-1980s, the fertilizer subsidy has been continued; by October 1985, it was costing the government K8 million per annum.[111] As a flat-rate subsidy, it offers the largest cost savings to the largest users, and the poorer peasant, who obtains little to no fertilizer, gains next to nothing.

The government's *Guidelines* for the formulation of the Fourth National Development Plan, published in March 1985, contains an unusually explicit statement on policy. In the section on agriculture, it says that "investment resources will be channelled to the following . . . programmes on a higher priority basis," the very first of which is "provision of irrigation facilities on a much larger scale . . . particularly in existing agricultural areas along the old line of rail . . ."; and the second is "acceleration of the pace of development of large scale farming and ranching in the high rainfall areas . . . ."[112] The state's increased commitment to highly capitalized farming seems to be intended.

There are a number of indications of the government's support for large-scale farming. The Mpongwe Development Company, Ndola Rural, is owned 51 percent by the state and the remainder by a consortium of international organizations and private companies. By late 1984, Mpongwe had become one of Zambia's largest single producers of wheat, soya beans, and tobacco, and when it received a loan totaling K15.4 million from a number of international bodies and the Zambian government, President Kaunda referred to the company as a shining example of cooperation between private enterprise and the state in the agricultural sector.[113] Joint large-scale agricultural projects between foreign investors and the state seem attractive to the government. The Nakambala Sugar Estate, comprising some 10,000 hectares at Mazabuka in Southern Province, was Mpongwe's forerunner in this field. It represented British interests and the Zambian government and was highly productive.[114] An executive of the ZIMCO (Zambian Industrial and Mining Corporation) conglomerate stated in December 1984 that the government wanted foreign investment in agriculture and that it "worked hard to ensure that conditions were favourable to the outside investor." Shortly afterwards, General Chinkuli called on private investors to enter into joint agricultural projects with the state.[115]

The state also seems to have a growing and clearer appreciation of the importance of private commercial farmers. President Kaunda told the Commercial Farmers Bureau in November 1985 that it was the government's wish that the number of commercial farmers should increase.[116] His own actions through the year have reinforced his views, especially as regards the position of large-scale capitalist farmers. A most interesting case first appeared in February, when members of parliament took note of a new and very large-scale commercial farm owned by a Briton, J. H. Williams, and a Kenyan, F. Mbulu. Their company was called A. G. Zambia Ltd., and they had acquired 20,000 hectares in Chief Chiyawa's area of Lusaka Rural, fronting on the Zambezi River. The two foreigners intended to invest K68 million in the farm, which would use irrigation to produce wheat, cotton, and other crops: Expected wheat production was 5,000 to 9,000 metric tons annually.[117] Many parliamentarians, however, opposed such a large allocation of good land to foreigners, and a private motion was passed in March, by fifty-five votes to forty-two, calling for a stop to the project. Amidst much furor, Prime Minister Mundia declared before and after the vote that the government did not intend to interfere with a legal contract.[118] Other leading ministers also participated; the speaker called Mundia's comments improper and unparliamentary;[119] but the last words were the president's. In April he briefly and firmly stated: "I want investment in Zambia so the Chiyawa issue is going ahead."[120]

As if to establish the continuity clearly, Kaunda reiterated his strong support for capitalist agriculture in July, when he visited the 2,800-hectare Zambezia Farm, owned by an American, Eric Winson, which utilized a supposedly new irrigation system. The president acknowledged that opposition to such large-scale farms existed, but that he hotly disagreed with it; critics of the farms owned by foreign investors were ordered to "shut up or be whipped." The government and UNIP appreciated the efforts of Eric Winson: "God has sent you to us," the president told him. Turning finally to the labor force at the farm, the president told the workers to be disciplined and work hard.[121]

The government's warm support for capitalist agriculture was strengthened through the personal involvement of members of the bureaucratic bourgeoisie in large-scale farming. Lusaka Province was particularly notable in this regard. It was estimated that large-scale commercial farms represented no less than 21 percent of all farms in the province,[122] a figure far above the national percentage. A report of the Lusaka provincial government also noted that there was a "relatively high proportion of commercial farmers" in the area and attributed this to the fact that 75 percent of the best land in the province was classified as state land,[123] as such disposable through grant or lease to individuals and groups by the commissioner of lands. Of further importance was the historic development of commercial agriculture, associated infrastructure, and the bureaucracy in the area. A large part of the state land in Lusaka Province is owned by the government and various parastatals, but of the state land that is held by private landowners, professional commercial farmers form the minority. Instead "politicians, businessmen and civil servants in Lusaka" constitute "a substantial share" of commercial farmers in the province.[124]

Other big capitalist farmers have received significant assistance and support from the state in the mid-1980s. A reportedly prominent Lusaka businessman, Abe Galaun, had purchased a 1,200-hectare farm in Chamba Valley, Lusaka Province, in November 1982 but had been unable to develop his property because of squatters who had occupied a portion of the land for many years. The stalemate was, however, terminated in May 1985, when the Lusaka Urban District governor, Michael Sata, told the 500 or so squatters that they had until June 30 to leave or be evicted by the police. Sata, who had been appointed governor in the previous month, blamed the district party leadership for past inaction: "Mr. Galaun is legally resident in Zambia and the party and its government gave him the farm. If the people respect the party, they should respect the title deed of Mr. Galaun."[125]

Members of the bureaucratic bourgeoisie appeared strongly to favor the wider involvement of their class in commercial agriculture. The 19th National Council of UNIP in December 1984 called for changes in the Leadership Code so that the amount of land that a party or other top official could own would be increased commensurate, they aptly said, with the emphasis on agriculture.[126] The code purportedly proscribed landownership of more than 10 hectares for a leader, but the mechanisms for the implementation of the limit were clearly ineffective.[127] Landownership by the bureaucratic bourgeoisie, in a society guided officially by humanism, remained controversial. Nevertheless, Enock Kavindele, a Lusaka businessman and district party official, suggested in late 1985 that government leaders should be allowed to go further into farming because, he argued, they had the means to boost agriculture.[128] These calls appeared not ineffective, and in October the chairman of the party's political and legal committee, Daniel Lisulo, announced that the code would soon be amended to allow leaders to go into large-scale farming.[129]

Despite the promptings of the Zambian bourgeoisie, bureaucratic and other, there is not now a coherent policy of state support for large-scale capitalist agriculture; possibly there would never be a truly coherent program. Many negative influences were affecting agriculture at the end of 1985, among them high bank interest rates (about 26 percent per annum), rapid inflation, and the escalating costs of imported farming inputs.[130] But there was nevertheless a fairly clear and increasing commitment to this sector from the state and the bureaucratic class.

Zambia's main international linkages encouraged its orientation to capitalist agriculture. The government expressed hostility to South African racism, but also imported heavily from that country—mining equipment, food and beverages, medical supplies, automobiles.[131] In 1982, the latest year for which statistics are available, South Africa was Zambia's number one supplier, ahead of Britain and the United States.[132] Zambia tended to turn to South Africa to obtain key commodities during more or less regularized crises, such as for wheat, diesel, grain bags, and gasoline during 1985. South African capitalists seemed ready to offer more. A group of South African businessmen, led by David Graham, visited Zambia in November 1985 in order to meet representatives of both the private sector and the government, and they declared that business in their country was keen to assist Zambia's agricultural development.[133]

Britain and the United States have already assisted agriculture in Zambia. Britain saw the Nakambala Sugar Estate as "highly successful"—evidence that British aid was "being put to good use."[134] The United States was a particularly important source of loan funds for the importation of food and agricultural commodities, such as diesel and grain bags purchased in the mid-1980s from South Africa.[135] The U.S. government saw President Kaunda as a conciliator in the strategically important and increasingly volatile southern African region. It praised such steps as the raising of official producer prices and, as former U.S. ambassador to Zambia Frank Wisner said in July 1985, tried "to encourage a more open and efficient system for marketing maize and fertilizer." U.S. loan funds to Zambia's agriculture were specifically designed to further this end.[136]

The impact of Zambia's linkages with the IMF, the World Bank, and other international lending agencies and institutions was similar but sharper. Much of the country's international indebtedness had been incurred to maintain the copper monoeconomy; in consequence, foreign-debt-servicing payments absorbed 47.6 percent of Zambia's export earnings in 1982 and 55 percent the following year.[137] In 1983 debt repayments to the IMF alone accounted for 44 percent of all the country's foreign-debt repayments and 26 percent of its export earnings, but by 1985 the IMF commanded 40 percent of export revenues.[138] Zambia's total annual foreign-debt repayments exceeded its export earnings.[139] The IMF, by early 1985, wanted many changes in the Zambian government's policies, and thanks to the borrowings of the state-supported copper economy, it was in a strong position to promote them. Proposals that directly affected agriculture included a much lower and flexible exchange rate, higher interest rates, increased official producer prices, and greater efficiency by parastatals.[140]

A more procapitalist agricultural strategy by the Zambian state was supported by important internal and external forces. Such a strategy would seem to entail an even greater neglect of the mass of the rural population. Dangers for the production of food could also result. Maize growing was done chiefly by the poorer and middle-level peasantry; if many of these farmers were further disadvantaged, maize output might remain below consumption levels. Large-scale commercial farmers were less committed to maize than were smaller peasants and were far more free to select the crop that promised the best return at the particular time. The government's expectation appeared to be that increased wheat production would result. But Zambia's wheat output in the mid-1980s was far below national consumption levels. The gap seemed unlikely to be bridged in the near future, and increased output might still have to contend with rising urban levels of bread consumption.

The state's new agricultural orientation promised deepening poverty for the peasantry and uncertainties for domestic food production. On the other hand, whether agricultural exports would eventually result, and costly food imports cease, was at best problematic—it was not a question of the efficiency of large-scale farmers in Zambia, but of the smallness of their total number both in absolute terms and relative to the poor and middle-level peasantries. This orientation offered few potentialities for national development. The strengthening of the weak Zambian state through improved agricultural productivity could not be readily expected. Instead, the established and debilitating interlinkage between weak state and backward peasant agriculture would almost certainly continue unbroken.[141]

• NOTES •

This chapter is adapted from the author's paper, "Systemic Agricultural Mismanagement: The 1985 'Bumper' Harvest in Zambia," *Journal of Modern African Studies* 24, no. 2 (June 1986).

1. *Zambia Daily Mail*, February 15, 1985, and *Times of Zambia*, May 14, 1985.

2. Perhaps the provincial cooperative marketing unions could be best described as quasi-parastatal. They are in large part funded by the state and work in close collaboration with it on both the input and output side of marketing. Zambian peasant farmers seem to see cooperatives as agents of the state. The minister of state for agriculture, Justin Mukando, told a seminar on cooperatives in late 1982 that peasants tended to look at cooperative unions and the Zambia Cooperative Federation as organizations created by the government to serve its interests. He said that since the 1950s the cooperative movement had operated as an instrument for the implementation of government policies. *Zambia Daily Mail*, December 18, 1982.

3. Zambia, Central Statistics Office, *Monthly Digest of Statistics* 21, nos. 4-5 (Lusaka, April-May 1985), Table 8, p. 6.

4. Zambia, Ministry of Agriculture, Planning Division Study No. 4, *Nationwide Study of Zambia's Storage Requirements for Both Produce and Inputs* (Lusaka: Ministry of Agriculture, March 1984), Summary and Introduction. (Hereafter *Zambia's Storage Requirements*.)

5. *Times of Zambia*, July 6, 1984, *and Zambia Daily Mail*, July 30, 1982.

6. *Economist*, February 11, 1984, pp. 74 and 76.

7. *Zambia Daily Mail*, October 31, 1984.

8. *Times of Zambia*, November 20, 1984.

9. The general manager had received a letter from President Kaunda sending him on indefinite paid leave with no reasons given. *Zambia Daily Mail*, December 14, 1984.

10. Zambia, *Budget Address* (Lusaka: Government Printer, January 1985), p. 8.

11. The minister's reference to "cooperatives as in the past acting only as agents of Namboard" was unhelpful, as Namboard had supposedly been in a process, after 1981, of handing over part of its operations as the distributor of inputs and purchaser of produce to the provincial cooperatives. The overall marketing responsibility had been Namboard's, but after 1981 the intraprovincial responsibility, it was said, was that of the cooperatives, whereas the interprovincial trade remained with Namboard (*Zambia's Storage Requirements*, p. 5).

12. *Zambia Daily Mail*, February 6, 1985. The five ministries were Finance, Cooperatives, Agriculture, Works and Supply, and Commerce and Industry.

13. *Times of Zambia*, February 25, 1985.

14. Clemens Bokosi, "Co-ops Our Only Survival," *Zambia Daily Mail*, January 3, 1983.

15. *Zambia Daily Mail*, December 14, 1984, and *Times of Zambia*, December 12, 1984.

16. *Times of Zambia*, November 26, 1982. The period during which the loss was accumulated was not specified.

17. Details of the misappropriations from all nine cooperatives were contained in the report in parliament. *Zambia Daily Mail*, March 20, 1985.

18. *Zambia Daily Mail*, March 26, 1985.

19. *Times of Zambia*, May 13, 1985.

20. *Times of Zambia*, May 29, 1985.

21. *Times of Zambia*, February 11, 1985.

22. *Zambia Daily Mail* and *Times of Zambia*, February 15, 1985.

23. He was reported as speaking over the weekend of February 2–3 at a primary,

multipurpose cooperative in Western Province. *Zambia Daily Mail,* February 5, 1985.

24. Editorials of January 30 and May 23, 1985, and report, May 23, 1985, in *Times of Zambia.* Namboard is one of the oldest state agencies in Zambia, having been established in 1969 by the merger of two previous marketing parastatals.

25. *Zambia Daily Mail,* January 30, 1985.

26. *Times of Zambia,* February 8, 1985.

27. *Zambia Daily Mail,* March 4, 1985.

28. Editorial, *Zambia Daily Mail,* April 29, 1985.

29. *Times of Zambia,* April 19, 1985.

30. His predecessor, Nalumino Mundia, was to be deployed in the foreign service, said President Kaunda. *Zambia Daily Mail,* April 25, 1985.

31. It was on this occasion in Kabwe that the prime minister predicted a harvest of 10 million bags of maize. *Times of Zambia,* May 14, 1985.

32. *Times of Zambia,* April 20, 1985.

33. *Times of Zambia,* May 31, 1985.

34. Editorial, *Times of Zambia,* May 14, 1985.

35. Following the removal of Chabwere as general manager in December 1984, Stephen Kani had taken over in an acting capacity. However, Chabwere was not finally dismissed by President Kaunda, for "alleged misconduct and negligence," until November 1985. *Zambia Daily Mail,* May 21 and November 12, 1985.

36. *Zambia Daily Mail,* May 28, 1985.

37. *Zambia Daily Mail,* June 4, 1985.

38. *Times of Zambia,* April 4, 1985.

39. *Times of Zambia,* April 22, 1985.

40. *Times of Zambia,* April 29, 1985.

41. *Zambia Daily Mail,* March 4, 1985.

42. Reference to the bureau's monthly journal, *Productive Farmer,* in *Zambia Daily Mail,* July 16, 1985.

43. *Times of Zambia,* May 31, 1985.

44. *Zambia Daily Mail,* June 12, 1985.

45. *Zambia Daily Mail,* July 3, 1985.

46. *Zambia Daily Mail,* July 11, 1985.

47. *Times of Zambia,* July 26, 1985.

48. *Zambia Daily Mail,* July 31, 1985.

49. This fuel was being imported despite the belief that a better arrangement would have been to resell the fuel in Zimbabwe and use the proceeds for the purchase in that country of spare parts for Zambian truckers. *Zambia Daily Mail,* August 21, 1985.

50. *Times of Zambia,* August 14, and *Zambia Daily Mail,* August 21, 1985.

51. *Zambia Daily Mail,* September 29, 1985.

52. *Times of Zambia,* October 30, 1985.

53. Kamanga declared on April 14 in Lusaka that part of the consignment from Bangladesh had already arrived and that Namboard and the cooperatives were all set to start hauling maize next month. *Zambia Daily Mail,* April 10 and 15, 1985. The estimate of 13 million bags required for all crops nationally in 1985 was Kamanga's.

54. The chairman of Central provincial cooperative, Lodge Kambelo, pointed out that the bags from Bangladesh would at best not arrive until June, when the harvest was under way: "Someone somewhere in Zambia is not doing his work properly," he declared, "because the harvesting period of all crops . . . is known even to blind persons. . . ." *Zambia Daily Mail,* April 23, 1985.

55. *Zambia Daily Mail,* June 6, 1985.

56. *Zambia Daily Mail,* June 27, 1985.

57. Ibid.

58. *Zambia Daily Mail*, July 16, 1985.

59. *Zambia Daily Mail*, September 5, 1985. The province required more than 2.5 million bags.

60. *Zambia Daily Mail*, August 16, 1985.

61. *Times of Zambia*, July 8, 1985.

62. *Zambia Daily Mail*, July 11, 1985.

63. *Zambia Daily Mail*, July 16, 1985.

64. Namboard placed advertisements in the press on that date. Implementing the move across the country was slower still.

65. Mkushi district governor stated that grain bags remained unsold because of the high price. *Zambia Daily Mail*, July 20, 1985.

66. *Zambia Daily Mail*, July 20, 1985.

67. *Times of Zambia*, July 26, 1985.

68. *Times of Zambia*, July 27, 1985.

69. *Zambia Daily Mail*, August 28, 1985.

70. Ibid.

71. Nyirenda was briefing Lusaka Province central committee member Bautis Kapulu when the latter called on him at Namboard headquarters. Nyirenda noted that the consignment of grain bags that had been received with financial assistance from the United States and West Germany were imported from South Africa. *Zambia Daily Mail*, September 6, 1985.

72. *Zambia Daily Mail*, September 9, 1985. The committee under the prime minister may have been the "ministerial task force" announced in early February and apparently rather inactive or at least ineffective since then.

73. *Times of Zambia*, September 18, 1985.

74. *Times of Zambia*, October 8, 1985.

75. *Zambia Daily Mail*, October 11, 1985.

76. *Times of Zambia*, October 12, 1985.

77. *Zambia Daily Mail*, November 1, 1985.

78. *Zambia Daily Mail*, October 29, 1985.

79. *Zambia Daily Mail*, November 1, 1985. The Northern provincial political secretary, Wilson Chakulya, said in Kasama on November 6 that thousands of bags of maize were still lying exposed at rural depots awaiting collection. The situation with regard to transport and sometimes "impassable roads" was "disparate." Farmers in the area, he said, had marketed only 542,000 bags of maize against a projected figure of 800,000, and many were still awaiting payment for their produce. *Times of Zambia*, November 7, 1985.

80. *Zambia Daily Mail*, August 28, 1985.

81. Figures given by a government spokesman, *Zambia Daily Mail*, September 13, 1985.

82. Figure given by a spokesman at the British High Commission, Lusaka, who was highlighting the value of a British loan to Zambia for purchase of tarpaulins. *Times of Zambia*, August 15, 1985. Zambia, Ministry of Agriculture, *Quarterly Agricultural Statistics Bulletin* (July-September 1985) (hereafter *Agricultural Statistics Bulletin*), Table F11.0 ("Minimum Producer Prices").

83. Thus, marketed maize in Central Province in 1984 represented about 50 percent of the province's total maize output, and in Eastern Province "retained" maize production was substantially greater. Maize not marketed through the official agencies represented in good part, of course, the home consumption of the small and middle-level peasantries. But the large quantities of retained maize, and of groundnuts and wheat, also constituted a vote of no confidence by farmers in the state's monopolistic buying agencies. *Agricultural Statistics Bulletin*, p. 15, Table C1.0, and *Zambia's Storage*

Requirements, p. 26. In addition, according to figures presented by the UNIP central committee member for Southern Province, Mungoni Liso, for his region in 1984, farmers produced 20,400 (90 kilograms) bags of wheat, but sold only 1,117 bags to the provincial cooperative. *Zambia Daily Mail*, December 28, 1984.

84. *Zambia Daily Mail*, September 5, 1985, and *Agricultural Statistics Bulletin*, Tables C1.0 and 1.5.

85. The new system represented minimum official prices, permitted farmers to negotiate for higher prices, and included all controlled agriculture products except maize. Announcement by General Chinkuki, *Times of Zambia*, May 21, 1985. The system effectively discriminated against small peasant maize growers and advantaged large and organized farmers in negotiations for higher prices.

86. *Zambia Daily Mail*, September 12, 1985, and *Agricultural Statistics Bulletin*, Table C1.5.

87. *Times of Zambia*, April 30 and August 12, 1985.

88. ILO, *Basic Needs in an Economy Under Pressure* (Addis Ababa: International Labour Office, Jobs and Skills Program for Africa, 1981), p. 47.

89. The class of the small, or poor, peasantry embraces all those officially classified as "subsistence" farmers and overlaps with those officially termed as "emergent" farmers. "Subsistence" farmers are defined by the government as those who market half or less of their output. These two categories of farmers together produced, in the early 1980s, around 60 percent of all marketed maize.

90. The two crops were not entirely the same in that some middle-level and perhaps small peasants have engaged in cotton production in Southern Province.

91. *Times of Zambia* and *Zambia Daily Mail*, August 30, 1985.

92. Zambia, *Report of the Committee on Agriculture, Lands and Cooperatives*, for the Second Session of the Fifth National Assembly (Lusaka: Government Printer, 1985), pp. 18–19.

93. *Times of Zambia*, November 13, 1985.

94. *Times of Zambia*, December 5, 1985.

95. The Northern political secretary, Chakulya, stated on January 7 that he could not say when the buying season would end. *Times of Zambia*, January 8, 1986.

96. *Zambia Daily Mail*, January 28, 1986.

97. ILO, *Narrowing the Gaps: Planning for Basic Needs and Productive Employment in Zambia* (Addis Ababa: International Labour Office, Jobs and Skills Program for Africa, 1977), p. 79; and Robert Klepper, "Zambian Agricultural Structure and Performance," in Ben Turok, ed., *Development in Zambia* (London: Zed, 1979), p. 147.

98. *Zambia's Storage Requirements*, p. 1.

99. Ibid., p. 26.

100. ILO, *Narrowing the Gaps*, pp. 339–341.

101. *Zambia Daily Mail*, June 12, 1985.

102. *Times of Zambia*, July 12, 1984.

103. *Times of Zambia*, September 29, 1983.

104. *Zambia Daily Mail*, July 8, 1985.

105. *Zambia Daily Mail*, July 6 and 20, and August 30, 1985.

106. Zambia, *Report of the Auditor-General*, for the financial year ended December 1983 (Lusaka: Government Printer, 1984), p. 19.

107. *Times of Zambia*, November 1, 1985.

108. For example, the moderate judgment of the ILO says that in contrast to the state's declarations about the need to transform the rural sector, "one is struck by a neglect of agriculture, by the low priority given to rural development in national planning, by the low priority . . . in the allocation of economic resources and skilled

manpower, and overall, by the absence of a clear and coherent framework for rural development. . . ." *Narrowing the Gaps*, pp. 78–79.

109. The selling of the Japanese farming machinery may, of course, have placed this equipment in the hands of individual commercial farmers who were able to obtain good and quick advantages from their acquisitions.

110. The ILO has useful comment on earlier producer prices in *Basic Needs in an Economy*, p. 62.

111. *Zambia Daily Mail*, October 21, 1985. Additional incentives with similar effects are a foreign-exchange allocation for large producers and allowances on the depreciation of farm machinery.

112. Zambia, Office of the President, National Commission for Development Planning, *Guidelines* (Lusaka: Government Printer, March 1985), pp. 7–8.

113. *Zambia Daily Mail* and the *Times of Zambia*, October 9, 1984.

114. A recent yield was 13.9 metric tons of sugar per hectare. *Times of Zambia*, September 20, 1984.

115. *Zambia Daily Mail*, December 10, 1984; *Sunday Times*, March 24, 1985. The Zambia Industrial and Mining Corporation is the country's largest state conglomerate.

116. *Times of Zambia*, November 2, 1985.

117. *Times of Zambia*, February 13, 1985; *Zambia Daily Mail*, March 14, 1985.

118. *Zambia Daily Mail*, March 9 and 14, 1985; *Times of Zambia*, March 14 and 15, 1985.

119. *Zambia Daily Mail*, March 28, 1985.

120. *Times of Zambia*, April 25, 1985. The name "Chiyawa" is also rendered as "Chiawa."

121. *Zambia Daily Mail*, July 25, 1985.

122. *Zambia's Storage Requirements*, p. 73. Lusaka Province was until 1980 a part of Central Province.

123. Zambia, Provincial Planning Unit Lusaka Province, *A Blueprint for Agricultural Development in Lusaka Province* (Lusaka: Government Printer, November 1984), p. 11. The full extent of state land was about 6.5 percent of Zambia's total area.

124. Ibid.

125. *Zambia Daily Mail*, December 14, 1984, and April 10, 1985. Galaun had bought the farm for K340,000. *Times of Zambia*, April 30, 1985.

126. *Zambia Daily Mail*, December 18, 1985.

127. Manifestly so with regard to the landownership of many top government figures; and also in the admission of the member of the central committee for Lusaka Province, *Times of Zambia*, November 1, 1985.

128. *Zambia Daily Mail*, October 12, 1985. Kavindele is managing director of Woodgate Holdings, which is, among other things, an automobile importer and distributor.

129. *Zambia Daily Mail*, October 12, 1985.

130. Rising interest rates and inflation were rapidly negating the higher official producer prices.

131. Official statistics are scarce in this area, but the automobiles that are imported are often luxury ones for the use of leading members of the parastatals and ministries.

132. Zambia, Central Statistics Office, *Monthly Digest of Statistics* 21, nos. 4–5 (Lusaka, April-May 1985), Table 23, p. 22.

133. *Zambia Daily Mail*, November 22, 1985.

134. Words of the Foreign and Commonwealth Office Minister of State, Malcolm Rifkind, who added that cooperation between the two countries was "very good" and Zambia would "continue to be an important beneficiary of British aid." *Times of Zambia*, September 20, 1984.

135. By July 1985, U.S. food aid to Zambia exceeded K264 million in value. *Times of Zambia*, July 10, 1985.

136. Wisner was a State Department official and former ambassador to Zambia and was speaking at a conference on the Zambian economy in New York. *Zambia Daily Mail*, July 6 and November 1, 1985.

137. Allast Mwanza, "Export Instability and the Public Debt: The Case of Zambia" (University of Zambia [UNZA], Humanities and Social Studies Staff Seminar, January 3, 1985, mimeo.), p. 11. The mining industry, he said, was "the heavy borrower and also the guarantor of Zambia's borrowing" (p. 8).

138. *Times of Zambia*, July 22, 1985, and *Economist*, June 8, 1985.

139. J. Wulf, "Policy Targets of the IMF Package" (UNZA, Economics Department, Staff Seminar, February 6, 1985, mimeo.).

140. Ibid., p. 1.

141. The interrelationship between weak state and backward agriculture, and the significance of the government's failure to develop the potentialities of the smaller peasantries, are examined in Kenneth Good, "The Reproduction of Weakness in the State and Agriculture: The Zambian Experience," *African Affairs* 85, no. 339 (April 1986): 239–265.

·PART 3·
Coping with Crisis

·9·

Crisis and State Reform

MICHAEL FORD
FRANK HOLMQUIST

In popular parlance referring to the Third World, the term "food crisis" denotes life-threatening shortages of food supplies, whereas in referring to North America the same term is used to indicate recurring food surpluses causing lower crop prices, sharply reduced returns to farmers, and foreclosures when farmers are unable to repay their debts. In North America advanced technology, skilled agricultural workers, and plentiful capital inputs are said to lead to overproduction. In the Third World, and especially Africa, underproduction and a resulting scarcity of food is presumed related to a lack of technology and skilled manpower, poor management, and insufficient agricultural capital.

These pictures of two different worlds described by a single label have in common a focus on production—too much in one case and far too little in the other. For many decades the most important policy response to the dual nature of the food crisis has prescribed that food producers in North America should be paid not to produce, whereas in the Third World production should be expanded. But both crises have only grown worse. The world is literally awash in grain, while the absolute number of the world's malnourished continues to rise.[1]

Casting the food crisis as a problem of production gets at only part of the difficulty, and not even the most important part. There are persistent observations that even in the midst of the worst famines, past and present, there has been adequate food within affected nations to meet the needs of all.[2] And hunger remains a massive problem even in those Third World states that manage to produce a surplus of grain for export.[3] Thus, in Africa and the rest of the Third World, the more serious crisis of differential access to power and food underlies the presumed crisis of insufficient production. The need to focus upon access to power and food is clearly evident when we consider hunger in the United States in the context of today's crisis of overproduction. There is now ample documentation of the return of hunger despite the fact that it was all but eliminated through several income and food-maintenance policies in the 1970s. It is clear that hunger in the United States is not caused by food scarcity. Instead, hunger, once removed by politics, was subsequently revived by

213

politics. This process resulted from changing access to state power. In the late 1970s and early 1980s, a new coalition of ruling forces poked innumerable holes in the food safety net until, by the mid-1980s, according to the only comprehensive study of hunger in the United States, about 20 million people suffered from chronic hunger.[4]

Explanations of hunger amidst record food production in both the United States and the Third World demonstrate that hunger is above all a product of poverty and associated powerlessness.[5] We gain an important perspective on Africa's crisis by recognizing that in the United States poverty and hunger can exist alongside an abundance of food. There is a widespread, if often unconscious, belief that Africa's food problem is the product of rampant irrationality—of a continent and a people run amok. The horrifying pictures and instant analyses emerging from the recent Ethiopian disasters reinforce the belief that uniquely poor policy, mismanagement, and simple venality have caused the crisis. Without ignoring African responsibilities for the crisis, it is necessary to guard against the old racist assumption that Africa is simply incapable of doing anything right. The reality is that food crises have nothing to do with defects of character or irrationality and a lot to do with who has power and who does not. In other words, food crises are about state-society relationships, poverty, and unequal access to state power in Africa, the United States, and the rest of the world.

Although we emphasize the state-society relationship and access to power and food, we acknowledge that matters of production are crucial. Naomi Chazan and Timothy Shaw and several of the other authors rightly point out in this book that supplies of food in Africa are sometimes very limited and that, at those times, it is the poor whose access to food is most at risk. Also, because the majority of Africans are smallholders, rising peasant agricultural productivity means improved food and income security for the majority, whereas greater supplies of food on the market are likely to mean lower prices to the poor, including many peasants, who must purchase food. Nonetheless, to help right a very lopsided imbalance in the literature on Africa's food crisis, our focus is on access—access to power, because state policy is a key factor structuring the environments of production and distribution, and access to food, because food availability, even abundance, is no guarantee that all members of society will be able to satisfy even a minimal level of nutritional needs.

Despite a decade of literature on the food crisis in Africa, little is known about the ways different sectors of African society respond to the crisis. This book addresses this deficiency. In this concluding chapter, we will look at the essays in broad comparative terms in relation to what we believe is a first principle in any discussion of food crises—namely, the relationship between state and society, which, in both the short and long run, greatly influences access to food. We will discuss four major postindependence trends in the state-society relationship. Then we will review the essays with an eye to whether and how the coping strategies of international, national, and local popular forces alter political trends and affect policies biasing access to power. Finally, we will close with a critical assessment of proposals for reform of the African state.

· THE POSTINDEPENDENCE STATE-SOCIETY RELATIONSHIP ·

Four crucial developments in postindependence African politics explain the growing distance between states and their societies—a root cause of the African food crisis. These are: the unraveling of nationalist political coalitions; departicipation, or a distancing of the state from its population; coups d'état; and civil strife. The first two are elements of the process that created the gulf between state and society in Africa, whereas coups d'état and civil strife are a product of that separation. When channels of participation and conflict resolution were blocked, there remained no legitimate outlets for political discontent. Groups wishing to press their claims on the state or protest policy often saw coups or political violence as the only options available.

Soon after independence, nationalist coalitions began to fall apart. In retrospect, it is easy to see that nationalist parties were fragile to begin with. Nationalism required an uneasy merger of class, ethnic, and other interests in the pursuit of independence. Consequently, the discussion of crucial issues such as the character of the economy and the structure of the state was postponed. After assuming power, African governments had to allocate resources and respond to popular expectations, which meant rewarding some people and withholding privileges and benefits from others. Tensions and hostilities multiplied as spokespersons for different interests were arrayed against each other, and competing ideologies of development were voiced amid a flowering of popular and intellectual media. As deep differences emerged, old constellations of interests were reinvigorated and the national consensus with its institutional expressions were put in jeopardy.

A second feature of African postindependence political life was departicipation. Unraveling nationalist coalitions did not necessitate state suppression of democratic practice. But most African leaders chose not to abide by democratic rules because they had so much to lose and because they could get away with this as a result of generally weak political organization in civil society.Elite status was often a by-product of political access and the use of the state for private purposes; the elite decided that they could dominate society only by virtual permanent control of the state. Thus, regimes did not give political ground to the majority. Instead, they protected themselves by gradually undermining many popular democratic rights won in the struggle for independence.

Departicipation involved an erosion of many autonomous, mass-based, if not mass-led, institutions. Most political parties became more centralized, more bureaucratized, and generally less responsive to declining memberships. Some became virtual arms of the state, and some tended to atrophy and all but disappear only to reemerge on symbolic and candidate-nominating occasions. Legislatures that were hastily set up in the waning days of colonial rule were arenas of lively debate, if not effective policymaking authority. But as years passed, they gradually lost that vitality as the fragile democratic fabric began to loosen. There was a steady erosion of civil liberties indicated by the growing use of preventive detention laws to silence and punish opposition spokespersons. Elections became irregular and were sometimes abolished altogether. When they were held, they were rarely competitive between parties, nor was there competition for the top spot. Local government structures weakened as central government ministries usurped their financial bases citing corruption and inefficiencies.

Trade unions were brought under state umbrellas, and thus a good deal of their political autonomy and clout was lost. Marketing cooperatives were also subject to increasing state regulation and control in the name of protecting members from occasionally inefficient and corrupt leaders. But member vigilance declined, rather than grew, because external controls were so pervasive. More or less direct state control and censorship of the press was used to suppress dissent, and as a result the ideological spectrum of debate was forcibly narrowed. The vibrant development debate that only began after independence was all but ended. It was argued that such debate, along with opposition parties and other popularly based structures, stood in the way of national unity and undermined the singularity of purpose required for development. Departicipation, however, probably fostered greater disunity by repressing grievances rather than allowing them to be voiced and resolved, or contained. In summary, then, after a brief political opening around the time of independence, departicipation severely narrowed avenues of access to the state.

A third fact of African political life in most, if not all, states is the coup d'état.[6] There are several reasons for coups d'état. At the most general level, it appears that they are a natural by-product of the growing autonomy and illegitimacy of civilian regimes. Departicipation put the distance between the state and much of its population in sharp relief. As state corruption, social inequalities, and insecurity spread, there was growing popular dissatisfaction, which the military acted upon, usually to the momentary cheers of the population. These cheers should not be taken as popular approval of military rule—coups simply appeared to be the only way to remove unpopular regimes. Chazan and Shaw argue that as food insecurity became more severe in the early 1980s, there were a correspondingly greater number of coup attempts. Class and ethnic tensions pervaded the independent state, and weak civilian governments depended upon the military to keep them in power because they had little or no popular support. Consequently, the military became partisans in the wider struggle. Colonels and generals soon awoke to the realization that if they were the essential props of regimes, they could replace them if they chose.

Were military regimes more successful than the regimes they replaced? Not noticeably. The anticorruption mission of many coups sometimes changed the locus but rarely the fact of corruption. There is also no evidence that military rule has effectively dealt with class and ethnic divisions. With few exceptions, the military has not challenged dominant class forces. Because the military also lacked popular roots and was unable to generate long-term legitimacy for itself, there was an inevitable tendency to rule through subordinate powers that be. No obvious stimulus to the economy resulted from military rule. In fact, there has been a net drain of resources, because the military tends to expand its establishment when it controls the state. In the long run, this expansion is a threat to the revival of democratic practices, whereas in the short run, military regimes tend to be more coercive and abusive of the population. In short, military regimes frequently worsen the character of the state-society relationship.

Recently, there have been a few populist coups d'état, and they may become more frequent in the future. Good examples may be the two coups of Jerry Rawlings in Ghana. Rawlings came to power on a sentiment to remove corrupt politicians, enhance the democratic process, and revive a declining economy, as well as encourage a more equitable distribution of income. In many predominantly agrarian societies, land reform policies that redistribute agricultural holdings would be a sure way for new regimes to gain legitimacy. The problem with this form of "revolution from above" in Africa is that unlike land reform revolutions elsewhere—those of Attaturk in Turkey, 1921; Nasser in Egypt, 1952; the colonels in Peru, 1968; and with the possible exceptions in Sub-Saharan Africa of Zanzibar in 1964 and Ethiopia in 1975—most African regimes cannot find instant popular roots through land reform. There are places like Kenya and Zimbabwe where land reform has enormous popular appeal. But in most cases land is not that unequally held or that scarce, although rapid population growth and a closing of the land frontier will soon change that situation. But for the moment there is little that populist regimes can quickly redistribute in order to gain mass support. Jon Kraus documents for Ghana the brief, impossible to sustain consumer subsidies introduced by successive regimes. The case of Ghana also illustrates that despite a good deal of institutional and ideological experimentation, the "revolutions from above" have remained centralized affairs of rival elites and have not substantially broadened access to power.[7]

A fourth political reality for some states is severe civil strife and sometimes actual warfare. There are various causes of this phenomena, ranging from internal guerilla challenges to the central government, such as the Southern Sudanese movement and Yoweri Museveni's takeover in Uganda; to secession attempts, including that of Biafra in 1967 and the more than twenty-year effort of Eritrea to secede from Ethiopia; and, finally, to the challenges sponsored or aided by South Africa to the regimes of Angola and Mozambique and other neighbors. The agricultural and general economic destruction from such conflict is extraordinarily high. Also, over one-half of the world's refugees are in Africa, although the continent contains only 10 percent of the world's population. Large refugee populations tend to breed political tensions between states and great friction with host populations as well.. The cost of maintaining refugees is an enormous burden upon states, despite international aid and relief efforts. Meanwhile, the human misery is incalculable.

The cumulative effect of the first two, let alone all four, facts of postindependence African political life, coupled with well-documented economic stagnation or decline, has been to rupture the relationship between states and societies; to restrict radically access to power; and sometimes, as Chazan and Shaw point out, to bias severely short-run, as well as long-run, access to food. In addition, the relationship between economic decline and these political factors created two debilitating processes that make almost any creative and effective response to the general economic crisis very difficult. In the first place, as the case of Zaire illustrates most graphically, state fiscal crises and political uncertainties led to a partial decay of state personnel infrastructure. The general crisis brought more lax personnel management and a decline of bureaucratic morale, especially when salaries were occasionally delayed or frozen, material support grew scarce, and absenteeism and corruption increased. As Chazan and Shaw indicate, the combination of economic deterioration and political upheaval may also spur migration, with a resulting loss of technical personnel. The end result of this process is that vastly expanded postindependence bureaucracies may experience declining productivity at a time when the situation calls for enhanced efficiency and effectiveness.

Second, fiscal crisis and political uncertainties also led to a partial decay of physical infrastructure, as in the cases of Ghana, Tanzania, Zaire, and Zambia. Limited investment in rural infrastructure and lack of spare parts, equipment, and skills brought the decay of some roads, railroads, ports, electrical facilities, telephones, etc. This, of course, raised hidden costs to users and hurt the poor the most. It also directly interfered with the marketing of agricultural products and the general servicing of the agricultural sector.

This backdrop of political economy crisis sets the stage for discussion of the coping strategies of actors in the international arena, the state, and at the local level. We will pay particular attention to the question of whether the rift between states and societies is being repaired or exacerbated. Because this relationship has been at the center of the crisis, it will also be a principal feature of successful reform.

· COPING: INTERNATIONAL ACTORS ·

Sub-Saharan Africa has been described as increasingly dependent because of the political and economic developments of the 1970s and 1980s. Yet it could also be argued that Africa has grown more self-reliant in that same period. This apparent contradiction is characteristic of the general social position of the needy. The poor are subject to the dictates of institutional almsgivers—dependency is a reflection of a lack of resources. But when aid is insufficient or not forthcoming, then self-reliance results because there is no alternative. The late 1970s brought bad news from the international arena: world recession, soft markets for Africa's products, inflation and higher costs for manufactured goods from the West, and the second oil shock of 1979. The 1980s brought more bad news: International private capital was less interested in Africa because of political uncertainties and economic stagnation; aid flows declined; and there is no prospect for substantial relief from debts that quickly mounted in the late 1970s and early 1980s. Amidst Africa's debt difficulties and the problem of debt recovery for major world banks, loan capital is not readily available to Africa as it was in the 1970s. The result is a self-reliance less chosen by African states than foisted upon them. But the self-reliance has a deeply dependent character to it, because, as Carol Lancaster points out, Africa's debt and the resultant donor-recipient "policy dialogues" allow considerable international agency leverage across a broad range of policy, in the form of IMF policy mandates and donor criteria for aid.

The international aid donor community has coped with the food crisis with the clearest objectives and the most detailed agenda, which has, in turn, helped maximize its political leverage. The major document guiding donor community policy is the World Bank's *Accelerated Development in Sub-Saharan Africa: An Agenda for Action* (1981), otherwise known as the Berg Report after its principal author, Elliot Berg. The Berg Report has had an extraordinary impact, probably more than any other single piece of writing about the continent. This report, and the OAU's *Lagos Plan of Action for the Economic Development of Africa 1980–2000* (1980), has spawned a remarkably well drawn economic debate about Africa's future development.[8] The ultimate impact of donor policy direction upon issues of poverty and access to food is unclear partly because the effect will be so far-reaching and because state situations and responses are so diverse. Lancaster carefully reviews the debate surrounding aid and economic reform, and we will not repeat that discussion here. Instead we wish to register two anxieties.

First, in most of the literature, smallholder production in preferred, and we agree with that sentiment. But the economic crisis has also given rise to a sense of emergency and an ethos of production first, which has provided a mistaken rationale for betting on large producers. A World Bank official for the Eastern Africa Projects Division points out that although the World Bank's focus is on smallholders, it is not dogmatic about it:

> There is a certain trade-off between catering to the very poor farmer who feeds his own family and has only a marginal surplus and assisting somewhat larger farmers with a more noticeable effect on surplus production. We are open to

assisting larger farmers, which does not mean turning Africa over to Unilever and similar multinationals; it does mean aid, for example, to a farmer with [20 hectares] because he is likely to be innovative, willing to bear risk, and produce quick results—a marketable surplus—and that is what we are after in this period.[9]

With this classic rationale for betting on the strong, the primary intent may easily become production first. Needless to say, a farm of 20 hectares is very large in most African contexts. And short-term biases toward large producers are likely to prove very difficult, if not impossible, to reverse through normal administrative policy. In other words, there is usually a long-term political result of a bet-on-the-strong policy that is not likely to be compatible with generating broad-based access to power or food.

Second, the highly influential international donor community is coping with Africa's food crisis by ignoring the political breach between states and their societies. One cannot help but be struck by the absence of the 1970s language of providing "basic needs" or of popular "participation" in current international aid dialogue. Although both terms were admittedly honored more in the breach than in practice, they were useful language tools with leverage for personnel interested in poverty alleviation. The current language for state reform basically refers to an in-house reform of the administration. There is little reference to structures of accountability or participation, let alone real structures of democracy. The reforms are highly economistic, and, where they refer to the state, they usually recommend a smaller and wiser state. It is assumed that state structures may be reformed—that is, can manage their economies better—without expanding society's access to power.

The question remains how states are coping with the crisis and the extent to which states mirror the international reform effort or chart their own directions. As we look at the case studies, we will pay particular attention to the state-society relationship.

· COPING: THE STATE ·

The case studies illustrate the diversity of state response to the crisis because of the deeply political nature of food policy choices. Each policy responds to, or ignores, specific international and domestic interests. In the case of Tanzania, Michael Lofchie points out that policy debate brought about the rise of informal "red" versus "expert" factions with strengths in different institutions of the state and with different relations to international and domestic interests. In relation to Ghana, Kraus details the rise and fall of several regimes and the variety of policy changes that accompanied them. But rural interests were not prominent in any one of them, including the second coup of Jerry Rawlings. The very nature of coups makes their connection with the peasantry unlikely. Zaya Yeebo echoes Kraus's point that the Rawlings regime was prone to "consumerist" urban policies. Yeebo writes: "One fundamental difference between a coup (a mere change of power at the top) and a genuine people's revolution is that coups tend to concentrate on winning immediate support by making populist appeals to the working class while ignoring the rural areas where patient and painstaking organisational work is often required to win the support of the peasants." He goes on to say that given the peasant majority in the country, it is "inconceivable that a genuine social revolution can be waged without their participation, and in particular that of the poorest strata. The response of the peasantry to the December coup was slow, suspicious and generally cynical. Unlike their urban counterparts, many of them saw it as 'these soldiers again.' Moreover, since the peasantry is not homogeneous, their responses differed at various stages." Meanwhile, the poor and landless peasants who wanted the state's support over land battles never got it.[10]

Food policy corresponds to interests rooted in the state-society relationship, and peasants are among the least well represented—even in regimes that have an ideological affinity with the peasantry, such as Tanzania and Rawlings's Ghana. In the cases of the Ivory Coast and Cameroon that have had reasonably successful agricultural production policies, it is likely that larger farmers are reasonably well represented in the state, with the result that producer price and servicing policy is broadly compatible with peasant interests. But, following the research of Robert Bates, we suspect that subsidy and input policy will be heavily biased toward large producers.[11] Peasant, and in general rural, political weakness has implications for other policy as well. Agricultural investment may be low. Lofchie notes declining agricultural investment in Tanzania, from 35 percent of capital resources in 1975/76 to 11.5 percent in 1981/82. Kenneth Good cites a financially starved agricultural sector in Zambia, and he discusses at length the mismanagement attendant upon maintaining state-controlled marketing structures despite their well-known poor record of performance. Barbara Lewis reports that in Cameroon, state-controlled food marketing was attempted only on a trial-and-error basis. Here there was a certain flexibility because the venture was not seen as an important revenue producer and because private traders—presumably many of them rural—had a certain amount of political clout. But again, the peasant majority did not figure in the national political equation.

Cyril Daddieh and Lewis, writing on the Ivory Coast and Cameroon, respectively, are only guardedly optimistic about the future of food production despite the relatively good performance to date. The authors argue that vested interests in export production, led by the larger producers and state institutions, have made it difficult to turn toward food production should that be necessary.[12] One suspects that the turn toward food will be necessary because the land frontier is closing, and because Green Revolution technology has not been created for the full array of staple crops in the African diet. Also, unless there is an equitable distribution of income and a strong domestic market for food, large producers who have the ear of the state will opt for high-value export crops over lower-value food crops for domestic markets. Meanwhile, none of the case studies mentions any serious efforts to gear policy and extension to women who, in the cases of Ivory Coast and Cameroon, are said to bear increasing responsibility for food production. The lack of attention to women in production no doubt reflects the limited role of women at national, as well as lower, policy levels.

Another striking feature of most of the cases is the attraction of large producing units for frustrated policymakers. This echoes, as we have suggested, a sentiment in the international donor community. The "big is beautiful" attitude is brought out strongly in the case of Zambia, where the food crisis appears to have devalued peasants as producers. Policymakers tend to blame the victims rather than fault their own policy or other circumstances. Large state or private, foreign or local, capital is then seen as possible salvation in times of production shortages.[13] Good, writing on Zambia, describes a bureaucracy wishing to end the restraint of the Leadership Code in order to ensconce itself in the private sector, diversify its economic roots, and make use of benefits from the state in the form of fertilizer subsidies and irrigation. Betting on the strong in Zambia takes state attention away form majority peasant interests in maize production and improved marketing infrastructure. This is similar to long-term historical processes that occurred wherever European settler and mining interests competed with peasant production in Africa. Betting on the strong is also probably counterproductive from a production-first point of view. Kraus documents an expensive trail of wasted resources that were lost on both private and state-run large production ventures. Betting on the strong ultimately affects the political character of state power. It is likely to foster a ruling coalition unfavorable to food production and unreceptive to policy designed to alleviate poverty. In Kenya, policy biases toward large producers, coupled with rapid population growth and increasingly scarce land, means that land reform is necessary for both welfare and production; but the idea is firmly rejected by the state, and land reform advocacy is repressed.[14]

The case studies indicate a marked absence of state-initiated changes of political structure aiming to bridge the state-society gap. We found this true of international initiatives as well. Lofchie points to the revival of local government and cooperatives in Tanzania, but this has had uncertain results.[15] In the case of Ghana, there has been a great deal of institutional experimentation, but coercion continues undiminished with no indication of expanded peasant access to power. Looking at the continent as a whole, Chazan and Shaw find that repression has expanded in the wake of food crises in Sudan, Ghana, Kenya, Zaire, Guinea, Angola, Central African Republic, and Uganda. Periodic crackdowns may also be expected in order to quell disturbances in hard-hit urban areas experiencing inflation and high food prices. In summary then, the case studies provide no indication of fundamental improvements of the state-society relationship initiated from above. The question remains whether there are sufficient pressures for change from below.

· COPING: POPULAR RESPONSES ·

Choice of coping mechanisms depends upon position in the structure of power. The case studies point to the political weakness of the peasant majority that is evident across a wide range of food and general agricultural policy, including issues of subsidized inputs, producer prices, state services, and credit availability. But although the peasantry has great difficulty influencing state policymaking in a systematic manner, peasants are not without leverage. From their position at the productive base of their economies, and given their control of land, their exit from state-planned cropping patterns and state-controlled marketing structures can all but bring regimes to their knees.[16] Janet MacGaffey points out that although the Zairian peasants are not courted as producers in the political process, there are some limits to the extent to which they can be abused. The weapons of the peasantry are several, and they are detailed in the case studies: use of parallel markets, which effectively deprive the state of revenue; smuggling; cropping strategies (Chazan and Shaw mention that peasants sometimes switch from export to food crops); migration; and, in some cases, more self-reliant communities that are created in a process of encapsulation. These are all classic peasant strategies, but they are as much declarations of political weakness as of strength—demonstrations of powers of veto rather than of initiative. Power-as-exit is an accurate reflection of peasant distance from state power. Although peasant weakness is partly a product of the social structure of the peasantry—in particular its isolated and sometimes divided character—peasant political weakness is primarily, as we have argued, the result of political departicipation engineered from above.

We know very little about peasant political consciousness, and especially about consciousness around food crises. In theory, one might assume that Africa is in a revolutionary situation. James Scott tells us that subsistence crises galvanize peasants of the moral economy into, at least momentarily, a class for itself.[17] And Theda Skocpol tells us that revolutions happen when states fall as much as when they are pushed.[18] But what is the African situation? South Africa is in a revolutionary situation, but there is no peasantry. Most of Sub-Saharan Africa is not in a revolutionary situation because peasant control of land and exit options often provide a means of survival, if not redress. Chazan and Shaw and several contributors point to the fact of protest in response to the food crisis. But sustained rural organization is rare primarily because it is repressed by the state. And very little is known about how the food and general economic crises affect everyday political forms and institutions.[19]

What is peasant political consciousness today?[20] First, there are deep feelings of political impotence, apathy, and cynicism: "Why vote and change leaders if they all act the same?" There is hoarding of political affection from the state and the regime.[21] Hoarding and apathy mean that politics beyond the community is pursued only half heartedly. But this response only allows leeway for the powers that be to do what they have been doing. Protest by apathy does not fundamentally challenge existing structures.

Second, there is a strong anti-elitism among the peasantry that takes many forms. "They take our money," murky though the process may be, and, "they even refuse to drink with us." The system is unfair and rude. Here we have classic populism juxtaposed with apathy. Regarding agriculture policy failure as well as virtually all other policy failures, the main popular explanation tends to be "They are corrupt." Failure is not explained by policy paths not taken, partly because policy options often cannot be discussed in the wider political realm. Instead, failure is personalized even though the actual culprit may be unknown. This attitude amounts to an indictment of the state, and it defines a crisis of legitimacy. But the character of anti-elite protest is often clothed in communal garb. Chazan and Shaw suggest that encapsulation processes and parallel markets may enhance local loyalties. This further encourages the expression of class-based sentiment in nonclass forms—ethnic, lineage, religious, village, and region.[22] These forms of expression occur partly, however, because these ideologies are "available." In the face of state repression, class-based ideological forms, as well as related organizations with specific policy proposals, are not likely to see the light of day.

Third, there is a certain irony that state weakening or decay may lessen the impulse to confront the state. The rise of parallel markets gives rise to a politics of protection and control of those markets. As the state grows more ineffective there is less incentive to lobby the state. Indeed, when extension workers are grounded by lack of transport and as the morale of state workers declines, it may be difficult to even find the state. Meanwhile, the state loses "intelligence" because civil society is simply "out there," unstructured, inchoate, and vaguely threatening. As a result, the state is less likely to know how to respond creatively even in its own interest. This is a situation in which the reproach to incompetence goes beyond complaint about momentary failure to a structural truth: Some states do not, almost cannot, know how to rule.

· CRISIS, REFORM, AND THE STATE-SOCIETY RELATIONSHIP ·

The case studies document a general absence of state effort to positively reshape state and society relationships either in the process of coping with the food crisis or as a general process of reform. There are, however, a variety of proposals in the air for reform of African states in the hope of their embracing and implementing economic reforms. This discussion is muted and elliptical, and sometimes more is assumed than clearly voiced. We want to counter several of these proposals because they ignore postindependence political trends that are a fundamental cause of the current crisis.

The problem of the African state is usually connoted by the term "soft state." This state is seen as heavily patrimonialized, which inhibits its performance as a strong bureaucracy; it lacks internal coherence, and hence it cannot provide clear policy direction; it cannot penetrate society to effect reforms; it cannot act as the primary engine of development in lieu of the role historically played by a strong capitalist class; and it is unable to gain sufficient distance from society in order to chart and systematically implement policy. It is said that societal demands intrude on the African state in ways that make a mockery of a smooth policy process. The political need to dispense patronage, find jobs for family and friends, distribute public projects and state largesse for selected constituencies, and also expand popular social services results in a state more adept at consumption than at fostering production. The reform prescription seems to logically follow from the diagnosis. If the state is too "soft" and too ridden by particularistic societal pressures, then the solution must be to make the "soft" state "hard." The state must become more autonomous from society in the short run in order to become more useful to society in the long run. The state must be liberated from its social and political context in order to pursue a more rational policy direction.

The question "What is to be done about the crisis of the state in Africa?" prompts responses ranging from vague sentiment to more precise recommendations. At one extreme is a nostalgic turn to the past that is rarely openly stated but is hinted at in conversations about the state past and present. The state in Africa that was most autonomous from the pressures of African society was the state that contained few Africans—the colonial state. A longing for the presumed order, authority, and clarity of colonial policy direction is, in conversation, occasionally revealed through critiques of the "messy" postindependence state. But the colonial brand of "hard" state is obviously no longer available. The state in Africa has irrevocably become the African state.

A second suggestion is literally no response at all. This view regards careful thought about the character of the state's relationship to society a luxury because of the economic crisis and political instability. The apparent emergency requires immediate action, to save the state and foster production, rather than any debate concerning access to the state. There is an unexamined assumption that current structures of power are irrelevant to the cause, and adequate for a solution, of the food crisis.

Those who hold a third position say that the situation will eventually take care of itself because the political rationale for agricultural policy that led to the crisis no longer holds. In other words, some regimes pursue policies for short-term advantage that eventually become a liability for those at the top: Prices paid to producers are too low; parallel-market activity deprives the state of revenue; imported food is too costly; parastatals may drain off too many resources, etc. States can be expected to adopt better policy if only as a matter of self-protection. Thus, the state-society relationship need not be reformed.

Some of what is presented in several of this book's chapters indicate that self-preservation and stark reality do bring some policy change. But it is also evident that broad access to power and food are not priority considerations. And policy conversions form the top beg questions of whether new and consistent long-term policy is possible without different ruling coalitions and whether regime stability and economic recovery are possible without broad-based access to power and food.

A fourth suggestion is in keeping with the central thrust of international aid and African state policy since independence. It is thought that the state grew "soft" as a result of a lack of expertise and technical ability. If state personnel knew what to do and how to do it, the job would be done. A great deal of aid money has been spent for training and advice in an effort to create the "developmental" state, and a great deal of ink has been spilled writing about "development administration." But as Eqbal Ahmad notes, in Third World postcolonial contests between inherited colonial structures of rule and burgeoning organizations of civil society, international economic and military aid helped ensure the triumph of colonial state structure.[23] International diplomatic sympathy was clearly with the state rather than with society. Although education and training are obviously useful, it is far less clear that ignorance, rather than concrete interests, is the crux of the problem. The management-training position is also undermined by evident declining state performance over time despite funds devoted to bureaucratic training and education.

In a fifth suggestion, opportunity for reform is seen in the fact of the state's severe dependence upon outside aid sources. In today's circumstance of exceptional external leverage, it is said that the aid community could act as policy reform designer and initiator and take some pressure off the state by absorbing any short-term political heat that reform policies may generate. But dependent states even more responsive to external powers will only further distance themselves from their own societies, exacerbate problems of state legitimacy, and postpone the creation of structures of rule affording broader access to power. It is somewhat ironic, perhaps, that only new structures of access could provide states with sufficient popular legitimacy and strength to make difficult short-term decisions and survive. But we can doubt whether the aid-as-leverage scenario is even possible. States are adept at dodging external demands that are most at odds with governing-class predilections.[24] And as Chazan and Shaw point out, as populations cannot "get at" the IMF or the World Bank, political heat is, quite logically, channeled against their own regimes.

A sixth suggestion follows from a widely shared, and largely accurate, belief that African state structures have been more parasitical than developmental because they are both large and ineffective. Hence the state should reduce the number of functions it currently performs, the numbers of personnel it employs, and the amount of wealth it consumes. In the process, more efficient market forces, as well as cooperatives and nongovernmental organizations, will come to the fore. There is a tendency to see the shrinking state obviating the need for careful consideration of the state-society relationship and issues of access to power. In this rather fanciful scenario, the state will simply bulk less large in society, making the arena somehow less political. Our case studies imply, however, that it is unlikely that the state will shrink. Instead, in lieu of a large private sector, the state will hulk extremely large in African economies for a long time to come. Focusing on markets may also ignore broader power issues. Markets can be quite compatible with repression. Chazan and Shaw point out that although states have provided more leeway for market processes, these same states, rather than loosen political controls, have exerted more repression. Also, an expansion of markets would not necessarily expand rural access to food or power. E. A. Brett reasons that in "a context in which there is already a substantial degree of inequality, in which the dominant strata in the countryside are capable of using their social and economic power to enforce the support of the rest, market forces, too, could act to reinforce inequalities and hasten the disintegration of the property rights of a large proportion of the poor."[25]

Shrinking the state will, it is sometimes argued, allow it to regain lost legitimacy by doing fewer things but doing them better. But to the extent that social service expansion is held back and higher user fees act as a rationing device, there may be even more popular dissatisfaction with states. State expenditure does require pruning, but cutbacks need not center on popular victories—despite departicipation—in areas such as education and health, functions that the state performs routinely and quite well. Instead, rapidly growing military expenditure should be the major candidate for budget cuts.[26]

Those making a seventh suggestion select practical models for the reformed African state: the newly industrialized countries (NICs), and especially South Korea and Taiwan, but also historical Japan. It is presumed that these states were quite autonomous and well insulated from society; that they acted as effective catalysts for development; that they nurtured, created, and continued to work closely with a strong bourgeoisie; and that ultimately they fostered revolutions from above. Leaving aside for the moment the empirical accuracy of these observations, and the assumption that these states were optimal for growth rates as well as for broad-based welfare, the question remains whether such a state—ultimately a Weberian model of rational bureaucracy—is possible in the African context. There is plenty of room for doubt. In the first place, it is unclear that African states will allow greater play for markets and, ultimately, for capitalism. John Ravenhill suggests that when bureaucratic and capitalist forces are virtually one, as in much of Africa, "there is the probability that state power will be used not to promote market efficiency but to sustain oligopolistic advantages and generate economic rents."[27] At the very least, capitalist development and the arrival of a strong bourgeoisie will be a long process.[28] Meanwhile, military bureaucracies have not provided disciplined rule any better than have civilian regimes. As a result, there is little likelihood of the autonomous Asian developmental state emerging in Africa.

Richard Sandbrook, however, sees possible African roots for this model, although he notes the absence of a traditional oligarchy, cultural homogeneity, as well as long-term external national threats that were present in the Asian cases. He finds that he "cannot rule out the possibility that nationally minded and modernizing bureaucracies led by far-sighted political leaders will emerge here and there. Boigny and Kenyatta have played that kind of role. What this role demands is a finely honed realism, including an ability to seize opportunities presented by the operation of the world-economy and to shield the administrative apparatus from the corruptive might of neo-patrimonialism"[29]—and, one might add, the likelihood of shielding the state from all other societal claims as well.

Even in the unlikely event that the NIC model could be diffused throughout Africa, there is no real expectation that it would foster expanded access to power or food. Although Sandbrook understands the need for state legitimacy and the long-term dangers of repression, and even though he is tempted to recommend more democratic forms of rule complete with contending political organizations and free speech, he ultimately rejects the idea of democracy for Africa. "Realistically speaking . . . our analysis does not suggest that democracy has any real prospect in the limiting conditions of contemporary Africa. What is the best feasible alternative? Decent, responsive and largely even-handed personal rule."[30] Thus, the hope of Africa lies in the lonely dictator. This recommendation implies that current structures of power and access in Africa are a given. All that can be hoped for are better leaders provided by the luck of the draw. Democratic forms of rule may be appropriate for other people, places, and times, but not for Africa now.

These suggestions for state reform in Africa lead to a dead end. Instead of change, they offer more of the same. Two observations are necessary before we can go forward. In the first place, the autonomous state in Africa is not something to be sought; it has already arrived. As we pointed out, departicipation, coups d'état, and civil wars effectively distanced states from their societies. It is also clear that citizens did not withdraw from the state; they were pushed out, and access to power was severely restricted. It is not proven that all this was necessary for rule in general so much as it was necessary for the survival of particular regimes. It is the ruling class, broadly defined, that has opposed democratic politics in Africa and has gone to great lengths to restructure institutions, putting itself beyond the reach of much of civil society. As a result, the African state has grown dangerously autonomous to the point that it lacks legitimacy and, partly as a result, efficacy in development.

Second, we must emphasize the importance of state repression that makes politics, organization, and widespread debate over programs all but impossible in most states. Patronage politics around a variety of parochial, including ethnic, claims is sometimes all that is allowed. People pursue this form of politics not just because it is traditional, but because it is possible and it sometimes "works."[31] The state also uses a patrimonial style in order to make minimal connections and exchanges with the population and garner some legitimacy. Robert Bates relates the fact of repression to political practice that marginalizes the peasantry and results in agricultural policy harmful to its interests.

> Through coercion, governments in Africa block the efforts of those who would organize its attempts to achieve structural changes; only the advocacy of minor adjustments is allowed. Moreover, through the conferral of divisible benefits, they make it in the interests of individual rural dwellers to seek limited objectives. Political energies, rather than focusing on the collective standing of the peasantry, focus instead on the securing of particular improvements—subsidized inputs, the location and staffing of production schemes, the allocation of jobs, and the issuance of licenses and permits. Rather than appeals for collective changes, appeals instead focus on incremental benefits. The politics of the pork barrel supplant the politics of class action. Debates over the fundamental configuration of policies remain off the political agenda of the African countryside, and individual rural dwellers come, as a matter of personal self-interest, to abide by public policies that are harmful to agrarian interests as a whole.[32]

Thus, agrarian policy is the outcome of a real structure of power. René Lemarchand sees the root of the food crisis in similar political terms when he concludes "that rural poverty is fundamentally related to the powerlessness of the peasant sectors. Not only do the rural poor lack minimal control over their immediate environment and economic circumstances, they also lack all opportunities for taking part in the elaboration of the policies that affect their livelihood most directly."[33]

The postindependence autonomous state is at the root of the food crisis and the broader crisis of African political economies. Any reform of agriculture will require a major change in the relationship of states to their societies, including more broad-based access to power. Although the precise causal connections remain unclear, one cannot help but note the strong correlation between processes of states distancing themselves from societies, on the one hand, and growing agricultural and general economic crises, on the other. Peter Anyang' Nyong'o writes that "political demobilization, in most African countries, contrary to what some other political science literature would suggest, did not lead to effective government in terms of undertaking modernization tasks; it led, instead, to socio-economic and political decay in almost all spheres of life. One is therefore tempted to draw a correlation between lack of democratic practices that institutionalize public accountability and the deterioration of socio-economic conditions in Africa.[34] Following political demobilization, or departicipation, the interests of the peasantry were given little consideration, rural political organization was often prohibited, criticism could not be channeled in programmatic directions, and policy responded to only a narrow range of national and international, and usually nonagricultural, interests. Economies ultimately based on agriculture faltered, and, as we have seen, state legitimacy declined. Military regimes did not prove to be effective modernizers, nor were they hospitable to rural interests. The state often lost its rural "political legs" and grew increasingly ignorant of the agricultural setting—in some cases unable to pursue policy even in its own interest—as it lacked sufficient political "credit" to elicit rural cooperation for otherwise well-considered policy.

Most states became both weak and repressive—characteristics that at first glance appear contradictory but, in fact, are complementary because repression rises in direct relation to the decline of popular support. Some authoritarian states in Asia and Latin America have been successful modernizers, but the major preconditions for a successful parallel effort in Africa are absent: considerable foreign capital; military establishments exerting substantial social power; and a large middle class willing to support the authoritarian state as long as it delivers the goods of consumerism.[35] Most African states have not been able to effectively discipline and organize themselves or society for development, let alone encourage broad distribution of the fruits of development. The authoritarian state cannot organize society in the midst of only limited capitalist development because the peasantry, as the productive base of the economy, is able to escape some state demands.

All this suggests that a more equitable state-society relationship is required to break the impasse. The more African states have leaned on society, the weaker states have become. Meanwhile, limited capitalist development has also meant that organizations in civil society are weak and have difficulty influencing the state. But although both African states and societies are weak, each needs the other—societies need state impetus and policy direction in order to modernize forces of production, and states need to modernize society in order to strengthen themselves. But society cannot depend upon the state to become enlightened out of abstract self-interest. In other words, political space will not be given—it must be taken. Ultimately organizations of civil society must gain sufficient strength to make themselves heard and strengthen themselves vis-à-vis the state. We agree with Crawford Young that "a stronger civil society is not antithetical to a restructured and stronger state, better able to fulfill its role of guidance and orientation of the development venture."[36]

The question remains whether the weak can become stronger, whether peasant political consciousness, broadly characterized by anger, apathy, and anti-elitism, can be organized and effectively voiced in policy channels. In other words, where is the opportunity for progressive politics amidst crisis and repression? We would like to note three trends. In the first place, although we should not be overly optimistic about reform, there are some lessons to be learned from two examples of peasant leverage on the state in East Africa. The case of Bugisu in Uganda, discussed by Stephen Bunker, indicates that the peasant majority had, until Idi Amin, real leverage on state coffee-growing policy because the district grew a high-value export crop, the state wanted revenue from it, district political leaders were influential at the center, and a decentralized cooperative marketing structure, coupled with local government, was able to define local priorities and exert real leverage on the state.[37] Frank Holmquist argues that peasants in Kenya's self-help movement sustained strong initiative from below through a tacit alliance with successive presidents and a decentralized and competitive electoral structure that held leadership somewhat accountable to peasant-defined needs in basic social services. As a result, the state spent more money on social services than it otherwise would.[38] These two cases illustrate the need to take political structures seriously with their several incentives for alliances and action by both leaders and followers. The cases also illustrate the necessity of peasant alliances across social classes and economic sectors. And they indicate the need for political space at some distance from state institutions—not to stew in political isolation, but from which to organize and exert direct pressure on state institutions.[39]

Second, in several of the chapters it is implicitly indicated that rural and urban protest in and around the food situation has rarely been joined. This is probably true for a broad range of political issues in which urban and rural interests appear to be in conflict. Until this division is bridged, however, peasant political clout will be minimal. This begs the question of whether leadership may emerge to span the gap. One bright spot may be the political impact of the postcolonial explosion of secondary education. Large numbers of high school leavers are in the countryside unemployed or partially employed, poor, often very disaffected, and they think as much in terms of policy and program as they do in terms of communal loyalties and clientelism. These young people may be the rural intellectuals who will act as liaisons with urban counterparts who, in turn, will gradually take to the countryside and organize. Already there is evidence of ad hoc rural organizing by this secondary-school-educated population, which has been central to the election of several left-wing populist politicians in Kenya and has been known to have a significant impact upon Africa's extremely young electorate. In the years ahead, reactions to the food crisis, and local populism in general, may be poured into new political molds.

Third, we should also remember that African society is undergoing profound change that may bring about democratic opportunities sooner than some evolutionary analysis predicts.[40] It is ironic that both capitalist development and state decay are likely to foster a new state-society relationship. The capitalist development that is occurring in some of the more advanced states like the Ivory Coast and Kenya inevitably creates strengthened organizations within civil society. In other cases, state weakness, decay, and even collapse allows for unprecedented local initiative in the economy, processes of class formation less mediated by the state, new organizational forms, and, ultimately, new relationships with states.[41] In the opposing cases of steady capitalist advance, on the one hand, and state weakness in the face of poor growth, on the other, new political spaces are created as are possibilities of negotiation from some strength from below. The state may not successfully dominate the countryside as it has in the past. Both situations yield a novel institutional complexity with the possibility for a more equitable and productive state-society relationship.

• CONCLUSION •

Needless to say, these trends provide only a minimal foundation upon which to predict a changing state-society relationship. But, sobering as reality is, we believe it is, above all, necessary to challenge the dominant rationale for the autonomous state. We began our discussion by retreating to a first principle noting that state policy highly conditions access to food whether the context is Africa, the United States, or any part of the world. Hence, the state-society relationship is a central consideration in any discussion of the genesis of the crisis or of subsequent reform.[42] As Chazan and Shaw, quoting Amartya Sen, assert at the outset: There is no such thing as an apolitical food crisis.

We saw that in discussions of policy reform the cause of state failure is often wrongly laid at the door of parochial—read popular—demands on the state in the form of patronage considerations and expanded social services. The interests of elites are acknowledged, but it is thought that prior elite policy preferences may be reformulated in ways that are coincident with their real interests. Meanwhile, the "soft" state must be reformed, not by opening the state to new social forces, but by further shielding the state from these forces. As a result, the mild reform language of the 1970s—"participation" and the provision of "basic needs"—was jettisoned in favor of an alleged clear-eyed awareness of what was possible at this juncture of Africa's evolution.[43] If the bureaucracy was to lead private capital along the development path in the 1960s and 1970s, now private capital would take the lead with the support of a scientific bureaucracy willing and able to provide and implement rational policy and harsh political discipline. Thus, the leading edge of state factions would change, but the peasant majority would remain politically marginal to the development of its society.

In the dominant view, popular forces cannot, do not, and should not have an important political role to play. This argument is highly economistic, harkening back to archetypical modernization and Marxian forces-of-production theory. In either case, it is said that Africa simply needs capital, technology, and skills. The approach implicitly declares a moratorium on politics. Africa is told to patiently wait for a bourgeoisie, which will mechanistically initiate dynamic capitalist development; modernize the forces of production; create a proletariat; through an inevitable elaboration of the bourgeoisie's social and political power, discipline the patrimonial state; and last, and far off, lay the groundwork for democratic structures of rule. Popular politics prior to the bourgeois coming risks diverting scarce resources from "rational" investment decisions known only to national and international bourgeoisies and their bureaucratic allies.

This intellectual environment is very hostile to democracy. In policymaking circles, advocacy of democratic forms of rule may be dangerous, whereas in some academic and donor-aid circles it is considered simply daft. It is curious that in the face of widespread regime illegitimacy and ineffectiveness African leaders, foreign advisers, and many academics continue to debate the appropriateness of varieties of authoritarian rule. The fact that the popular majority almost certainly prefers democratic rule and has a very sophisticated sense of its political preferences carries little or no weight. People repeatedly come out in large numbers for elections when viable alternatives are presented.[44] Rather than retreat from state policy, peasants do so only selectively when states leave them no alternative. In our East African experience, peasants often have a sound set of well-grounded policy preferences. The populist array of peasant and working-class attitudes found in Africa today does not connote populism without program so much as populism with a program but lacking a precision that can only be provided by competing leaders and parties, which are, however, rarely allowed to compete.[45]

Because the dominant approach to Africa's crisis is deeply antidemocratic, it is also positively utopian. The received wisdom ignores several obvious facts: The interests of powerful forces—domestic and foreign—in and around the state in large part created the crisis; the state grew weaker as it progressively cut its ties to civil society; the forces that created the problem will not readily usher in serious reform; fundamental policy change in food production, let alone distribution, will require a new coalition of ruling forces afforded by broader-based access to power; thus, the character of the state-society relationship must become more democratic.

We have tried to make a very simple, albeit often forgotten, point: that structures of power have policy consequences. We have argued that a major cause of both the food crisis and the general crisis of African political economy is the autonomous state and the narrow set of interests it serves. We recognize that our suggestions for state reform are very sketchy, and we are aware that there is a major difference between democratic form and democratic content.[46] We also understand that current features of the political landscape, like patronage, will remain for a long time to come. We know that there will be regime failures, but we must be careful not to accept at face value the multiple "failures" declared by ruling classes, international forces, and military establishments who never subject their periodic moratoriums on democratic procedure "for public benefit" to public opinion.[47] We also, of course, cannot be sure what coalitions of forces might rule in less authoritarian environments. What is clear is that the autonomous state, with much of the population—and especially the peasant majority—held at arm's length, played a central role in the process leading to the food crisis. Obviously reform suggestions built upon this paradigm of failure lead nowhere. Our suggested democratic opening is, then, decidedly less utopian than a repackaged version of the state-society model that has already failed. Democratic forms of rule in Africa are not luxuries to be casually entertained or dispensed with on the road to development. On the contrary, they are necessary for development.

· NOTES ·

1. World grain surpluses are discussed in Barbara Insel, "A World Awash in Grain," *Foreign Affairs* 63 (Spring 1985): 892–911. Growing malnutrition amidst expanded production is discussed in Frances Moore Lappé and Joseph Collins, *World Hunger: Twelve Myths* (New York: Grove Press, 1986). The World Bank has acknowledged the dual crisis in the recent *Poverty and Hunger: Issues and Options for Food Security in Developing Countries* (Washington, D.C.: The World Bank, 1986).

2. Amartya Sen, *Poverty and Famines: An Essay on Entitlement and Deprivation* (New York: Oxford University Press, 1982).

3. "World Hunger Found Still Growing," *New York Times*, June 28, 1987.

4. Physician Task Force on Hunger in America, *Hunger in America: The Growing Epidemic* (Middletown, Conn.: Wesleyan University Press, 1985); J. Larry Bowman, "Hunger in the U.S.," *Scientific American* 256 (February 1987): 37–41.

5. Carl K. Eicher, "Facing up to Africa's Food Crisis," in Carl K. Eicher and John M. Staatz, eds., *Agricultural Development in the Third World* (Baltimore: Johns Hopkins University Press, 1984). Of course, powerful influences over access to food, aside from social class, include gender and age and sometimes religion and ethnicity.

6. There are many coup attempts that do not succeed but nevertheless unsettle the political system.

7. The promise and limitations of the first years of Thomas Sankara's populist regime in Burkina Faso is outlined in Guy Martin, "Ideology and Praxis in Thomas Sankara's Populist Revolution of 4 August 1983 in Burkina Faso," *Issue* 15 (1987): 77–90.

8. For a comprehensive bibliography on the development debate, see Joan C. Parker, "Bibliography on the World Bank Report on Sub-Saharan Africa," *Rural Africana* 19–20 (Spring-Fall 1984): 131–137. See also the several essays in this issue and especially the summary article by David F. Gordon and Joan C. Parker, "The World Bank and Its Critics: The Case of Sub-Saharan Africa," pp. 3–33; the special issue of the *IDS Bulletin* 16 (July 1985); and John Ravenhill, ed., *Africa in Economic Crisis* (New York: Columbia University Press, 1986). For literature on agriculture, see Lynette Rummel, "African Agricultural Development: A Bibliography of Recent Works," in Stephen K. Commins, Michael F. Lofchie, and Rhys Payne, eds. *Africa's Agrarian Crisis: The Roots of Famine* (Boulder, Colo.: Lynne Rienner Publishers, 1986), pp. 210–229. Jon Kraus, in his essay on Ghana in this volume, nicely reviews the several causes that have been offered to explain the food crisis.

9. Rolf Gusten, "African Agriculture: Which Way Out of the Crisis?" *Rural Africana* 19–20 (Spring-Fall 1984): 60.

10. Zaya Yeebo, "Ghana: Defense Committees and the Class Struggle," *Review of African Political Economy* 32 (April 1985): 69. A good discussion of the tenuous popular roots of coups is in Bjorn Beckman, "The Military as Revolutionary Vanguard: A Critique," *Review of African Political Economy* 37 (December 1986): 50–62.

11. Robert H. Bates, *Markets and States in Tropical Africa: The Political Basis of Agricultural Policies* (Berkeley and Los Angeles: University of California Press, 1981).

12. Jon Kraus, in his article of Ghana, doubts that there is a necessary conflict between export and food crops. Gusten, "African Agriculture," p. 59, also sees a synergistic effect rather than trade-off.

13. Ben Wisner argues that agribusiness is currently, and wrongly, seen as a quick fix. See his *Power and Need: A Reassessment of the Basic Human Needs Approach in African Development* (London: Earthscan Publishers, forthcoming).

14. Diana Hunt, *The Impending Crisis in Kenya: The Case for Land Reform* (Brookfield, Vt.: Gower Publishing Co., 1984); Ian Livingstone, *Rural*

Development,Employment and Incomes in Kenya (Brookfield, Vt.: Gower Publishing Co., 1986). Biases toward large producers in Kenya are discussed in Stephen Peterson, "Neglecting the Poor: State Policy Toward the Smallholder in Kenya," in Commins, Lofchie, and Payne, *Africa's Agrarian Crisis*, pp. 59–83.

15. A discussion of the background and implications of these moves can be found in Frank Holmquist, "Tanzania's Retreat from Statism in the Countryside," *Africa Today* 30 (1983): 23–35.

16. The best extended discussion of peasant exit options in Africa is Goran Hyden, *Beyond Ujamaa in Tanzania: Underdevelopment and an Uncaptured Peasantry* (Berkeley and Los Angeles: University of California Press, 1980). For a critique, see Nelson Kasfir, "The Notion of an Autonomous Peasantry," *Mawazo* 5 (June 1984): 35–46.

17, James C.Scott, *The Moral Economy of the Peasant: Rebellion and Subsistence in Southeast Asia* (New Haven: Yale University Press, 1976).

18. Theda Skocpol, *States and Social Revolutions: A Comparative Analysis of France, Russia and China* (New York: Cambridge University Press, 1979).

19. If the 1930s and the Great Depression are any indication, one might expect growing engagement with churches and religious movements. See Terence O.Ranger, "Religious Movements and Politics in Sub-Saharan Africa," *African Studies Review* 29 (June 1986): 50.

20. This is obviously a broad, cavalier, and all-too-brief sketch. Work on peasant political consciousness attuned to differences of strata and general and local political economy is rare. A good study is David Brown, "The Political Response to Immiseration: A Case Study," *Genève-Afrique* 18 (1980): 57–74.

21. The term is from Alan Wolfe, *The Limits of Legitimacy: Political Contradictions of Contemporary Capitalism* (New York: Free Press, 1977), pp. 343–344.

22. Brown, "The Political Response to Immiseration."

23. Eqbal Ahmad, "The Challenge of Democracy," paper delivered to a conference in Penang, Malaysia: conference sponsored by the Third World Network on Third World Development, November 1984.

24. John Ravenhill,"Africa's Continuing Crises: The Elusiveness of Development," in John Ravenhill, ed., *Africa in Economic Crisis*, p.29.

25. E. A. Brett,"State Power and Economic Inefficiency: Explaining Political Failure in Africa," *IDS Bulletin* 17 (January 1986): 29.

26. The political rationale for shrinking the state in Africa in the 1980s echoes rather strikingly a prominent conservative argument in the United States and Western Europe in the 1970s in reaction to the political mobilization of the 1960s. The problem was defined as the "overburdened" state resulting from expansion in the prior decade. The "overburdened" state was a product of an excess of democracy, and as a result the state required protection from excessive popular demands for social services and social welfare. Ultimately, popular apathy and lower expectations were necessary to save democracy. The state needed distance in order to set priorities more rationally, which usually turned out to be greater military expenditure. An example of this point of view is Samuel P. Huntington, "The Democratic Distemper," in Nathan Glazer and Irving Kristol, eds., *The American Commonwealth 1976* (New York: Basic Books, 1976), pp. 9–38.

27. Ravenhill,"Africa's Continuing Crises," p.28.

28. The best discussion of the bourgeoisie in Africa is found in Paul M. Lubeck, ed., *The African Bourgeoisie: Capitalist Development in Nigeria,Kenya,and the Ivory Coast* (Boulder,Colo.: Lynne Rienner Publishers, 1987).

29. Richard Sandbrook,*The Politics of Africa's Economic Stagnation* (New York:

Cambridge University Press, 1985): p.156.

30. Ibid., p.157.

31. Robert H. Bates, "Modernization, Ethnic Competition, and the Rationality of Politics in Contemporary Africa," in Donald Rothchild and Victor A. Olorunsola, eds., *State Versus Ethnic Claims: African Policy Dilemmas* (Boulder, Colo.: Westview Press,1983).

32. Bates, *Markets and States in Tropical Africa*, pp.117–118.

33. René Lemarchand, *"The Political Economy of Food Issues,"* in Art Hansen and Della E. McMillan,eds., *Food in Sub-Saharan Africa* (Boulder,Colo.: Lynne Rienner Publishers, 1986), pp.37–38.

34. Peter Anyang'Nyong'o, "Struggles for Democracy: State and Popular Alliances in Africa," *Eastern Africa Social Science Research Review* 2 (January 1986): 111.

35. Frederick S.Weaver, *State and Industrial Structure: The Historical Process of South African Industrial Growth* (Westport, Conn.: Greenwood Press, 1980), pp. 166–175.

36. Crawford Young,"Africa's Colonial Legacy," in Robert J.Berg and Jennifer Seymour Whitaker,eds.,*Strategies for African Development*(Berkeley and Los Angeles: University of California Press), p.48.

37. Stephen G. Bunker, *Peasants Against the State: The Politics of Market Control in Bugisu, Uganda, 1900-1983* (Urbana: University of Illinois Press, 1987).

38. Frank Holmquist, "Self-Help: The State and Peasant Leverage in Kenya,"*Africa* 54 (1984): 72–91.

39. Frank Holmquist, "Defending Peasant Political Space in Independent Africa," *Canadian Journal of African Studies 14(1980): 157–168.*

40. Thomas M.Callaghy, "Politics and Vision in Africa: The Interplay of Domination, Equality and Liberty," in Patrick Chabal,ed., *Political Domination in Africa: Reflections on the Limits of Power* (New York: Cambridge University Press, 1986).

41. Nelson Kasfir, "State,Magendo, and Class Formation in Uganda," in Nelson Kasfir, ed., *State and Class in Africa* (London: Frank Cass, 1984); Michael Whyte, "Crisis and Recentralization: 'Indigenous Development' in Eastern Uganda," typescript,n.d.

42. Our discussion is centered on the question of state power—whom it embodies and to whom it responds. A different focus on projects is the centerpiece of a very useful book by Paul Harrison, *The Greening of Africa: Breaking Through in the Battle for Land and Food* (New York: Penguin Books, 1987). By way of pointing out that there have been many successful and innovative agricultural projects in Africa, the book is a breath of fresh air amidst pervading gloom. But the project approach does not systematically address the broader question of state power.

43. A powerful case for the necessity of a strong basic-needs and participatory approach to rural development, in general, and for alleviating the increasingly severe reproduction crisis for peasant women is found in Wisner, *Power and Need.*

44. Ahmad, "The Challenge of Democracy," p.13, surveying Third World popular participation in democratic processes, writes that "voters' turn-out has been invariably excellent in contested and free elections. The voting pattern indicates a marked preference for progressive parties and reformist programs. Secular parties and leaders have been favored over religious fundamentalists; socialist and social democrats over conservative candidates, civilians over soldiers, independents and nationalists over the aligned pro-Western or pro-Eastern parties."

45. The populist character of working-class political consciousness is well described and analyzed in Richard Sandbrook and Jack Arn, *The Labouring Poor & Urban Class*

Formation: The Case of Greater Accra (Montreal: Centre for Developing-Area Studies, 1977).

46. Jibrin Ibrahim,"The Political Debate and the Struggle for Democracy in Nigeria,"*Review of African Political Economy* 37 (December 1986): 38–48; Mahmood Mamdani, "Contradictory Class Perspectives on the Question of Democracy (The Case of Uganda)," *Eastern Africa Social Science Research Review* 2 (January 1986): 26–47.

47. Ahmad, "The Challenge of Democracy."

Acronyms

ADB	Agricultural Development Bank [Ghana]
AFRC	Armed Forces Revolutionary Council [Ghana]
APPER	African Priority Programme for Economic Recovery
ARPB	Association of Recognized Professional Bodies [Ghana]
Ashanti NLM	Ashanti National Liberation Movement [Ghana]
CCCE	Caisse Centrale de Coopération Economique (Central Fund for Economic Cooperation) [Ivory Coast]
CDC	Cameroon Development Corporation
CDC	Commonwealth Development Corporation [Ivory Coast]
CENEDEC	Centre National du Développement des Entreprises Coopératives (National Center for the Development of Cooperative Enterprises) [Cameroon]
CFDT	Compagnie Française pour le Développement des Fibres Textiles (French Company for Textile Fiber Development) [Ivory Coast]
CIDT	Compagnie Ivorien pour le Développement des Textiles (Ivorian Textile Development Company) [Ivory Coast]
CMB	Cocoa Marketing Board (after 1981, Cocobod) [Ghana]
CPC	Cocoa Purchasing Company [Ghana]
CPI	consumer price index
CPP	Convention People's Party [Ghana]

239

CSSPPA	Caisse de Stabilisation et de Soutien des Prix des Produits Agricoles (Agricultural Products Stabilization Fund) [Ivory Coast]
ECA	Economic Commission for Africa
EDF	European Development Fund
EEC	European Economic Community
EIB	European Investment Bank
FAC	Fonds d'Aide et de Coopération (French Aid and Cooperation Fund) [Ivory Coast]
FAO	Food and Agricultural Organization
FDC	Food Distribution Corporation [Ghana]
FER	Fund for Extension and Renewal
FONADER	National Fund for Rural Development [Cameroon]
FPC	Food Production Corporation (formerly WB) [Ghana]
GAM	Groupement d'Agriculteurs Modernes (Modern Agricultural Associations) [Cameroon]
GBA	Ghana Bar Association
GDP	gross domestic product
GNRC	Ghana National Reconstruction Corporation
GNTC	Ghana National Trade Corporation
IFCC-GERDAT	Institut Français du Café, du Cacao et Autres Plantes Stimulantes (French Institute for Coffee and Cocoa) [Ivory Coast]
ILO	International Labour Office/Organisation
IMF	International Monetary Fund
IRCT	Institut de Recherche sur les Cotons et Textiles (Research Institute for Cotton and Textiles) [Ivory Coast]
IRHO	Institut de Recherche de l'Huile et Oléagineux (Research Institute for Edible Oils) [Ivory Coast]
LINTCO	Lint Company of Zambia
MIDEVIV	Mission pour le Développement des Vivriers (Food Development Authority) [Cameroon]
MP	member of parliament
MWU	Mine Workers' Union [Ghana]

Namboard	National Agricultural Marketing Board [Zambia]
NCZ	Nitrogen Chemicals of Zambia
NMC	National Milling Corporation [Tanzania]
OAU	Organization of African Unity
OCPA	Office de Commercialisation des Produits Agricoles (Commercial Office for Agricultural Products) [Ivory Coast]
OFY	Operation Feed Yourself [Ghana]
ONATRA	Office National des Transports du Zaire (National Transport Office for Zaire)
ONPR	Office Nationale de Promotion Rurale (National Office for Rural Development) [Cameroon]
Palmindustrie	Palm Oil Industries [Ivory Coast]
PDCI	Parti Démocratique de la Côte d'Ivoire (Democratic Party of the Ivory Coast)
PDCs	People's Defense Committees [Ghana]
PNDC	Provisional National Defense Council [Ghana]
PNP	People's National Party [Ghana]
PP	Progress Party [Ghana]
RC	regional commissioner [Ghana]
SATMACI	Société d'Assistance Technique pour la Modernisation Agricole de la Côte d'Ivoire (Technical Assistance Company for Agricultural Modernization in the Ivory Coast)
SF	State Fisheries Corporation [Ghana]
SFC	State Farms Corporation [Ghana]
SMC	Supreme Military Council [Ghana]
SODECAO	Cocoa Development Corporation [Cameroon]
SODEPALM	Société d'Etat pour le Développement et l'Exploitation du Palmier à Huile en Côte d'Ivoire (State Company for Oil Palm Development in the Ivory Coast)
SODERIZ	Société d'Etat pour le Développement et l'Exploitation du Riz (State Company for Rice Development) [Ivory Coast]
TAZARA	Tanzania-Zambia Railway Authority
TUC	Trade Union Congress [Ghana]

UGFC(C)	United Ghana Farmers' Council (Cooperatives)
UMOA	Union Monétaire Ouest Africaine (West African Monetary Union)
UNIP	United National Independence Party [Zambia]
URADEP	Upper Region Agricultural Development Project [Ghana]
USAID	U.S. Agency for International Development
WB	Workers Brigade [Ghana]
WDCs	Workers' Defense Committees [Ghana]
ZAPI de l'est	Zones d'Action Prioritaires Intégrées (Integrated Zones of Priority Action) [Cameroon]
ZIMCO	Zambian Industrial and Mining Corporation

Index

Accra, 96
Acheampong, I.K., 90, 93, 95
ADB. *See* Agricultural Development
    Bank
AFRC. *See* Armed Forces
    Revolutionary Council
Africa's Priority Programme for
    Economic Recovery (APPER), 3, 19
Agenda for Action, 3, 19
Agribusiness, 2. *See also* Agroindustry
Agricultural Development Bank (ADB),
    87, 93, 102
Agricultural Products Stabilization Fund
    (CSSPPA) (Côte d'Ivoire), 127, 128
Agroindustry; Côte d'Ivoire, 119-120,
    122-123, 131-134; palm oil
    production, 122-123. *See also*
    Large-scale farming
A.G. Zambia Ltd., 200
Aid, 2, 8, 47, 101, 191; debates, 41-42;
    development, 49, 51; donors, 18, 38,
    43, 48, 218-219, 226; free market,
    42-43; impact, 49-50; policy reform,
    43, 52(n9); structural, 44-45. *See also*
    Donor community
Angola, 11, 12, 40, 217, 222
APPER. *See* Africa's Priority
    Programme for Economic Recovery
Armed Forces Revolutionary Council
    (AFRC) (Ghana), 76; production, 96-
    97; reform, 95-96
ARPB. *See* Association of Recognized
    Professional Bodies
Ashanti National Liberation Movement
    (Ashanti NLM), 83
Ashanti NLM. *See* Ashanti National
    Liberation Movement

Association of Recognized Professional
    Bodies (ARPB) (Ghana), 94

Banana production, 130
Basic Import Strategy (Tanzania),
    162-163
Belgian Congo. *See* Zaire
Belgium, 170-171
Black market, 9, 11, 63, 95. *See also*
    Informal economy; Second economy
Botchway, Kwesi, 101, 104
Burkina Faso, 11

Caisse. *See* Agricultural Products
    Stabilization Fund
Cameroon, 15, 73(n8); agricultural
    policy, 70-72; cocoa production,
    56-57, 58-59, 74(n20); cooperatives,
    57-58; food production, 55-56,
    73(n1), 74(nn 13, 17), 221-222;
    market structure, 60-62, 67-68, 69;
    palm oil production, 62-63; truck
    farming, 63-64; women as farmers,
    64-66
Cameroon Development Corporation
    (CDC), 62-63
Cash crops, 2, 4, 5, 7-8, 80; Côte
    d'Ivoire, 120-121, 130, 131- 132, 134.
    See also Agroindustry
Cashew nut production, 146, 157
Cassava production, 66, 78, 97, 102
CCCE. *See* Central Fund for Economic
    Cooperation
CDC. *See* Cameroon Development
    Corporation; Commonwealth
    Development Corporation
CENEDEC. *See* National Center for the